The West

An insider's tales

A romping reporter in Perth's innocent '60s

Connor Court Publishing Pty Ltd
PO Box 7257
Redland Bay QLD 4165
sales@connorcourt.com

www.connorcourtpublishing.com.au

Phone 0497 900 685

ISBN: 9781925826128

Cover design: Maria Giordano

Front Cover Photo:Bike-borne and clad in shorts, Tony Thomas in pursuit of a scoop for 'The West Australian'. Author's collection, 1964.

Printed in Australia

This book is dedicated firstly to my loved and forbearing wife Margaret. Secondly to 'The West Australian' which published so many of my off-beat pieces in the 1960s and hence preserved tales of Perth life, people and peculiarities for posterity.

CONTENTS

THE LIVES OF OTHERS

GARDENS AS A WORK OF HEART

FOOLING ABOUT IN PROSE

EXTRACTS FROM THE FAMILY FILE

PREFACE

I've had 60 years' joy from journalism. What a privilege to be paid to learn about people and society and then to pass on that knowledge in print!

I finished Perth Modern School in Perth in 1957 and went straight to a cadetship on *The West Australian*. My dad Pete was a well-respected reporter there pre-war and a pal of to-be-editor Griff Richards and to-be-managing director Jim Macartney, both in office when I applied. So a touch of nepotism greased my entry into Newspaper House in St George's Terrace.

I'd already taught myself touch-typing and Pitman's New Era Shorthand. But *The West's* shorthand teacher Mrs Sadlier took one look at my scraggly word outlines and ordered me to start again at Lesson One, with the vertical strokes for T and D. So I became one of the few Pitman's writers who learnt the system twice. Later when I interviewed, neither of us were conscious of my hand shuttling across a notebook held at navel level. You can trust my direct quotes. Because I didn't need to remember material, I lost a lot of my memory skills. I must have seemed stupid over this … but I never lost a notebook.

During my decade on *The West* I studied literature part-time at WA University, planning to become a lecturer. By working 3-11 p.m. shifts and weekend police and emergency rounds, I could get to morning lectures and have two weekdays off work for study. Burning the candle at both ends sent me at 22 to six months in Gairdner Hospital with TB. Thereafter the slow work pace in those days (how different in media today!) left me loose time to do offbeat features about unrecorded life in Perth. At the time these were just my entertainment but they now seem the most enduring part of my 1960s reportage.

I think of the 74 essays in this book as 'The Lost City of Perth' because they light up lifestyles and eras now extinct. Still, the themes like earning a crust, planning a city or making a fool of oneself may have evolved but they're timeless. You won't meet today, as I did 50 years ago, an old seaman who sailed seven times around Cape Horn and got wrecked in the West Indies, living on turtles' eggs. All he lacked was a parrot on his shoulder.

My strangest profile (*'Toiling inside a drain pipe'*) is of a pair of small fecund Italians whose job was to dig out dirt from 3ft concrete pipes as the pipes, with their human cargo, were jacked under rail and highway embankments. Health and safety codes? - what were they?

Other little-celebrated Perth workers I befriended included a chap marshalling trucks into his rubbish dump; a diesel train driver (my excuse to ride at last upfront in a train), a speedway motorbike rider; the visiting wrestlers Brute Bernard and (momentarily) Gorilla Monsoon; a horse vet; and a private eye specialising in midnight raids on errant Perth spouses' love-nests.

Another aspect of "lost Perth" is that our sole morning daily, "*The West*", is not searchable electronically by keyword for the 1960s, because of some copyright glitch. Searching "*The West*" via tangles of microfilm in a State library is a horrible business and I suspect this is why Perth's 1960s are a relatively neglected era.

Luckily, my then wife Carolin around 1972 transferred my "*West*" cuttings books to several big hardcover volumes. These went with me between houses, cities and marriages for the next 45 years. Generally I chucked them in corners of cupboards and wardrobes. While drafting a different book this year, I prised those yellowed volumes open and began reading. Of the news stories, 98% were passé and of little interest. But many feature stories seemed to have a timeless interest, with their focus not on news but on human variety or historical value. Maybe Perth today would be interested, I thought.

This was Perth just before the mining boom, when living standards were modest and the State government was tight as Scrooge in spending our money, especially on discretionary items like waifs, the environment and the arts. Top official priority then was Development, e.g. knocking down the bush to grow things or encouraging new industry. Flip to the essay, *"The Yellow Sea isn't just near Korea."* Macbeth feared he would *the multitudinous seas incarnadine, Making the green one red.* Laporte Chemicals at Binningup went one better, making the green seas yellow, as I demonstrated by diving in wearing singlet and underpants. Sir Dave Brand's government wasn't fussed.

This was the era before media management by public relations stalwarts. I could chat up folks high or low, go where I pleased, and tease our civic guardians with good-natured witticisms.

At one stage I was promoted to *"The West"* leader writing team but I couldn't get the hang of gravitas. Over a couple of lunchtimes I relaxed by profiling dummies in Hay Street clothing stores. My feature, *'Their figures are always fashionable'* would today be titled *'Clothing for Dummies'.* It annoyed the chief leader writers and for this and other incompatibilities they sent me back to the reporters' pit. I never again worked in management and kept my family fed by pen alone.

After Perth I switched abruptly in 1971 from English-lecturing aspirations to economics, and reported from the Canberra Press Gallery for *The Age* and then for business weekly *BRW* in Melbourne until I retired from paid work at 60 in 2001. Most highlights from 1970-2000 are in my 2016 book *That's Debatable.*[1]

In my clan, writing seems a family affair. I've included samples at the end of the book of my parents Joan and Pete, my uncle Geoff Allen the Perth jeweller and my daughter Ros Thomas. I hope their fine prose justifies this indulgence.

Readers here will wince at crass terms in my pieces from the '60s. This applies particularly to Aborigines whom I often described as "natives" or even (when quoting others) as half or quarter-castes. No disrespect was then or now intended. Keep in mind, for example, that public servants then worked for the "Native Welfare Department".

---

[1] *That's Debatable* - 60 Years in Print. Connor Court, Melbourne, 2016.

The essays are also an unsafe space for those, including me, who today scorn sexist worldviews. In the 1960s we male reporters referred to humans as "men" and women were commonly airbrushed out of our mental landscape. In extenuation I wrote quite a few female-friendly articles, such as on married women teachers' woes and institutions like kindergartens and homes for waifs. They're not republished here, but trust me. Perth was also homosexual-intolerant. I have included an essay from *That's Debatable*, titled *"Pretty Perth: pity about the "perverts"*. Again, the quoted words are offensive to modern times.

At the last minute I decided to repeat here another piece from *That's Debatable*, "Not so intrepid: I miss a big story", because it has so much about older Perth, "The West" and my youthful love-life.[2]

In 2016 I'd imagined *That's Debatable* to be my farewell to the world, given a late-stage diagnosis of multiple myeloma (blood cancer). But the chemotherapy regime from my smart haematologist Annabel Tuckfield has worked a treat and I've embarked now on a third book of essays.

My thanks to a newfound friend and volunteer editor Tony Andrews, who cleaned up this manuscript. Thanks to *"The West"* which published my original stuff, perhaps sometimes with misgivings. Thanks to *Quadrant* which revived various pieces. And above all, thanks to my dear wife Margaret for her loving support while I spent my days among laptops, press cuttings and books sprawled sacrilegiously on her kitchen table.

---

[2] My current archive is at *https://tthomas061.wordpress.com*

INTREPID REPORTING

When the "highway" to the West is "good" and the dunnies are studded with gems

13 August 1968

The Eyre Highway was called "good" when we drove home. Motel keepers said that when the track was "bad" one car in every 20 was cracking up with smashed sumps and petrol tanks and broken suspensions.

The track has four lanes, each worse than the other. The two main ones often become impassable, disappearing in muddy lakes, soil dumps or precipitous chasms. Cars detour until the main road re-appears.

One learns to live with ordinary potholes that merely produce a "Clang!" as the suspension bottoms. They cannot be avoided on many stretches but one tries to hit as few per minute as possible.

The 400 miles of dirt track are dotted with the hulks of abandoned cars. One traveller reported seeing an owner strip his car last year and set it alight, so that he could at least enjoy the bonfire.

Our ordeal ended a hundred miles inside WA when we came upon big yellow road-making machines straddling the road. This was a blockade to stop cars climbing on to a few miles of surfaced but not quite sealed road that ran alongside the old track.

To smash something on those last few potholes - like getting killed on the last day of a war - was quite a possibility but we survived to kiss the bitumen ahead.

In the peak summer period, about 300 cars a day do the crossing. In July the average was about 20.

It seems an impertinence for any government to subject its citizens to such a road - the sole road link between Perth and Adelaide. All States agree that the Commonwealth should give some help to seal the highway. As South Australia points out, few of the cars using the road are South Australian, so it is not SA's job to pay the $6 million needed.

Civilisation has arrived on the Nullarbor with a $160,000 motel at Eucla, as luxurious as any in Perth. A desalination plant takes water from the sea just over the hill; a tape-recorder plays hi-fi music; pebble-beds keep the Nullarbor dust from the spongy carpets.

This nine-month-old motel has taken the place of an older one. The owner told me his motel was going well - practically filled each night and a beer garden to open at Christmas. He was using the old motel to take any overflow of guests.

He was prepared to wait for the sealing of the highway to see his investment really pay off. The motel would then be in a commanding position for the heavy traffic.

On the SA side we found a motel of asbestos and tin looking as if it had been transported into the desert by a willy-willy. There were lavatories of the thunderbox sort, a café decorated with pin-ups from men's magazines, a display of snakes pickled in bottles, rubbish tins improvised from half drums and a paperback library for diners.

The owners served good bacon and eggs and, if they demanded room money in advance, it was doubtless a wise precaution. A chequebook buys nothing once you reach the outback. We found this sign - more tactful than most - in one garage:

"Yes Sir, we cash all cheques - on producing birth certificate, marriage licence, driver's licence, social security card, bank statement, reference from employer, rent receipts for five years, two character references, services discharge - and then you're in business FOR WE DO TRUST YOU."

Addendum about some gem-studded lavatories

Soon we pulled into a garage at Coolgardie, hastened to the lavatories and found them out of order. This was a good thing.

Otherwise we would never have discovered Coolgardie's gemstone studded lavatories. They are over the road behind the garage of Mr Ben Prior.

The first garage owner told us his lavatories had closed for repairs. In fact they dried up with envy of the lavatories opposite.

These look ordinary from the outside - cement walls, silver painted roof of corrugated iron, "Gents" and "Ladies" in red on white signboards.

But the inside shimmers with the glint of quartz, glows with the lilac of lepidolite and bottle green of chrysoprase, warms with the reds and browns of ochre and galena, rejoices in the candy strips of halloysite.

Centrepiece of the Ladies, when it opened a month ago, was two magnificent specimens of black opal. Mr Prior's cheerful face darkened as he told me how two local residents (he named them) had prised the opals from the cement and made off with them.

The four walls of both lavatories are studded with hundreds of gemstones. The effect is beyond words. Sunbeams come in above the door and set the walls sparkling.

I felt bound to question Mr Prior about it. He's been in the town 34 years, seen it rise with the gold and fall with the abandoned mines. He gets around in an old blue jumper and blue denims putting petrol in tourists' tanks. He's bald and nuggetty though nuggets have eluded him all his life. He has a passion for preserving relics of the town's great days.

Round his garage he's created an outdoor museum. There are 1913 trucks, wheelbarrows made from tin and tree trunks, a machine that sank a shaft 10ft and showed the way to 10,000oz of gold. There's a wagon wheel with an inscription *"To Warden Finnerty, Leader of Mankind"* and he's trying to recover the wagon used by Plugger Bill Place and Bob Holden, the only teetotallers among 600 teamsters on the Goldfields in 1895.

When weary travellers arrive from the Nullarbor seeking a new home in the west, he greets them with this encouragement: "You are welcome to the West. You are in a mighty land. This town is no longer the centre of the State, but we have a government here that is 50-50 Labor and Liberal and will be the greatest of all."

What did people think of his lavatories? He didn't know; they hadn't been open long.

The tourist potential, of course, is fantastic. My RAC Guide for Victoria has entries like this: "Buangor (pop. 216) - A pastoral district. It has its own cartage contractor."

I can visualize this entry soon in guides to WA: "Coolgardie - a ghost town. It has gem-studded lavatories."

Correct a big mistake: shift Perth to Cottesloe!
July 1964

Perth should be at Cottesloe. To put it where it is was the biggest mistake ever made in WA.

So says Dr Frank Crowley (39), a jovial, beer-drinking historian whom WA will lose to SA in a few weeks.[3]

Dr Crowley's two books, *A Short History of Western Australia* (1959) and *Australia's Western Third* (1960) are studied by nearly all WA schoolchildren.

Tired of teaching and administration, at the WA University, he is going to Adelaide University to do what he wants to do - research, and writing history books.

In WA he saw only more teaching and lecturing ahead. Adelaide was keen to provide him with research facilities, he said. (By implication, UWA was not).

He gave one more reason for leaving: "Nobody suggested I should stay."

He gets eloquent about how, he says, people bungled Perth. He said it was founded by a naval captain who tried to get it as far inland as he could to protect it from naval bombardment.

"Damn it all, what do you do if you sail up to an enemy capital?" thought Captain James Stirling in 1829. "You bombard it."

To the captain it did not matter that the site was by a swamp, on an un-navigable river ten miles upstream from the port.

In any case, Perth should at least have been on the south side of the river, Dr Crowley said. Stirling's orders were to put Perth either at Point Heathcote or at Cockburn Sound. But Stirling did not like the look of them. Cottesloe would have been ideally close to the port.

"Just think of the skyscrapers straddling the spur between the ocean and the river," he said. "How cool."[4]

---

[3] He died in 1983 aged 88.
[4] I think he meant "not-hot". I don't think "cool" in 1964 had the meaning "classy".

Our railway line to Fremantle was on the wrong side of the river, he said. But the north-side people had not wanted it to by-pass Perth.

The decision meant that two costly rail bridges had to be built over the river. The planned standard-gauge line to Fremantle would bypass Perth and take the south-side route. That proved his point, he said.

Why did Perth still have no suburban railway system linking all suburbs?—Because the State Parliament had been dominated by farmers who wanted railways for the bush. They got them. Now we were closing them down - and still had no suburban railway system.[5]

A proper system would have been an inner rail ring Perth-Claremont-Melville-South Perth-Perth, with spur lines to outer suburbs such as Scarborough.

Dr Crowley believes in first-hand work. To write about the North-West, he got a basic wage job anonymously with a Main Roads road gang, feeding stones into a cracking machine. He also helped to paint the Onslow Town Hall to find out about social attitudes, the native problem and how a government department functioned.

Writing of John Forrest's 1869 exploration, he followed in the expedition's steps from Mt Margaret to Perth. "The country is still the same. Dismal low scrub, sand and spinifex," he said.

I suggested it must have been an arduous trip for him too. "It was," he said. "We went by car and got stuck in the mud."

Dr Crowley made a list of what he thinks about controversial subjects.

He is **AGAINST**: State aid for religion and church schools; Indonesian confrontation; knighthoods for Australians; non-Australian Governors and Governors-General; kindergartens for his own children; his wife working for someone else; spiritual wickedness in high places; topless dresses in university classes; self-publicists; and pomposity.

He is **FOR**: the White Australia policy[6]; American aid for

---

[5] Today Perth has its north-south line but no spur-lines east and west.
[6] Yikes!

Australian defence; restrictions on student entries to universities (they are too crowded already); Federal cash for all government primary, secondary, technical and tertiary education; an increase in financial and other powers of the Federal Parliament; a bigger minimum wage; professors retiring at 60 from university departments; abolition of the Country Party; family planning; the pool in the park; bank overdrafts; trotting, night and day; and Subiaco winning the Grand Final.

On Kings Park, he added: "Personally, I would get a couple of bulldozers, start at one end, and …".

My tête-à-tête with Mr Gorilla Monsoon

12 January 1968

Brute Bernard, a primitive wrestler from Quebec, gave a roar of rage, climbed up on the ring ropes and made punching motions at the crowd at Perry Lakes stadium.

Someone had thrown a green plum at him. His reaction provoked another missile. Brute charged into the grandstand, shoulders pumping like pistons. The shrieking crowd parted like the Red Sea and Brute returned in triumph to meet his principal opponent for the night.

The combatants always felt free to leave the ring, either head first in pursuit of missile-launchers, or on the heels of a panic-stricken opponent disappearing into the darkness.

Brute, getting the worst of his slugging match with a 7ft Texan, tumbled through the ropes and crawled furtively up and down in the hope of climbing back in unseen. Tex evicted him twice more with elbow and toe.

That made Brute mad. He jumped onto the ring steps until they collapsed. Then he seized the stoutest piece of timber remaining, and tried to hit Tex's head. Tex grabbed it, whacked Brute, and sent him overboard again. This time Brute found a piece of white cord, and in no time had wrapped it around Tex's neck and was pulling on each end.

Brute does not speak while on duty in the ring, but utters cries like "Aw aw AW AWAW!"

He was hardly recognisable later in his dressing room, in a tweed sports coat and dandling a felt money purse.

I tried to think of a winning line of conversation.

"How do you feel, Brute? I may call you Brute?"

"Tah-yed [tired]," he croaked.

"How is Skull?"

(His wrestling partner, Mr Skull Murphy, has hurt his back on active service).

"Not too good."

Pause.

"Is your head naturally bald?"

"When I was a kid, rheumatic fever, I lost hair."

Snarling (from the wrestlers) and roaring noises (from the crowd) floated to our ears across the night air.

Emboldened by my recent tête-à-tête, I headed for Gorilla Monsoon, 32 stone, who was sitting moodily on a wooden bench. Shortly before, he had been pitted against 16-stone Len Holt. Mr Monsoon simply planted his elephantine legs, let Mr Holt climb over and under him for a while, and then fell on him, ending the bout. Having been declared the winner, Mr Monsoon trod on the throat of his supine opponent.

"Where do you come from, er ar?" I asked, tactfully sidestepping the first-name problem.

He favoured me with a bitter glance through black spectacles and sat.

"Gorilla's a mystery man," volunteered the manager. "I don't get buddy-buddy with the wrestlers."

Gorilla's former opponent, combing his hair in the dressing room mirror, seemed little the worse now for the squashing and trampling.

Killer Karl Kox, a notorious bad guy in wrestling, was lounging outside the dressing shed. He specialises in a hold called a 'brain-buster', in which he lifts his opponent shoulder-high and drops him on his head.

"I'm not a bad guy all the time," he explained. "But when I climb through the ropes, I'm in business. I invest my winnings in a feed and grain company in Texas. I got tired of fighting for nothing."

His bout with Mario Milano, a huge Italian, was the *piece de resistance* for the night. Killer won the first round by twisting Mario's fingers, and Mario won the second with an abdominal stretch.

In the third round, both parties abandoned finesse to hit each other mighty blows on the head. Mario got Killer tied up in the ropes, and every time the referee went to untie him, Mario leaned on the ropes on the opposite side of the ring, to Killer's discomfort.

In time, they wound up brawling in the grass some distance from the ring. Killer was able to run Mario's head into a steel light pole. Mario kept punching, so Killer did it again. Mario began stumbling around in circles, while Killer returned in triumph to the ring.

Mario put his hand to his forehead, and discovered it was bleeding profusely. With a wild cry he hurtled back into the ring and after knocking the surprised Killer almost senseless, lifted him into the air and began to choke him.

The referee, who was on the smallish side, ran in to separate them. Mario threw an uppercut that sent the referee his own height into the air. Picking himself up off his back, the referee returned to the affray and collected another punch from Mario that threw him 10ft. The 15 policemen on duty began to consider taking action but several wrestlers who happened to be nearby rescued Killer and the referee.

The announcer announced a win to Killer Karl Kox, on a disqualification. "That is it for tonight in World Championship Wrestling," he concluded blandly.

Actually, it's since emerged that all such bouts were rehearsed and choreographed. When Mario, as I wrote, "put his hand to his forehead", he was possibly concealing a capsule of blood which he broke on his skull.

Exploring strange Perth Customs

My liqueur-chocolate phase as a Perth reporter was good for two features. The first in The West Australian was about the alcohol in the chocolates and the ambience in a nameless chocolate shop. Keep in mind that I am personally a choc-aholic but in those days couldn't afford to actually buy liqueur chocolates. This first article led to feedback in the form of a Customs Officer wanting me to disclose my liqueur-chocolate interviewee. This sequel led to a second feature. For some reason I published that piece in an obscure literary monthly of WA University called "The Critic". Possibly The West had rejected it or maybe I thought it too weird for the morning daily. Amazing that Customs officials took seriously the issue of alcohol content of chocolates. It gives added spice to the truism: "We're from the government and we're here to help you."

Part One: Hand, Soft or Alcoholic?

11 December 1967

I didn't expect to find danger in a chocolate shop, but you're not safe anywhere.

The chocolate shop man reached into a recess behind the door and pulled out a 100gm block of Swiss chocolate.

"*Ne doit pas etre remis aux enfants*," the label warned. "Keep out of children's reach."

"Liqueur chocolates," breathed the owner. "Real liqueur. They are good chocolates. We keep them out of sight. If anyone asks for them specifically, OK, we are guided by that."

"But haven't all liqueur chocolates got liqueur in them?" I asked in genuine perplexity.

He looked canny.

"If they do have liqueur, you'll have to be careful of Customs. If they don't, people could say they are wrongly titled. We could assume there is not much liqueur involved."

In any case, he said, there would be the danger of a cured alcoholic getting them by chance. Parents could unwittingly feed them to children…

The most expensive box comes with an original oil painting of a lot of flowers and costs $50. You could also choose an oil painting of Montmartre by a French artist.

"Such an oil painting in its gold frame is good enough to grace any home," he said.

Quite a conversation piece, too.

"Is it an original?" asks your admiring guest.

"Yes, it came with some chocolates," you reply…

Part Two: Heroic Reporter Defends His Sources
26 February 1968

The press lives by disclosures, fearless of the consequences. But little did I expect that my disclosures in *The West Australian* about liqueur chocolates would bring the Customs Department down on me.

My investigations had showed that nearly all the liqueur chocolates on sale in Perth are liqueur-less, but that connoisseurs know how to get them with real liqueur in them.

I was brushing my teeth the next day when the phone rang from the office. "There's a Customs man been here wanting to see you about the liqueur chocolates," said a colleague, with suppressed excitement.

I threw down my toothbrush and sped fearfully to work, but the Customs man had left. We met on the telephone soon after.

"We are having an inquiry throughout Australia from central office to see whether we should revise our ban on imported liqueur chocolates that are more than 2 per cent proof strength," he said. "Can you tell me which shop you found the liqueur chocolates in, so we can talk to the owner?"

"Never!" I shouted. "I'd go to gaol first."

"We're not going to make a pinch. We're just checking up," he said soothingly. "As a matter of fact, I had a look round Perth myself. You said in that article that the shop had a $50 box of chocolates in the window. I found two shops in that category."

I inquired whether Customs was trying to crack a liqueur-chocolate smuggling ring. He said the smuggle-busters at Fremantle Customs were a bit worried. Chocolates often came in described as 'sugar confectionery'. His fellows had not suspected these might sometimes be liqueur confectionery.

"If they are invoiced as liqueur confectionery, we always sample them - chemically, I mean. The law says that they mustn't be more than 2 per cent proof strength, in case children get on to them."

"They'd have to eat a hundredweight to even get tipsy."

"I don't make the laws, Mr Thomas."

He said agonising complications had set in lately because local chocolate-makers had started making real liqueur chocolates, allowable under State laws. There wasn't much point in Customs getting upset about the imported ones when local ones were on sale anyway.

And then he made his own disclosure. The Customs is thinking about smashing the alcohol barrier on chocolates, allowing them to pack a real punch to the sweet tooth. "More lenient…in the light of changing times…prohibition rather silly…" he continued.

Bold thinking, Customs! But I foresee a new crime being added to the statutes - *driving under the influence of chocolates.*

Customs' Censors Pounce on the Bishop's Wife

The Customs Branch in Perth was not wholly fixated on liqueur chocolates. It also kept a vigilant eye on titles of imported books. The inspectors' job was to make sure that we didn't read imported books that were "obscene, indecent, offensive, profane, blasphemous, libellous, unduly emphasizing matters of sex, cruelty or violence or was likely to deprave or corrupt." Any literary merit was irrelevant.[7]

Booksellers nationally were driven mad by having popular new books piled up in shops' back rooms awaiting Customs' approval to put them on sale. In Melbourne one Elizabeth Street shop manager rebelled and shifted books prematurely to "on sale". A Customs inspector arrived and in front of all the customers shouted, "If you continue doing this I will shut your shop down!"

The Victorian Chief Secretary in 1972 was John Rossiter, in charge of the Vice Squad. This squad hounded any book shop which sold a book containing the word "fuck". Michael Zifcak, president of the Booksellers Association, went to see Rossiter to complain. After a wait, Rossiter arrived and snapped, "What the fuck can I do for you?"[8]

I was already on to the long-standing book controversy from my Perth perch. Here's what I turned up eight years earlier.

Censors Selections Puzzle Booksellers
March 1964

Demands from the Customs and Excise Department to inspect such imports as Rudyard Kipling's Just So Stories and George Bernard Shaw's plays for censorship purposes are puzzling Perth and Fremantle booksellers.

The managing director of a Perth book store, Mr E. R. Kent, said yesterday that Customs had queried between 100 and 200 imported titles this year.

---

[7] Locally produced books were subject to police scrutiny under the State's Indecent Publications Act.

[8] Zifcak, Michael, My Life in Print. Lothian, Melbourne, 2006, p. 137.

Customs were given invoices showing titles of all books imported. Customs passed most books immediately but if a clearance was refused the books could not be sold until a man had inspected them at a shop's bulk store. Nearly all were then passed. Titles recently queried included:

"They Do It with Mirrors" (an Agatha Christie mystery); "Forever Free" (about a woman who raises lions); "The Terrible Dog"; "The Bishop's Wife"; "The Greek Experience"; "Tales After Supper"; "Confidential Living" (an inspirational religious book); "Great Hunter"; "Hold Your Hour and Have Another" (Brendan Behan's latest book); "Sex and the Single Girl"; and "The Boilerplate War" (a book on tank warfare). Even "The Golden Bough" a 19th Century pioneer anthropological text, was called in.

Books on mathematics were often inspected because the word "Figures" appeared in the titles.

Mr Kent said some titles could arouse suspicion, but he could not understand why such books as "Stream of Music" (a young person's guide to orchestras), "The Berlin Wall" (a political book) and particularly Kipling's "Just So Stories" should be queried.

Another Perth bookseller said titles "Bedtime Stories" (for children) and "Between Overs" (on cricket) had been queried.

Mr J. G. Dodd, a Fremantle bookseller, said two editions of Bernard Shaw's plays containing "The Doctor's Dilemma", "Getting Married", "The Showing Up of Blanco Posnet", "The Dark Lady of the Sonnets" and "Fanny's First Play" had just been queried, though the books were published in 1932.

A semi-religious work, "The Witch's Horn" by Elizabeth Goudge, was also queried.

Mr Kent said the same title could be passed one month but queried when the next shipment arrived. This had been going on for years.

Titles with the word "sex" or even "marriage" were highly suspect. Books dealing with puberty, courtship, childbirth and serious sex information were always queried.

A book called "Sex Control Today" by Marie Stopes was queried although it was more than 50 years old.

He said the present system was inefficient because it was managed by men who obviously lacked literary background.

Officers had power to interfere with trading in books that were innocuous and long known to the public. This dislocated trading and warehouse arrangements, though generally the invoice system was helpful.

The Collector of Customs in WA, Mr W. R. Lawson, said yesterday that if book merchants put the complete title and author on the invoices, the number of books queried would be reduced. The number was in any case very small —- one in a hundred or more.

Customs had the power to stop the books at the wharf until they were checked, but instead permitted booksellers to take them to their bulk stores, where they could get on with listing and pricing. Customs wanted to speed up delivery of books.

But with only titles to guide them, the Customs checkers had no choice but to query some books until they had inspected them.

The checker was guided by the Commonwealth's list of banned books. Some of the banned books were listed in the Commonwealth Gazette, but this was not the full list.

"The checker might see a bare title resembling a title on the list," he said. "He inspects the book, checks the author, and usually finds it is not the banned book."

Desecrating Leighton with billboards
23 October 1967

The Australian journalists' Code of Ethics includes that journalists' union members identify themselves and their newspaper before obtaining any interview for publication.

I violated the code in a shocking way for a piece published in late 1967. I got on the phone to a Perth railways bureaucrat and posed as a potential customer for yet another big advertising hoarding by the rail tracks along the beachfront.

I was riding the Fremantle-Perth train a lot and was always infuriated by ad hoardings that blocked my view for about a mile of the scrubby sandhills, golden beach and sparkling blue sea on the Leighton Beach-Mosman stretch.

Never one to suffer injustices meekly, I resolved to give the railways a public caning. I didn't pay any heed to my profession's Code of Ethics about identifying myself. Did the end justify the means? You be the judge. (My story flashes forward to witchcraft, prostitution, police corruption and murder, details of which I include as a gratuitous extra).

On a sadistic impulse I thought of desecrating the landscape at Leighton or Mosman. The quickest and best way would be a 20ft by 10ft hoarding by the railway line. I rang the railways and was put through to the hoardings promoter. "I'd like to put up a big hoarding," I said. "How much would it cost?

"We'll put it up for you," he said. "You'll only have to pay about $100 a year rent."

"How long will I have my hoarding for?" I asked eagerly.

"As long as you like."

"But don't you have to limit the number of hoardings along that coast strip? It's got a lot there already."

"Many people say it's over-cluttered but other people say it isn't. We don't have any limitation except when residents start objecting. It's the objectors that make me careful."

"What about motorists? Does a hoarding distract them?"

"That's all press propaganda. Drivers will take their eyes off the road to look at a girl in bikinis, and no one complains. But newspapers don't like competition. They want all the advertising. Anyway if you didn't have these sort of things Perth would be a dead city."

Dropping my role as a would-be hoarding renter, I made an official call to the Liberal's Railways Minister Ray O'Connor.

Why does the department erect hoardings? - To get money, the same as with other commercial undertakings, and to advertise its own businesses. Most railways in the world do the same.

How many hoardings has your department put up in the metropolitan area? - Four hundred.

How much money do they bring in? - In 1966-67, $44,769.

What aesthetic standards does the railways have about hoardings? - Structures are well built and of neat appearance. They are maintained in good condition and generally comply with the standards of the Outdoor Advertising Association.

My piece generated no reaction that I was aware of. My paper's advertising salespeople were doubtless happy to have me trashing a competitor, though that was not my motive. Whether Minister Ray O'Connor complained to my Editor (Griff Richards) I don't know; no one chipped me.

The only sequel worth mentioning is that Railways Minister Ray O'Connor rose to become, briefly, Liberal Premier of WA 15 years later but came undone via a conviction on a $25,000 fraud charge, served six months and had his Order of Australia revoked.

Even more sensationally, the ABC's Australian Story last year quoted Mrs Leigh Beswick, the driver of Ray O'Connor (who was then Police Minister), saying that O'Connor in 1975 was having an affair with brothel keeper, kickback payer to detectives and one-time witch coven member Shirley Finn. Shortly before someone killed Finn with four bullets to the head, she had threatened O'Connor that if she 'went down' over a $100,000 tax debt, he'd go down too, according to the driver Beswick. The case was never solved. O'Connor died in 2013.

Somehow all this later material makes my expose of the railways' aesthetic misconduct over the hoardings seem rather tame. I clearly wasn't the only player with an ethics deficiency.

"Mod girls" run rings around their Mums
14 July 1965

Before you start, you need to know what "Mod" girls were. Like other Australian cities, Perth in 1965 had a "Mod" fashion, derived from the Beatles look and the London scooter-borne Mods (moderns) who famously battled with motorbike-mounted Rockers at Brighton in 1964. Perth girls would get up in geometric and polka-dot patterned rigs, A-line skirts, shifts and flat T-strap shoes, style their hair in bobs and pixie-cuts, and put on eye-popping make-up. Perth was still staid and prissy and the Beatles had left Perth out of their Australian tour a year earlier. Perth teeny-boppers enjoyed blowing off steam in daring ways at concerts. But it was all utterly harmless compared with today's drug-laden and sexually explicit mass party scene. Unfortunately at age 25 I was in a prissy stage myself as you might notice in this piece, for example with my disapproval of dyed hair. It never crossed my mind, nor the sub-editors', that the 14-y.o. Mod I mention might be having an orgasm in public.

After a night spent listening to hundreds of little 'Mod' girls and Ray Brown & The Whispers (and others) at the Capitol, I reckon there's quite a gulf between parents and daughters.

I picked five fresh-faced and wholesome looking Mod girls (all aged 15) and asked them how they got on at home. One mother, it appeared, had burnt her daughter's black mod socks in a vain attempt to prevent her going to the show. A father had taken to one lass with a radiator cord when she was dancing in front of the television. The weapon indicates that the assault was unpremeditated. Another girl's father had thrown a tomato at her.

To get to such big-sound shows without maternal consent involves much planning. "It takes weeks," Julie said. "All your friends have to be in on the plan. I say I'm going to Bev's, Bev says she's going to Dawn's, and so on. If Mum finds out it's the end."

A more risky technique: Hide behind the door and then say, 'Ta-ta Mum' and before Mum can say anything, clear out.

The full text of the interview was:

Q: Why do you go to these shows?

The five girls (twittering and fluttering): "It's the boys' movements and the clothes they wear and the way they move their bodies. They are gorgeous. The way they shake all over and their feet move and the way their (long) hair goes. Their voices just go through you. When they talk from the stage, you feel like they are talking to YOU."

Q: Why do you scream while the singers sing?

A: To attract attention; everyone stares at you. The stars like it… You just go mad. You can't help it. Clapping is daggy [not good], you hurt your hands…You can't help yourself. You have to let yourself go and let off steam jumping and cheering. Girls can faint or cry. Some really howl…After the show you go home and can't sleep. Next day at school you just sit there all day, and talk about the show all day….

Q: Do you find the singers sexy?

A: That is the best thing about it. They are gorgeous.

Q: So that is what's behind all this?

A: Yes.

Q: Why do you wear Mod clothes?

A: We like to be different. You try to better everyone, you wear the same sort of things but more classy and expensive-looking.

Q: What should Mod boys wear?

A: Patterned waistcoats, mauve shirts and look like they are from England.

Q: Is the Australian look not acceptable?

A: No.

Q: How did you afford to pay for the tickets? (Prices 28/-, 18/-, 12/-)

A: You go without lunch the week before.

Q: Why, Dawn, are you holding that bus ticket?

A: Because Peter Hutton (singer) put it in his mouth twice, before he autographed it.

Q: Do you like boys who like science and all that?

A: No. They must have little surfie cars.

Q: How many of you have natural hair colour?

A: Only Lynette. I blonded my hair. I did it without Mum knowing…I bleached mine. I told Mum the sun did it.

Q: What do you all want to do when you leave school?

A: Stay a Mod. Be a beach bum. Go to Sydney. You get real surfies there. Work hard and go to England to see the true Mods.

Q: Aren't the Rolling Stones unworthy of admiration?

A: No. It makes it all the better if they are in trouble with the police. We have to be on their side…

Inside the theatre, the front and rear seats were full, and about 20 middle rows were empty, to be filled later by the back seat rushers.

A dark man in a white suit appeared in front of the curtain, the curtain was hauled back, and the little red lights on the guitar amplifiers could be seen gleaming in the darkness. A green spotlight falls on a youth with tossing hair and high-heeled boots. "I wanna be your lover baby, I want to be your man," he sings over and over again while the audience screams and girls leap up and down gorilla fashion and hurl streamers and Jaffas at the band while jackbooted night watchmen sweep the seats with torchlight beams.

"Bom bom bom," sings the singer. A girl 20 feet away watches him through binoculars, and another throws something at him that hits him on the head. The noise of the amplified guitars is like trains shunting in a marshalling yard.

"Tonight you're mine complete," the next singer, a girl, sings ambiguously, "to give your love so sweet…"

The drummer on his throne of boxes is an expressionless demi-god. A little blonde girl in a paroxysm of ecstasy lifts herself bodily a foot out of her seat with violent torso thrusts, whirling her hair like an African dancer. Momentarily she sinks back in her seat and listens with wide-eyed incredulity, as though she has reached heaven before her time.

"Yaaa Yaaaah!" she cries, clutching both hands to her head. After several hours she can still shriek hoarsely, "Sing it again, again, again!" and beat her fists helplessly against her knees. She looks about 14.

From backstage the audience was bathed in a dark smoky light, and handfuls of streamers were waving frantically like ostrich tails. Lollies became red and green sparks as they crossed the stage lights and fell on stage with a constant clicking sound.

The singer pointed and scores of girls in that direction leapt up screaming and waving. Other singing groups stood in the side curtains looking with professional curiosity at the skipping and shaking of the group on stage.

I talked to an amiable guitarist who a few minutes previously had enjoyed the all-oblivious worship of a theatre-full of teenaged girls.

"I'm an apprentice electrician," he said. "There's not enough of this sort of work to carry me full-time. We get union rates, three pounds ten shillings an hour but it works out at only about five pounds for tonight."

The screaming meant something, he said. He appreciated it.

When I left the theatre by a dark alley at the back, silent groups of shadowy figures stared. They may have been waiting for autographs, but they had a cutthroat air. Occasional screams could be heard faintly from the theatre.

Parents are advised to experience one of these shows for themselves.

Finer points of a bull
29 September 1967

Every year we reporters would be sent out to do "colour pieces" on the Royal Agricultural Show. This was not easy as just about every angle had already been written-up over the years. It was like the chore of writing about any hot day in Perth. I can still recite the standard intro from memory: "Crowds flocked to the beaches and ice-cream sellers did a roaring trade". Anyway, here's my 1967 Royal Show-piece.

There are those who pull and prod the bulls in the cattle section at the Royal Show and those who gape from a safe distance. Normally a gaper, I became a puller and prodder this week after some coaching from a wizened Scotsman in a black hat. I could tell he was an expert because when the Guernsey bull did a certain thing and we all jumped back, he just stood there.

He guided my hand to a flap of skin at the back of the bull and commanded me to pull. It was like lifting a carpet. "Ah, that's a lovely fine skin," he said. "Shows the breeding. Other bulls have hard thick skins."

He took me round to the front end. The bull drooled and rolled its eyes, showing the whites. "A beautiful head!" the Scotsman breathed. "Look at that wide jaw for cutting his tucker. A narrow jaw - we call it 'peaky'." At the top of the bull at the back were two knobs, which he called the pin and hook. The good length between them gave a good udder, I was told.

"Udder?" I queried.

"Udder on his daughters," he said with some impatience. "He'll have 50 daughters in one year."

The flap that I first pulled at meant that the daughters would have a built-in shutter to shield the udder, he said.

"It's a good bull all right," I said. "But his backbone is sticking up."

"'That's good. That's good. It means he won't be round-shouldered."

"What about his fat belly?" I asked.

"You don't want him like a racehorse do you? That's his furnace where he burns up his grass. On the cow that means a good milker."

He put three fingers between two of the bull's ribs to show the capacity. I pointed to a big cavity in the bull's side but he said that would fill out if the bull had a drink. Still in a critical mood, I complained that you would not get many steaks off his rump. The Scotsman, who had been breeding cattle for 40 years, explained that you didn't eat Guernsey bulls.

"Look here," he said, dropping his voice. "The stones are of equal size."

I thought this referred to the pop singers but it didn't.

"A judge knocked back a beautiful Corriedale ram of mine once, just because one stone was a little smaller than the other."

He continued, "Look at the ground he covers. Three families could picnic under there." He paused to scrape his feet. "I wish you'd keep your pens cleaner," he snapped at the young attendant. "I've got a boot-full now."

Then we set off to look at the cow that won a special prize for the most shapely udder.

Not So Intrepid: I Miss A Big Story
20 May 2013

I had an Oedipus Rex moment in 1963. If you recall the play, Oedipus goes looking for the man who killed his father and married his mother. On discovering the man is himself, he is so horrified he stabs out his eyes. (Incidentally, Oedipus killed his father in a prehistoric fit of road rage, involving chariots at an intersection).

I was an earnest but wayward reporter, aged 23, on *The West Australian*. My editor Griff Richards was troubled. A very illustrious gent called General Sir John Hackett had visited Perth. He was the son of an even grander Winthrop Hackett, who co-founded, edited and later owned *The West Australian* itself. Griff's problem was that he had picked up rumors that he, Griff, had seriously and deliberately snubbed General Hackett. I assume Griff had heard some elliptical references to the matter at the Weld Club in Barrack Street.

Griff had misplaced a lot of faith in me, and hence assigned me to get to the bottom of these rumors. They involved something about a magnificent speech Sir John Hackett had made where he had used his coat as a prop and declaimed about the sleeves. That didn't sound very poetic but I got the drift. Rather thrilled to get this detective-like assignment, I began my investigations.

To put all this in context, I intend to inflict on you some excessive detail about the Hacketts.

Winthrop Hackett, at times in league with Premier John Forrest, virtually ran WA for the decades straddling 1900. With his immense wealth and influence, he created most of Perth's institutions, including the free-of-fees and female-friendly WA University, the State Library and Museum, Kings Park, the Zoo, even Karrakatta Cemetery. Under his regime, *The West* was a 'paper of record' – it used to report verbatim the entire Sunday sermons of Bishop Riley at St George's Cathedral, for example.

For all that, Winthrop must have had a certain gleam in his eye. At the age of 57, the bachelor magnate married in 1905 the 18-year-old

Deborah Vernon Brockman, from WA's pioneer landed gentry. At one stage she ran a tantalum mine in the deserts of the Northern Territory. The tantalum became a crucial input to Britain's development of radar in World War II.

How and why Winthrop decided so late in life to wed a teenager is unclear (he did have a lifelong and probably innocent friendship with a chap named Leeper).

He wrote a fortnight before the marriage: "The place is so dull, and life so monotonous that I absolutely must have a new experience. Hence this determination. It seems to me as good a reason as most men have for marrying. What do you think? This is in the strictest sense a 'marriage de convenience' " [Pardon his French].

After marriage, he wrote querulously: "Did you find that marriage took at least a couple of hours out of your working day? It is my experience." This is very close to my favorite joke: When a tradie got married, he told a mate, "It's great, but long hours."

Winthrop even tried to run Deb's life from beyond the grave, putting a clause in his will that her inheritance would cease if she re-married. Deb not only re-married, twice, but became rich anyway, despite foregoing vast Hackett wealth.

Deb, sincerely or not, described her marriage to Winthrop as 'blissfully happy'. She was one hell of a snob too. She had to shift her *bric a brac* from Adelaide to Toorak when she embarked on her third marriage. The job took 12 pantechnicons. At the time, it was the largest family consignment ever to go by road in Australia.

She was also loathe to relinquish her title-by-marriage of "Lady", which she had enjoyed since her teen years. Her second husband, Frank Moulden, was plain "Mr" but Deb continued to call herself "Lady Hackett". One cheeky social reporter wrote that Lady Hackett and Mr Frank Moulden "were sharing a room at the Menzies Hotel". Mercifully, Frank got a knighthood later, so Deb could call herself Lady Moulden. Her third husband lacked a title so thereafter she called herself "Dr" Buller-Murphy, trading on an honorary doctorate she got from UWA. This used to be considered pretentious, but now a lot of Honorary Doctors adopt the title.

The Hacketts' only son John, amid four daughters, is the subject of my story and discomfiture.

Sir John, like his mother and father, had an astounding career. He joined the British Army after a not-so-good start in art and in the classics at Oxford. In every campaign, he did acts of heroism, accumulating war wounds and war medals at an equal rate. In Syria he was wounded and won the Military Cross. In North Africa he was in a tank blown up during an attack and he was seriously burnt climbing out. He won a DSO.

In 1944 he raised and commanded a parachute brigade, getting wounded again in Italy. Then he led the brigade into the airdrop on Arnhem, the celebrated Dutch 'bridge too far' which became an Allied disaster. He was severely wounded in the stomach and a German doctor was going to give him a mercy-killing injection, but a second doctor stepped in and saved his life surgically.

Hackett escaped with the Dutch resistance during a hospital transfer, after adorning himself with extra-bloody bandages. He won a second DSO for Arnhem.

After the war he rose to top ranks, including Palestine in 1947 and running the Northern Ireland campaign in 1961, both rather messy fields of conflict. His job from 1965 was as commander of the British Army of the Rhine and NATO's Northern Army Group but he was too abrasive politically to win the ultimate top job, Chief of the Defence Staff.

After the army he became Principal of King's College London, where he liked to join student marches for improved study grants, to the horror of other Dons.

After his years on the front line of the nuclear Cold War, he wrote in 1978 a fictional and best-selling scenario of World War III based on a Soviet invasion of West Germany seven years into the future (1985).

This big man came to Perth in 1963, a year or two before the zenith of his military career. This year was the 50th anniversary of the first courses of the WA University and the Uni Senate marked the occasion by conferring honorary doctorates on 15 alumni and bigshots, some with only tenuous WA connections.

As a further preliminary to my Oedipus moment, I will now describe my love life as at late 1963.

A young woman "Libby" and I were magnificently in love and eager to neck in secluded places. This was long before ardent young couples could hope for privacy in flats. My home was too inconvenient for trysts. Libby was still living with her mother, who made a point of never leaving us alone in her house, i.e. she was not stupid. At one point I tried a double-cross. I announced to Libby's mother that Libby and I would spend the evening at the pictures. Mother then felt it safe to organise a social outing of her own. At the last minute I announced that our movie was off and Libby and I would just have to entertain ourselves at home somehow. Mother showed such suppressed fury that Libby pulled the carpet from under me by discovering there was another movie she badly wanted to see.

The degree-conferring night found me seething with testosterone and fuming at the tedium of the ceremony. I had expected it would be all over by 9pm or so and that Libby and I could rendezvous and head down to the Crawley lover's lane in my car. But the uni felt that each conferee would want equal time and plaudits. Think 15 x 10 minute speeches, plus extras.

The chancellor, Sir Alex Reid, was in his peacock robes, along with all the Senators and profs. Each nominee got a speech about his accomplishments and was then presented with his doctorate.

None of the speeches so far were at all interesting, and of the 15, there were still three or four to go. The best to date was Fred Schonell, author of the famous *Schonell Speller*, lists of words which we as primary schoolers had chanted and spelled day after day, resulting in our cohort's superior spelling ability, compared to today's slack brats. Some recipients seemed to have no connection at all with UWA or Perth, such as Sir Charles Blackburn, chancellor of Sydney Uni, who by the time he retired the following year had himself conferred 31,194 degrees (true). Another was Freddie Alexander, a historian who had managed to bulk out his 50th anniversary history of the UWA to nearly 1000 pages. I had reported some other historian remarking bitchily that a 1000-year history of Oxford University had been a smaller volume. I hadn't given Fred any right of reply, and Fred carpeted me over it, with justice.

I decided to cut and run to Libby. Anyway, I reasoned, by the time the official ceremony finished, there would be little time to write the story, phone it through and still meet deadlines. Late night stories had to be particularly thrilling to justify the reworking of pages.

Libby and I managed to steam up my car windows and I thought no more about honorary doctors of laws and letters ... until my editor asked me to discover those rumors concerning our 'snub' to Sir John Hackett.

I began by checking our library files – nothing there.

I asked around, using my meagre list of Perth bigshots. Nothing much.

Finally, a uni contact said someone had told him something about a speech by Sir John. Maybe even at UWA.

An administrator confirmed, to my growing dismay, that the speech was at the Honorary Degree ceremony. "But wasn't all that just formal stuff?" I asked imploringly.

"No, I was there. It was terribly moving. You know that his father had also got an honorary degree? Sir John must have been wearing his own father's gown with all the academic stripes and trimmings, and he took it off and addressed it as though it was his father, still alive. We were all moved to tears, just about."

Well, that's cleared THAT up. All I needed to do now was break the news to my editor, Griff Richards. I'd just say…what would I say?

I could think of two precedents similar to this for breaking of bad news. As a boy I had once been caught by my stepfather, Vic, doing target practice on our chooks, using small stones. Reluctant to discipline me himself (although when I was about six he gave me a sudden slap on the bare bottom when he caught me peeing in the bathroom basin), Vic directed me to report my crime to Mum and take condign punishment at her hands.

I began by remarking to Mum on the smallness of the chook pen and the chooks' need for more exercise. Mum abstractedly agreed. In a few subtle steps I came to mention that I had even encouraged them to run around by tossing a few things at them. Mum abstractedly agreed...

The other occasion was when the local grocer-store owner caught me red-handed shoplifting a Cherry Ripe bar. Unwilling to discipline me and lose the family account, the grocer told me to report my crime to my mother. I trudged home, to find a serious Communist Party seminar in progress on the back lawn. Was this the right time for a general strike? How should we educate the masses (sometimes pronounced 'them asses') about the US war bases in the Indian Ocean?

As kids do (or used to do), I hung around Mum's skirts waiting for a break in the conversation. "Mum, I've got something I need to tell you," I whined. Mum was not interested. She was focused on the mood of the masses and the Soviet split with Tito of Yugoslavia. "Mum? Mum?" "Get out and leave us alone, we're busy!" I went off to play, with a clear conscience.

I couldn't visualise any comparable solutions for my present dilemma. Remarkably I decided to go the hang-out road, as Richard Nixon once put it, and do full disclosure.

Griff, by the standards of many modern-day editors, lived a remote existence in a panelled office off the reporters' hall. As I saw it, his senior people went in to report and came out to instruct. I never could reconcile this persona with the student Griff who was suspended from UWA over allegedly lewd material he published in the student newspaper *Sruss Sruss*. So "lewd" that the Student Guild had to literally burn the undistributed copies. ("*Sruss Sruss*" was onomatopoeia involving the rustle of female underwear).

I entered Griff's sanctum, apprehensively noting the subdued lighting and the important-looking desk.

"Mr Richards, Hackett made a big speech at the uni ceremony and I was there but it was getting really late. I'd been working long shifts and I was pretty tired and left a bit early and missed it."

Griff dismissed me from the office. He was not the emotional sort and I didn't know how annoyed he was.

But it so happened that he checked the time sheets and for one reason or another (perhaps I had done a day shift and then done a play review as well that evening), I did appear to have been over-worked. Very nicely, Griff gave me the benefit of the doubt and rounded on the chief of staff, Viv Goldsmith, for slave-driving his young reporter. Viv and I had never got on, but his hands were tied by the time sheets and he had to eat crow. I'm sure he liked me even less after that.

The Yellow Sea isn't just near Korea
5 March 1968

Binningup Beach, 16 miles on the Perth side of Bunbury, is a pretty settlement of 40 asbestos cottages set among green dunes.

The white beach slopes gently down to the sea, which some days, according to the weather, turns a bright yellow-orange in colour.

Yesterday the Yellow Sea was reverting to blue, though when a wave stood up there was a distinct yellow tinge.

A colleague spent two days early last week in a fruitless search for the yellow stain from the Laporte Chemical Works near Bunbury. The sea was a sparkling blue-green; a fisherman told him the pollution story was a myth, and that the yellow was merely sand churned from the seabed.

He found some circumstantial evidence by digging a foot-deep hole on the beach. On top the sand was white, but underneath it had a coppery hue.

Later the stain returned in full strength. The sea was the colour of beer, with wavelets providing a realistic froth.

Binningup people claimed the stain dyed their bathers, stung their eyes and spoilt their fun.

Rather nervously, I approached the deserted shore, put on a white T-shirt and waded in. The water turned an even, bright yellow in the sunlight and became opaque. Diving, I could see the bottom only when my nose was resting on it. I fished up a handful of sand and it had a cinnamon colour.

My T-shirt turned leopard-like with orange spots. My eyes tingled but I could not judge whether this was a result of the staining effluent or my own fault for open-eyed diving.

Binningup's chief fear is that the stain will accumulate and grow worse each time it reappears.

The Laporte people say their million gallons a day of effluent can make only a minute stain on the vast ocean. As for the stained sand, winter erosion would sweep it away every year.

The staining comes from iron particles in the effluent, which turn a rusty colour. It has not been found harmful, even to fish, and the iron concentration is said to be less than in some towns' drinking water.

But Binningup people still prefer their seawater blue. Somehow, a Yellow Sea is less refreshing to swim in.

I must say that this story was hardly normal fare in the news columns of The West. Reporters were traditionally fairly anonymous and didn't report on the effects of their chins on the seabed or admit to wearing singlets covered in orange spots (I spared them details about my literally or liberally stained underpants).

A sequel was that I long remembered my daring swim but forgot which company was doing the polluting, and in Canberra from time to time I blamed innocent companies like Alcoa. Readers today may wonder not merely at Binningup's pretty asbestos cottages but a State government which allowed its industrial developers to change the sea from blue to yellow, much like the Parisian art group Les Fauves (the "wild beasts") did in 1905, but only on their canvases.

Swamp and ruins in the heart of the city

21 July 1965

Perth before the Pilbara iron-ore mines was a sleepy town, typified by one of the prime blocks on St George's Terrace being left derelict for four years. I explored it in the style of a Boys' Own Adventure.

It was dark and messy in the undergrowth. Each time I put my foot down it sank through couch grass into water. To move forward I had to beat aside 15-feet-high spears of grass. Just visible through the swamp growth were concrete ruins – my destination.

The walls were 20ft high and a foot thick. They stretched in a rectangle the size of a city building. What was inside them I could not glimpse. The one entrance had to be reached through a spiky, spiny, anty morass.

An animal crashed and splashed somewhere in the thicket. A pig? Photographer Rodney Locke and I could only guess.

Birds twittered and screeched. Were it not for the roar of invisible traffic one would not guess that our expedition was taking place less than three blocks from the Perth Town Hall. Which ruins? The ruins of the still-born Chevron Hilton Hotel, next door to the former Christian Brothers College at the corner of Victoria Avenue and St George's Terrace.

The ruins have given themselves over to algae, reeds and slime. The vast foundations are hidden from the east by the crumbling CBC building; from the south by the swamp growth; from the west by the Governor's private grounds and from the Terrace because they are in a valley. At the back of the block is a patchwork of seedling nurseries for the Governor's garden.

The first deterrent to explorers is rubbish and weeds under which swamp water lurks to fill the shoe of the unwary stepper. The ruins are concealed behind razor sharp cane grass and who would march through marsh to risk the death of a thousand cuts? Only perhaps an inquisitive reporter who wonders at the desolate state of all land south of the Supreme Court between Barrack Street and Victoria Avenue.

I get through the cane grass in a prolonged flailing charge. What is this before me? An Aztec fort? A wartime fortification? The great wall rears unbroken from the middle of a sordid lake. Off, shoes, socks and coat! Plunge through the slime! Spring to the nearest orifice for my first peer in. Ugh.

The ruins are bare, a handball court floored with algae and muck. A dozen reinforcements for never-to-be-poured concrete pillars extend bony fingers to the sky. The furniture is a pile of rotting wood and a heap of mysterious tins, each snouted like a gas mask.

Four thousand tons of concrete are under my feet as I squelch across the floor to investigate a deep blue pool, hinting at extreme depths with perhaps a corpse at the bottom. I measure it with an unwieldy steel rod. Twenty feet long, it is too short for the job.

I see a doorway at the far end, and clamber on to the sill. Another bottomless pit of water. Yet another door, yet another pit.

No tourists had despoiled this hide-away with beer cans and lolly packets. I was congratulating myself on being its first visitor for several years when the photographer pointed out a little plank path over the marsh to the door. Someone must have been here since 1962.

So to civilization, creeping through a path between the massive walls and the CBC, which is tumbling down to make way for an 18-storey building for the tax men. We scramble up the 20ft slope to St George's Terrace, and have an eyeball to eyeball confrontation with a car as we leap over the crest. The family in the car, which is in the process of parking, stares with wild surmise as we pop up. On goes shoes, socks and coat, tie is straightened, and I revert from jungle explorer to denizen of the footpath, self-consciously trailing a big pickaxe handle.

So ended the adventure. On the way back, on the other side of the Terrace, compressors were furiously hammering down supports for another minor skyscraper. Around the procreant cradle of concrete, yellow scooper-machines scuttled, Italian workmen shouted to each other, piles of timber, wheelbarrows, yellow sand, white sand and cranes cluttered the site. An engineer with a train of younger engineers bustled his way through the confusion. This was how the Chevron Hilton must have looked the day before work stopped.

The ill-starred project began late in 1960, to give Perth a 19-storey hotel for the Commonwealth Games. Work stopped in April 1961, and the hotel's backers Stanhill Consolidated Ltd went broke officially a year later. The State Government now owns the land on which sit $60,000 worth of useless foundations, which may cost about the same amount to get rid of. The land is reserved for future public purposes.

The (Moscow) circus comes to town!

3 February 1968

Belatedly I got down to see the Moscow Circus people last week.

The performers' enclosure was littered with attractive Russian girls in microscopic bikinis, soaking up the sun. With circus interpreter Vladimir Zharikov (25) in tow, we called on the silver caravan of director Joseph Dubinsky, grey-haired and with the characteristic Russian row of gold teeth.

He assumed I was avid for statistics and before I could call a halt, I was informed of Russia's 100 circuses, 9,000 performers, 12 million spectators, tours of 20 countries and 50 new circuses to be built by decision of the government, with 50 new hotels for the cast.

"I've noticed a few slips in performances," I said. "Is this normal?"

(I'd seen one of the Bernadsky girls somersault into the air, not get caught and land on her chin. On Thursday, Nikolay Goncharov aged 15 who is bounced high into the air off a see-saw, failed to land on his chair-on-stilts).

The director said he didn't expect perfection. Sometimes electronic robots made mistakes - could more be expected of humans who were so complex? An opera singer who got out of condition could sing less loudly and with less emotion. But circus artists could not slow down as that could involve someone's life.

"What's the mortality rate?"

"There occur some casualties. Artists are good at surviving. Irina, from the Sputnik trapeze act, was performing in Tbilisi, Georgia several years ago and fell. She broke every bone. Doctors put every bone together but she was not allowed to move an inch for months. She took a special course of medical exercises and got better."

The director used to be an actor but broke his left leg and had to go into administrative work.

Strongman Vyachslev Anochin mentioned that another strongman had been killed when one of his heavy juggling balls hit him on the forehead rather than the neck.

The clown Andrei Nikolayev's arrival from shopping ended the morbidity. He said most people thought a clown was crazy all the time, though he did his best not to look like a clown when he was off-duty. He had a request from a powerful source, namely his wife, not to be so funny. He wanted to get his wife into his act, but would have to wait until she was older and less pretty.

"What's your theory of humour?" I asked. "Is it that pain gives pleasure to others?"

"That is so in overseas circuses. They have a point of view that the more a clown is beaten, the funnier it is. I don't agree. In my act, I beat, I am not beaten."

His tactics were to concentrate on the sourpusses in the audience; the others would laugh anyway. The people who laughed easily did not interest him.

One of the basic features of humour was the unexpected. Most people scratched their right ear with their right hand. He would bring his left hand round his back to do it. He would dust off a chair and sit somewhere else, or walk away from a balloon to aim at it, instead of towards it.

"Part of the soul of each clown is the soul of a child. I still learn from children, like the little girl I saw on the Black Sea, fighting with a plastic crocodile. May I meet only plastic crocodiles in my bath!"

Inevitably, we were drawn to the air-conditioned lair of Ivan Ruban, the animal trainer. Small, mild and wearing a clerkish pair of rimless spectacles, he was exclaiming at the beauty of new hardboard floors just installed in the cages.

He gave his lion, Leo, a caress through the bars, crooning something at it.

His personality guide to his wild beasts was:

Lion: Dignified but as eager for smooching as any cat.

Tiger: Not as strong but could probably outfox a lion in a fight.

Black panther: Temperamental, stubborn and slow to train.

Snow leopard: Reacts immediately if it dislikes something.

Sumatran tiger: Unstable, as likely to bite his hand as lick it.

Brown bears: Deceitful, capable of feigning friendliness in order to attack you. The biggest, the Siberian bear, has a head the size of a 44-gallon drum but it's so well trained that it carries Ivan's whip around for him. (Ivan's whip is more to impress the audience than the bears).

Polar bears: Jealous. It could be fatal to give one of the pair just one lump of sugar extra.

We have entrepreneur Michael Edgley 24, to thank for this 16-week Australian circus tour. He went through half a dozen circuses in Russia picking out their best acts for an ensemble. He's hoping for a million ticket sales to cover costs and make a profit.

The logistics alone are startling. The circus travels via 15 semi-trailers hauling, among other things, the (claimed) world's biggest tent of one-acre extent. Erected, it's green on top with red flags flying from four giant mastheads. The sides are red and blue.

This tent involves 4.5 tons of canvas, 2.5 miles of rope and (claimed) ability to withstand gales of 180mph. Now THAT'S a big top.

I can't let the clown stories pass without adding today the unfunny story of two Moscow clowns Bim and Bom at a performance in 1918. They were prone to making outrageous jokes like Bom toting portraits of Trotsky and Lenin, and Bim asking what he planned to do. "I'll hang one and put the other against the wall," Bom says. Whatever joke they made at this performance, some Cheka (Party police) present weren't amused and climbed on stage to arrest Bom.

People tittered, thinking it was part of the act. But when Bom fled, the Chekhists began firing their Browning pistols into the air, panicking the audience. Bom hid in the stables behind. Next day they were both interrogated, still in costumes including Bim with a giant chrysanthemum in the buttonhole of his tuxedo. Luckily, they survived their mistake.

The dangerous nature of clowning in Stalin's time is suggested by this joke: Stalin attends the premiere of a Soviet comedy movie. He laughs and grins throughout the film, but after it ends he says, "Well, I liked the comedy. But that clown had a moustache just like mine. Shoot him." Everyone is speechless, until someone sheepishly suggests, "Comrade Stalin, maybe the actor shaves off his moustache?" Stalin replies, "Good idea! First shave, then shoot!

A dazzling night at the circus

22 January 1968

Perth audiences can see the circus as an art as well as an entertainment at the Moscow Circus, which opened at the Esplanade last night.

The performers, with their grace, dignity and skill, create a warmly sympathetic atmosphere. Instead of normal applause, people were clapping in unison.

Ivan Ruban and his animals was a case of 'You watch the left of the cage, I'll watch the right'.

His bears made the big Ruban seem like a child in the company of adults. The act began with a polar bear climbing into the wire dome, up a swaying ladder and into its place. The second polar bear, with seal-like undulating neck, baulked and had to be hustled through.

There followed a wildcat as big as a kelpie dog, a snarling black puma, a tiger treading the ladder gingerly, two brown bears and a last, even-bigger bear.

A concentrated animal smell drifted through the vast tent as Ruban put his head in the lion's mouth, rode the bears, broke up fights and rescued the nervous wildcat.

The tension was lightened by the dainty appearance of the bears on their hind legs carrying things round for the trainer.

There was only one clown but he was a master. He was continually in strife with the ringmaster and did not force the slapstick. His big moment was when he hopped into his bathtub in the arena and found an alligator in it. His ensuing struggles might have come straight from a Tarzan film.

The performers made everything look easy, whether it was catching thrown plates till they were arm-high, catapulting four men high from a see-saw, standing on the wobbliest of wobble-boards, or merely demonstrating a rubber backbone.

One pair of musicians found innumerable instruments on their bicycle, starting with the pump on which they played folk tunes, and finishing with the carrier, which became a xylophone. The three chimpanzees played their jazz with authentic verve.

This is a Sputnik of a circus, a floodlit extravaganza that leaves you feeling a little dazed.

A damp look at bus stops

May 1967

In the fuss about preservation of the Barracks and nature reserves and so on, no-one seems to have spared a thought for our city's historic bus stops.

A bus stop built in the grand style at the corner of Stirling-highway and Broadway has just been demolished and replaced by an angular steel windbreak.

The old shed had a single disadvantage: you couldn't see the bus coming because there were no windows in the sides. Many times I have been tumbled from reverie by a bus thundering past the shed.

The old bus stop had been built, not assembled. Carpenters had whistled as they hammered on the weatherboards. Tilers had strode the rafters with stacks of tiles on their shoulders. Plumbers had soldered up gutters and downpipes. The new style comes in about three pieces.

I did some tests in a big storm on Monday, and found that the dry stops are the old ones. In the green and yellow concrete models in the Belmont area, the only way I could keep dry was to stand on the seat, which itself was wet from end to end.

A slot between the two slab sides and the roof lets rain in from the north and south; the eaves were not big enough to keep out eastern and western spray. The looking-out problem had been solved ingeniously by cutting portholes in the sides, but the holes let in wind and rain. There must be a better idea.

An advertising company supplies these shelters free to grateful local authorities. The councils let the rain and advertisements in together.

Our most unpopular models are those in St George's Terrace. They are designed to keep out the rain from one side only. They face in different directions all the way from the Causeway to William Street, as though the weather has a different pattern at each block. Elaborate glassed areas have been incorporated in the long side, but as often as not, they face away from the oncoming bus.

Those outside Council House give at most 25% protection, and people under them keep their umbrellas up.

The Perth City Council has rounded up its old park benches - the ton and half sort - painted them in white, red, blue, red and white stripes (some had white, blue, white and green) and installed them under the shelters. They were too wet to sit on.

Bus stops are not subject to the laws of demand. In outer suburbs exist gargantuan specimens capable of holding a football crowd; outside the Government Offices on the hill there isn't one, and people make 100-yard dashes to the bus from the ground-floor promenade.

In Dalkeith I found one with eight sides, two windows and electric light, with bench seating all round for 30 people. It could still be used for conventions. Someone had built another bus stop no more than ten feet away. If the big one ever fills up, people can spill across to the new concrete one. Dalkeith takes no chances.

It is worth a special trip any day to see our Taj Mahal of bus stops at the Thomas Street and Rokeby Road intersection. The biggest in the metropolitan area, it is 30ft long and made in brick, asbestos [!] and timber panelling. Carved rafters support the eaves rather like the figurehead below the bowsprit of a galleon. On the south side it has an annexe, but it was shut and I couldn't get in. Behind it a Ladies and Gents is attached, smelly but in working order. The whole building is called AMWAYS; the name is painted on one wall. AMWAYS was our summit of bus stop development. We have come a long way downhill since.

For a smooth shave, try a 6lb axe

September 1964

"I'm a bit nervous, my hand is shaking," said axeman Tom Brittain (26), of Manjimup, holding his axe in one hand and my chin in the other. He had claimed his 6lb. axe was sharp enough to shave me with, and I did not believe him.

Earlier, Ray Curtis, a Belmont van driver, had obliged by shaving my arm with a fresh-honed axe, and my calf with an axe he had just used to chop through a 12-inch jarrah log. (He came second in the heat).

But he did not care to try shaving my jaw and the task fell to Tom. He spent half an hour whetting and wiping his blade. He rested my head against a wooden beam in the back of the change shed and with four chops, off went my whiskers and the top layer of skin. Then he got rid of some whiskers around my bottom lip that had defeated my own razor that morning.

"Thanks," I said.

"No trouble," he replied.

Log-chopping is a uniquely Australian sport that has waned since power saws replaced hand-axes in timber-cutting. But the Henry Lawson flavour of the bush still lingers at log-chop meetings, even though choppers nowadays may drive bulldozers or even taxis.

"We don't chop for the money but for the spirit," Tom said. "Being of bush origin, I have learnt to love the simple things in life."

How to succeed? - Eat well, not too much starch. Live clean, go to church and don't be afraid of hard work.

About a dozen choppers sat on benches in the change sheds yesterday between heats, each casually honing his blades, yarning and reminiscing.

All the married men swore their wives chopped the firewood, except one who said his wife used to, but now his son did.

They could not chop that hardwood themselves, because they

might damage their axes, they said.

Accidents in contests are rare. One chopper at Donnybrook was standing on the log and sliced into his heel with his first stroke. Undaunted he chopped the log right through and then chopped an upright log through to finish his score.

A doctor sewed up his heel with 13 stitches, and he went back and finished the day's competition.

At Collie last year, Bob Dodd cut the toe of his sandshoe off but found he had only grazed his big toe. He had unconsciously wriggled his toes back as the axe fell.

Another time (this yarn caused some argument) a chopper was leaning over his block and his glass eye fell out. It fell in the cleft of his block and his oncoming stroke smashed it to bits.

Chopping had been taken up in the US but was not up to Australian standards, they said.

The gun US axeman, Dave Gear, flies to the Sydney Royal Show each year to compete, and local axemen such as Bobby Reynolds (27), a forestry worker, beat him there.

With 12in blocks being severed in 35 seconds or so, a single mishit will cost a man a place. The best men are put on handicaps but can win by faultless technique as well as power.

A novelty in Perth, these displays are a big drawcard at country shows during the year. Prize money ranges up to £50 and many axemen compete at every show.

The latest thing now is power-saw competitions. Men cut 25-inch logs up, down and sideways, with accuracy to a quarter of an inch. But the axemen, patiently honing their axes between their knees, were not enthusiastic about this development.

Tiger Snakes: handle with care

5 March 1968

I didn't care if handling was good for baby tiger snakes - I was discouraged by the sight of 28 of them in a mass in a tray, writhing their black tails and intermittently flashing their soft, green-golden underbellies. "Don't worry, don't worry," chorused Arthur Softly and Ted Cockett, who look after the snakes at the Royal Perth Hospital's animal house and keep them in good fettle for Professor N. Stanley's research work.

If they were handled a lot now they would be tractable under handling when they grew to full size, they said, assuring me that the fangs were probably too small to puncture my skin. The snakes had not tried to bite anyone yet, only a pair of forceps "which they struck at again and again".

Not wholly convinced by these sanguine arguments, I held out my palm gingerly and Arthur dropped into it a ten-inch tiger snake as thick as a pencil. It immediately headed for my finger-ends, its silky smooth motion setting my skin tingling. Before I knew what it was up to, it was over my fingertips and half dangling from the underside of my hand. "He needs more support," said Mr Cockett, plucking it away and returning it to one of three bundles of snakes in the tray. Picking one up by the neck was even more harrowing. With violence surprising in one so young, it lashed with its tail, got a purchase and tried to coil around my finger while I flapped my hand to shake it off.

No parents could be prouder of their babes than the two men were of their litter of snakes. Birth weights (taken by weighing them wholesale and dividing by 28) were chalked on the concrete wall, the charts showing how the snakes started life last month at 6.5 grams average, thinned down to 6.1 grams three days later, and fattened on a diet of live frogs, increased to 6.6 grams this week.

The attendants were grateful towards the public who brought in the live frogs. Frogs and news of frog-ponds showered on the animal house by mail, by phone and by small boy. They have enough for the time being.

The snakes have been too well fed even to bother one nervous sand frog since it was put in the cage a fortnight ago. I discovered it hiding in a corner of the netting and later noticed it squatting on a ridge only three inches from the nearest snake. About 90 frogs have led briefer, and perhaps happier, lives in the animal house.

The two attendants said snakes had to be fed live frogs at first because otherwise they might never learn to feed on freshly killed frogs. And the snakes were destined for important research on viruses which can make humans very sick. Professor Stanley wants to know if the snakes transmit the viruses to humans via mosquitos.

Meanwhile the much more sullen mother tiger snake lay curled in a stout wood-and-mesh cage. How did they get her? A girl who works in the hospital office has a father who many years ago sold milk machinery to a dairy farmer at Waroona, who told him, "If you walk down the irrigation channel and don't see a snake every 20 yards, I'll give you 5 pounds."

Mr Softly heard of this claim a few months ago, went to Waroona, found dairy farmer Tom Phillips-Jones milking a cow, and had his tiger snake in a sack soon afterwards.

Snakes are not inclined to mate in captivity and because this snake transpired to be pregnant, Mr Softly has been making the most of a chance to fill in some of the many blanks in zoologists' knowledge about snake habits.

Twenty-eight brother and sister snakes will be a boon to other research too, because researchers like to keep the heredity of each specimen as constant as possible. A tiger snake from Yalgoo may be quite different to one from the Swanbourne rifle range.

I asked Mr Softly how he came to be head of the animal house. In his Nottingham accent, he described how he left the forces after the war and got a job with a firm breeding rabbits for meat and pelts. They sold pelts for up to one pound until French and Belgian growers began exporting them at 3d each. "That's what you call the bottom dropping out of the market," he said. "But I stayed in the animal house line."

What he and his colleagues have learned about some snake habits is enough to make one blush. If a little tiger snake asks, "Where did I come from, Daddy?" then daddy snake is well advised to stick to the cabbage-leaf version or he will have a lot of explaining to do. Usually he cuts the Gordian knot and eats the curious offspring.

What happens to the snakes after the research? The harmless ones are let loose. The venomous ones' fate is obscure. I suspect they leave the hospital feet first.

Yo-ho-ho and a piece of wreck

22 January 1965

"Noah!" shouted the skipper of the Regina 11, soon after we left Fremantle on the way to see the newly found underwater wreck near Garden Island.

The black fin (Noah is rhyming slang for shark) was whizzing around in tight circles, and I felt sorry for whatever was in the centre. After wangling my way on to the skindiving expedition I now wished I could wangle my way back to shore, to face the lesser hazards of cars and the queues for Festival of Perth tickets. But everyone assured me that sharks were seldom seen near the wreck, and when we got to the spot we all jumped overboard without misgivings.

I felt near naked in my mask, snorkel and bathers. Professional diver Barry Martin not only had a neck-to-foot suit of watertight rubber but also a mask incorporating an underwater telephone. A compressor put-putted on the boat to supply air through a black hose for his underwater labours. The least of the divers had breathing equipment, and spouted lots of steel-grey bubbles that tickled those swimming overhead.

On one side of our boat the Indian Ocean drove its black and green southwest swells towards us. A hundred yards further on, the swells came up against a chain of high reefs and hit with a thud and spurt of foam. This was the route of that English sailing ship about 150 years ago. It was crushed between reef and waves just as a fly gets crushed against a wall by a swatter.

The seabed is broken into plateaus, holes, shelves and caverns. Nearly all of it is covered by a mat of brown flannel seaweed, which itself grows on an under-mat of white and pink gritty growth, and this growth grows on the rock and wreck beneath.

You have to be lynx-eyed to spot the wreck. The pointer to it is one rectangular beam jutting out of the reef - obviously a man-made object. For the rest, you have to scan the hundreds of seaweedy shapes for those with vaguely straight lines and right angles.

A curious woman once asked a Gilt Dragon salvager why he didn't just attach a rope to that wreck and tow it to shore? The answer is that these wrecks are just reefs. Pieces of metal and glass can be wrenched out of them, and an occasional cannon or rudder piece is movable - but there is no ship left.

From my herring's-eye view, the Garden Island wreck was usually obscured by the churning black figures of the skindivers. Finder Ross White lay curled in a cavern, as though back on his lounge-room couch, and he spouted bubbles as he tink-tinked at some iron with a little hammer. Masses of lead on his belt kept him in place.

Barry could usually be found half-in a cave, sifting the sand on the cave floor with gloved hand, and finding all sorts of nails, funny-shaped copper rods and other historic scrap.

Another diver, a Latvian from the Black Octopus Skindiving Club, swam around busily measuring things with a wooden foldout carpenter's rule, which was in a pretty soggy state by the end of the day.

Fat black rockfish and red-lipped morwong sulked among the same caves, apprehensive but too conservative to move to new quarters.

Guardian of one cavern was a little grey stingray. Barry noticed it and told Ross about it in sign language. Ross, misunderstanding, groped around the cavern regardless. How the stingray felt about this was not clear, but anyway, it didn't sting Ross.

Next to the reef is a picturesque island, with jagged 15ft cliffs at the base, a layer of yellow sand and a cap of green scrub. Some seals swam over from it to see what we were up to. They put their heads above the surface and peered at us like friendly old dogs.

Underwater they frisk around like jet-propelled sausages, zooming with wing-like side fins and twiddling their feet/flippers like Charlie Chaplin. Their colour is a black-grey-brown but we were charmed by their soft dark friendly eyes.

Their major vice is showing off, once they get an audience. They do forward somersaults, rolls, twists, power flights, arabesques and vertical take-offs, to the point of being tiresome. We foxed them with our backward somersaults - Ross said he once saw one seal retire a distance to practice them where he thought he could not be seen.

In this mercenary world it was nice to find seals performing for no reward other than a hoot of laughter through a snorkel, and faint underwater handclapping.

As practical jokers, the seals are no more lovable than the human kind. The previous time the Regina called, a seal gave a club member a powerful bump without warning, and the member was too fearful of shark attacks to see the funny side.

The seal is no fool. Handed a fish on a many-pronged spear, he will ease it off the barbs with his flippers - none of this grabbing!

When we set off for home, we had got a little pile of scrap from the wreck. There are many bits and pieces left, but the only way to find them is to pull up the seaweed, and the only way to get everything is to shake the whole reef through a sieve. No-one expects to find any treasure.

Pretty Perth: pity about the "perverts"

8 March 2016

What a nice town my hometown of Perth was in 1968! Optimism in the air as the Pilbara development got under way. Pretty Swan River, friendly tolerant folks. Classy intellectuals at the University of Western Australia.

I mean, Perth was a nice place for heterosexuals. For homosexual males, not so benign. Public or private sodomy earned you a maximum 14 years hard labour plus a whipping. Masturbation with another man, "gross indecency", attracted a milder maximum of only three years hard labour, plus a whipping. Nor was the legal threat an empty one. About 25 convictions had occurred from 1960-68, with three offenders currently doing time.

The Police Minister in 1968 was Jim Craig. He wasn't all that homosexual-tolerant, in fact he told me that personally, "I'd have their b's out!"

Today of course, we celebrate homosexuality (plus LGBTIQs) and from primary school onwards to UWA, the rainbow banner waves. Using Perth 1968 as a case study, it's amazing how social mores have changed in 50 years.

Perth's police style, 1968, was not to go hunting down homosexuals but if someone complained to the Criminal Investigations Bureau (CIB), then detectives had to follow-up and prosecute if evidence went that way.

At the time, Dr E.R. Csillag was senior lecturer in psychiatry at WA University, and he sought to 'cure' homosexuals via aversion therapy. This involved showing his client erotic homosexual pictures and texts followed by an electric shock and then showing an erotic female picture with no shock. "Dr Csillag tried the shock on himself once," I reported, and I quoted him, "I swore like hell!"

A consulting clinical psychologist, Mrs A. Creed, sought to correct "faulty attitudes towards women" through counselling. She told me, "To the homosexual I am the safe but warm mother-figure who cares, and all the sexual deviates I have helped have said that aspect was the most potent factor in their recovery." Good for Mrs Creed!

By now you may be wondering how and why I was getting up close and personal with Perth's homosexual set. You doubtless suppose that reporter Tony Thomas wrote a feature on the topic and my employer *The West Australian* published it. No, no such revelations ever surfaced in that sexually conservative newspaper.

So the back-story is worth telling. I liked writing odd stuff. These pieces would sometimes come back to me with the simple word "No" on the front of it, plus the Editor's initials.

Two miles to the west was WA University, where I was studying part-time. The Arts Faculty had a monthly journal called *The Critic* and I discovered *The Critic* was happy to run, without fee, my rejected pieces from *The West*. (Given that a 12-month sub to *The Critic* was only $1.75, *The Critic's* non-payment for work was understandable).

I was always a bit nervous when my pieces appeared in Crawley's publication, wondering if my paymasters at *The West* would view it as lèse-majesté.

It was investigating homosexuality that got me into big trouble at *The West*. My feature was rejected with fury and sanctions. If I hadn't slipped the piece to *The Critic*, an important slice of Perth life circa 1968 would have gone unrecorded.

To that date, May 1968, I confidently reported there had been no surveys or public analysis of the Perth homosexual community whatsoever. A cone of silence enveloped the topic. The only mentions of homosexuality in *The West* were occasional Magistrate's Court reports of a conviction. In polite company and the press, the topic was unspeakable.

During my high school years (1953-57) at Perth Modern, there was one lad "Geoff " in my year, who showed no fear of girls and had louche habits like removing a false tooth and menacing you with it. Geoff wound up in *The West* as a library assistant so we saw each other often.

In 1962, when I was in hospital with TB, I saw an item in *The West* to the effect that police had raided a party at a suburban house, arrested numbers of men dressed as nuns, and secured sodomy-type convictions. Geoff was among those convicted and hence was named and shamed to the world. I think he was fined. I wondered about this small-town tragedy, and felt I should contact Geoff in a friendly way. But I had no idea how to express my condolences, and never called.

A few years later I acquired a girlfriend "Trish" with a very conventional family that included Trish's older brother "Clive", a lifetime bachelor. Clive had a very close male friend "Ted" but the family tiptoed round the issue and assured each other that, one day, Clive would find Miss Right and settle down. Even though Clive and Ted behaved like a couple, Ted was always dubbed Clive's "best friend".

I felt motivated to lift the cone of silence by doing a solid feature on the topic. I suspected *The West* would disapprove, so I did all the work "off the books" between normal jobs. I thought that when I presented the Editor with my finished article, he would be impressed enough to give it an OK.

My first task was to locate and interview homosexuals ("gay" in those days meant cheerful). Easier said than done. First, I was unworldly and never involved in nightlife, drinking circles and other places where people acquire sophisticated know-how. Second, I could hardly ask a question like, "Are you homosexual? If so, may I interview you?" Might as well ask, "Are you a burglar? Done any jobs lately?"

I wandered around in the evenings keeping an eye out for any two or more men behaving unnaturally with each other, and even accosted groups of men in pubs and asked if they knew any homosexuals for my interview-fodder. No success: indeed looking back I suspect I myself was viewed as a shy homosexual trying to line up a rendezvous.

Finally someone told me about a nightclub involving cross-dressers and libidinous goings-on. I turned up and joined a table of rough-looking males, after explaining to them my reportorial mission. They were non-committal – but made frequent side-trips to the toilet or adjacent lane and discoursed in a coded way about incomprehensible (to me) activities. I departed none-the-wiser.

Word got out around Newspaper House about my project. A few colleagues dropped by, ostensibly to chat but really to try to sniff out what my line was. For all they knew, I could be preparing to "out" them or otherwise draw attention to matters hitherto undisturbed by media scrutiny.

I then did the rounds of some Perth professionals who dealt with homosexuals. They mostly viewed homosexuality as a pathological condition.

Only one of them, WA's Director of Mental Health, Dr A. Ellis, had a view then which has stood the test of time. He told me the law against homosexual acts was medieval and capable of making criminals out of a third of the male population (who according to Kinsey, had a same-sex experience at least once in their lives). The main problem was not the condition but the draconian laws and their potential for blackmailers, he said. A government solicitor opined that Perth would not be ready for any legal change to homosexual laws for ten years to come.

A Law Reform Committee had recently been appointed in Perth but it deliberately ignored the homosexual laws, saying those were for the State government to decide on.

I got an interview with the then Police Minister Craig, a Country Party stalwart, whose views would not be described today as "enlightened".

I wrote in the piece that Police Minister Craig had read some of the recent UK Wolfenden report proposing UK reforms, "but (he) considered the British eagerness to legalise evils like drug-taking, prostitution and homosexuality was largely responsible for the state of morals in Britain today."

The danger with legalising homosexuals was that they could start preying on youths, he said. I wrote, "Basically, he considered homosexuality unnatural. This was on personal grounds, not religious ones. Homosexuals were perverts, he said, and he had no intention of legalising their behaviour."

My punchline went: *"One cabinet minister said the government had an open mind on the laws. Another said bluntly: 'I'd have their [testicles] out!'"*

Feeling pleased with my draft feature, I dropped it in my Feature Editor's in-tray. Next morning I was summoned to the presence of the Editor himself, Griff Richards, who inspected me as if I was a blowfly on his blotter: "We are a family paper and this - [smacking my wad of copy against his desk] - is not what our readers want to read over the breakfast table!"

He followed up with some strictures to the Chief of Staff, Viv Goldsmith, to keep a closer eye on me, to keep me productively occupied and to ensure that no repeat offences of this nature occurred.

I certainly took a risk handing my manuscript to *The Critic* for publication. Luckily no one in Newspaper House was a *Critic* reader.

Perth no longer gaols and whips homosexuals, I'm glad to say. Attitudes have changed in the past 50 years, but I rather wonder what Perth social norms will be 50 years hence.

A clean fight with the washing machine touts
26 February 1968

The bazaars of Singapore are genteel compared with Perth washing-machine shops.

"How much?" I asked, pointing to one with at least 20 press-buttons.

"The normal retail is $550," said the clean-cut young salesman, looking me in the eye.

"I mean the real price," I said patiently.

His tone was a mixture of sincerity, confidence and friendship.

"We won't give you our price yet. Go around to all the other shops, and when they've given their prices, come back to us."

This seemed a good idea. I walked ten yards down Hay Street to the next shop.

The salesman there, middle-aged and fatherly, said: "We won't give you our price yet. Go around to all the other shops, and when they've given their prices, come back to us."

I told the next shop: "If you don't give me a price on that Slurpmatic with Power-Assisted Lint-Cleaner I'll walk out and never come back."

The salesman looked hurt.

"Have you decided you are really going to buy, now?"

"Depends on the price."

"I'm sorry, but I can't give you a price unless you're going to buy right now."

I got sick of walking around and seized a telephone.

"Give me a price on the Slurpmatic!" I shouted into the mouthpiece.

"I'm sorry," said the nice lady in the earpiece. "We can't give you a price on the phone. Come around and see us."

I went around to see them.

"I'm sorry, I can't give you a price on the Slurpmatic, only the manager can do that and he's out at the moment."

I began to feel like the character in a primary-school reader who does the same thing over and over.

I decided on new tactics. I collected all the pamphlets on washing machines that I could, and carted them home in a semi-trailer.

One washer pamphlet claimed its rinsing water came out so clean that a goldfish could live in it, though I had no interest in goldfish's welfare. That washer could also wash a rose without harming the petals. Another brand said it could wash your bridal veil - handy for divorcees. I was puzzled by the raptures over dirty washing water. "Save those precious gallons of sudsy water!" said one. (Perhaps you could bottle it and put it on the mantelpiece).

Some features like the Rinse Dispenser were so advanced that the manufacturers, whom I rang, could not explain them. Other washers claimed marvellous versatility. "Actually irons your permanent press garments," said one.

Illustrations were not helpful. One showed a female spy in raincoat, right hand on her fully semi-automatic washer and her left hand clutching a gun; perhaps seeking revenge on the manufacturer. The bladeless washers sneered at the others, for 'beating your clothes with blades'. The washers with blades found romantic names for them like 'wave-maker agilator'.

Every washer revelled in about six different models, with the differences (not to mention prices) cunningly confused. Several composed their own charts of differences, but could not bring themselves to admit that any of their washers lacked anything. This resulted in plenty of 'yes's' and ticks on their charts, but seldom a 'no' - only an ambiguous blank or a baffling code reference like 'KGB37'.

Finally I compiled a great chart of my own, listing important things I wanted. Then I rang each manufacturer to grill him on the unknown aspects.

Then it was back to the bazaar, this time armed with a wallet-full of money, drawn with some trepidation from my bank. A demonstration? So sorry. You must go to the manufacturer if you're that fussy about spending a miserable $300. The manufacturer was delighted to see me, but said he could only demonstrate with no water in the washing machine. I listened mournfully to the whirr of the solenoids and dry thrashing of the wave-maker agilator, pining for the slosh of those precious gallons of sudsy water.

Back in the shops, I began to hear horrible things about my prospective Slurpmatic. The bearings were weak; it tore your clothes to confetti, even rubbish dumps refused to accept them.

"Do you stock them?"

"No, we are agents for Press-Button Typhoons."

The price would be $270 with a trade-in and $270 without. Members of Knock-knee Sky-Divers Club were entitled to a discount price of $270. For cash, I could have it for $270. I laid siege to all 20 washer shops, and finally got my Slurpmatic for $269.

Thank heavens they don't sell bread that way.

The manufacturers and the retailers, it is now obvious to me, had cartelized the sector to prevent any price competition. Possibly, the manufacturers had even set a minimum retail price of $270. Sales above $270 (such as the $550 I was first quoted) would generate a super-profit to the retailer. In money of 2018, a $270 washing machine would cost $3,300. In Melbourne today, Fisher & Paykel washers sell for $600-1000.

Unionism's odd behaviour

3 June 2013

Around 1961 the WA branch of the Australian Journalists' Association (AJA) was dominated by right-wingers - probably Democratic Labor Party factionistas, although union politics at that time were way above my head. I was dimly aware of bad blood between the leadership and some left-wing rank and file members.

One day at home, Mum took me aside and said, "Do you know that the AJA has had a woman member arrested at the WA Museum where she worked, and taken off to the police station? Just because she hadn't paid her union dues?"

"Really?" I asked. I had already developed a native scepticism about wild stories like this.

"Yes, you can get in touch with her if you like. I think you should expose these union heavies for what they have done. But Annie (the woman – not her real name) doesn't want her case to be publicised because it's all been pretty traumatic for her."

So I rang Annie and we met at the Museum where she worked as a public relations person. She was of a certain age and seemed a bit fragile. She poured out a story of how she had been struggling financially and hadn't paid all her union dues for that reason. The union had got a bit threatening and next thing she knew, two policemen came to the Museum and took her off the police station as a defaulter.

I've forgotten what happened to her at the station, maybe she was formally charged with some offence, fingerprinted, whatever. Maybe she was just advised that the bailiff was now entitled to seize her goods and chattels and sell them to settle the debt. Either way, she did then find the money to pay her union dues.

This was 57 years ago, but even so I didn't think owing money could be cause for arrest - heavens, for that, who would 'scape whipping?' as mad Hamlet suggested.

And even 57 years ago, weren't unions in existence to protect their members rather than have them arrested at their workplace? Mightn't the worker's workplace manager consider such a tainted employee to be a liability and hence sackable? Or only slightly less worse, unpromotable? Might the employee's workmates form views about the oddness or moral turpitude of their fellow-employee, causing him/her to suffer opprobrium, ridicule, or at best pity or Schadenfreude (shameful joy, as the Germans have it)?

Naïve as I was, I still realised that debtors' prisons were or should be obsolete, even in Perth in 1961. On the other hand, police powers in those days often trumped civil liberties. It was then only a mere 17 years since the trial of Max Harris in Adelaide for having published the faked abstract poetry of the fictitious Ern Malley which a detective named Vogelsang ("Birdsong") considered to have immoral and indecent content.

Ern Malley had no friends. Perhaps his lonely existence drew him to write about parks at night, a subject that had Vogelsang fingering his truncheon. 'Apparently someone is shining a torch in the dark,' he said, 'visiting through the park gates. To my mind they were going there for some disapproved motive.' His clue was the symbolic iron birds with rusty beaks. 'The nature of the time they went there and the disapproval of the iron birds, make me say it is immoral. I have found that people who go into parks at night go there for immoral purposes,' Vogelsang told the court. 'My experience as a police officer might under certain circumstances tinge my appreciation of literature.'

(Magistrate Clarke) warned Harris that he displayed 'far too great a fondness for sexual references...'I cannot but regard it as an unhealthy sign even from a literary point of view. Boldness in sexual reference is too often mistaken for brilliance. I think that the defendant should either acquire that art of delicacy in the handling of sexual topics which is so necessary in Literature, or avoid the topic altogether." Harris was fined £5 in lieu of six weeks' imprisonment. Costs of £21/11/– were awarded against him.[9]

As I recall, in the 1930s left-wingers would sometimes be convicted and gaoled with hard labour for use of even such mild words as 'bloody'. Australians of that era through to about 1960 might be

---

[9] Michael Heyward, *The Ern Malley Affair.* Queensland University Press, 1993.

'young and free' but only within certain limits.

My problem, returning to my main theme, was what to do about Annie and her ugly experience, given that Annie didn't want herself identified. I decided to publicise the case within WA Newspapers, which employed maybe half the city's journos and certainly was the base of the AJA leadership.

In the big hall of the building on the south side of St George's Terrace was *The West's* reporters' and sub-editors' territory, a cacophonous scene of desks, typewriters, loud talk and telephones. Around the west side were glass-partitioned offices of executives, and on a wall on the west side was a green-baize union notice board, about 70cm square. This was in pristine condition and was only used for formal notices like changes to award conditions or date and details of the annual union picnic. As I recall, the union might also post there any management responses to union matters.

A corridor ran down the centre of the second floor and on the east side was a mirror-image reporters' hall, this one belonging to the *Daily News*, our sister paper that appeared in the afternoon, and was manned by a more louche set of journos. There they treated the union notice board with no respect and used it for pinning up ribald cartoons, car-for-sale notices and howlers that had got into print, both in the *Daily News* and *The West*. Any howlers involving sexual double entendres were highly prized for display.

I tapped out a note in the form of a signed letter to the union executive, wording it to disguise even the sex of the worker involved, but setting out the facts of the workplace arrest over non-payment of dues. Then I pinned it on the *West's* union noticeboard, and put a second copy in the pigeonhole of the union president, a man in late middle age whom I hardly knew.

I had work to do thereafter but from the corner of my eye I did notice a trickle of journos studying the notice board and a bit of a buzz about it. Strangely, no one came up to me and cross-examined me about the matter. They all knew I was Communist-affiliated and perhaps for that reason they stayed away. But the message was explosive enough, regardless of who threw the grenade.

With a few days everyone knew about the matter but how they viewed it, I knew not. A few *Daily News* lefties saw the affair as very legitimate stick with which to beat the rightist union leadership, and even asked me if I wanted to take part in some procedural coup against the executive. I was clueless about such things and there was no follow up.

After a week, everyone got in their pigeonholes an explanation from the leadership: The woman (they let that slip) had been recalcitrant about her dues. She had been given every opportunity to pay up. She had given undertakings but not upheld them. Sending in the police had been a last resort in this painful affair.

No one came up to me and discussed my complaint and the official union response, even then. It was as if I was radioactive - stand back! Plus the issue itself was incendiary – should our union seek arrest of a member?

The grand finale was that a day or two later I got an official letter in my pigeonhole from the union executive. I had breached union rules by misusing the official union notice board for non-official purposes. There was potentially some financial penalty or other applicable punishment but the executive would waive resort to this sanction. The executive seemed unaware of the desecration of the other union notice board with private material by *Daily News* reprobates, occurring a mere 10 metres away, as the crow flies. Strange times.

Deadline missed by 50 years

10 July 2017

Many journalists keep their scrapbooks of articles for inordinate periods. When cleaning out a cupboard, I found a volume of mine from *The West Australian* in the 1960s, the pages browned with age.

Something unusual fell out, a 'copy sandwich' of a story of 1 July 1967 that never got published. In those days we wrote each sentence on a separate half-page A5, so the subs could trim the story to length by throwing away pages. The stack of pages was called a sandwich.

On the top page was a note from the Chief of Staff, Viv Goldsmith: "Tony Thomas – see me about features and news cover (guideline for the future)."

Notes starting "See me" are seldom preludes to positive feedback. Strangely, the story had traversed the sub-editors' table and even acquired a note to the hot-metal compositors, 'Urgent'. This sub-editor was a clodhopper, turning my choicest bon mots into the English of phone books and railway timetables.

I suspect the chief sub had, in a spasm of caution, referred the sandwich upstairs to the editor, who sent it down to the Chief of Staff with advice to counsel me against levity and disrespect in news reporting.

My aborted story is about a fiery meeting between the semi-rural Armadale-Kelmscott Shire Council and hundreds of its electors. The council had summonsed and fined 500 of them for allegedly neglecting to clear 6ft wide firebreaks around their blocks. They were convicted whether or not the owners had conscientiously reduced other types of fire hazards. As is the way of the world, some council-owned blocks also lacked firebreaks but the council did not see fit to fine itself. The electors activated some clause in the shire's constitution to hold their councillors to account.

To set the scene, you probably know that Perth sits on the coastal plain and 30km to the east, running north-south, are the lightly settled Darling Ranges, rising to 600m. They're not exactly the

Alps. Armadale-Kelmscott is one of the hillside districts. I probably reported this meeting with special avidity because I lived on a half-acre nearby, on Gooseberry Hill.

The sandwich shows signs of poor typewriter hygiene. Each letter 'r' falls half below the line and the 'r's' stem is missing, leaving only a mark like a 'tilde' or curly hyphen. But no-one in Newspaper House ever kicked me about my r's.

A further point, which I've only just discovered, is that the Armadale-Kelmscott councillors included Ivor Birtwhistle, who retired from *The West* in 1957 after a long executive career. I don't know if his presence on the council had any bearing on why my story was spiked. My father Pete once told me that Mr BIRTwhistle hated above all things being addressed as "Mr BIRDwhistle". Warned about provoking such fury, one of Dad's fellow cadets compounded the felony by addressing him, once only, as "Mr Whistlebird".

Will I ever get round to the story? Here goes:

Next Best Thing to the Stake

We don't burn unpopular bureaucrats [subbed to read "we don't burn people"] at the stake any more, but an electors' meeting is the next best thing.

The smell of roasting councillors wafted through the Armadale Hall as 500 ratepayers asked questions and said things about last month's mass fining of firebreak defaulters.

All the Armadale-Kelmscott councillors attended, sitting in a row before the velvet curtains and red drapes of the antique hall. The only cheerful one was Mrs Julie Bethell, who had been elected after the council's fining sortie.

At 8 p.m. the meeting opened with the force of a wet match. President P. Kargotich announced that the sound-recording crew (who had decorated the fore-stage with teeming lianas of wires) had forgotten their microphones. Someone was speeding back to Perth (20 miles) to get them. The meeting would start when he got back.

This was like lashing the lions before the Roman games. The packed hall rumbled with discontent for 35 minutes. Some young blades started slow hand-clapping.

"Order," shouted the president.

"Time!" counter-shouted an angry woman.

At 8.45 p.m. a runner entered into the cheering hall carrying a box of microphones. The meeting started with a history of the controversy from the president, read fast and level. Then he called for questions and suggestions from the audience.

Here a misunderstanding arose. The shire thought the meeting had been called so that people could make sensible suggestions about how to reduce fire hazards in future. Most of the ratepayers thought the purpose of the meeting was to do the council over. This misunderstanding was never fully resolved.

The microphone fiasco was grist to the mill. Mr Kargotich disclaimed responsibility; Mr Hugh Leslie, of Kelmscott, said the equipment should have been tested long before the meeting started.

"What is wrong is the shire council, and the whole body of it," he said, after giving a different history of the fining. "If you can't lead, then get out and let someone in who can. And if they can't, we will kick them out."

Later, there was some confusion between Mr Kargotich and a redheaded youth from the sound crew about whose turn it was in the audience for a microphone.

"You're an employee of the meeting, not running it," Mr Kargotich said peremptorily.

Mr Chandler, of East Cannington, rose soon after.

"The way you treated that man gives an idea of how you treat employees..." *he began.*

Mr Kargotich (divining that this speaker may not be friendly): "Are you an elector?"

Chandler: "I'm a ratepayer."

Kargotich: "Are you an elector?"

Chandler: "I am not of the district."

Kargotich: "Well, will you sit down"?

Chandler: "I am being fined. Does that give me the right to speak?"

Loud cheering from the hall, and Mr Chandler spoke on.

Things got so hot after a while that Mr Kargotich had to remind a woman speaker that her remarks about a council employee were going on record and she might regret it if she continued (he was referring to the laws of slander).

Near the end of the meeting, the crisis point arrived, with a motion from an impassioned Mrs Mann of Roleystone that the whole council resign. Her family had collected seven summonses, reduced by the council later to one. The motion came unexpectedly, rather like the baby that popped out of Gargamelle's left ear.

[At the time I was doing post-grad English literature at UWA, where I would have picked up this bit of anatomical fancy in Rabelais' 'Gargantua' of 1550. In that pre-Google era, I must have had the book handy].

Mrs Mann first objected to the 'bombastic' manner of the chairman, Mr Kargotich. She thought he was paid by ratepayers and should be nice to his employers. Mr Kargotich said he drew no salary.

"What do the 3 per cents go to then?" she demanded.

Mr Kargotich explained that legally, this money could be spent at the council's discretion, and his shire spent only half of it, and that half was spent on worthy ends.

"I was told that at each council meeting cigarettes were passed around. Is this little enjoyment from the 3 per cents?" she asked meaningly.

Shouts to "Siddown!" came from around the hall.

"I would like to see the whole council resign," she finished.

This took everyone aback, but Mr Kargotich, unruffled, asked if she wished to move a motion. She did.

Mr Carlson, of Roleystone, tried vainly to cancel the motion, arguing that a vote against the council would be dangerous and that a vote for the council would be seized on by the council as evidence of popular support.

"If passed, the motion would be considered by ourselves," Mr Kargotich said. "We make the decision."

After a short speech or two against the motion, it lost by about 450-50.

Our next electors' meeting on 7 July concerns Paul Ritter and the Perth City Council. I advise the council to look to its microphones.

End of sandwich.

I went on to report that Perth council meeting. It sacked its town planner, Mr Ritter, soon afterwards. Ritter gazumped the council by getting elected to it for the next 16 years. He was runner-up as Perth citizen-of-the-year in both 1974 and 1976 but got a three-year stretch in 1986 for a dodgy application for a Commonwealth export grant. Doing time is an occupational hazard for Perth celebrities.

After yet more research the other day I discovered that Mayor Kargotich and I were not best buddies at the time. I quoted him refusing to speak to me on a follow-up about firebreaks, on the ground that "whatever he said would be misreported".

Well, that ends my amble down memory lane. I've just realised: it's the 50th anniversary of when I wrote the firebreak story. Spooky!

Diver versus a White Pointer
22 August 1967

Lee Warner did not know a shark could blink. He found otherwise in the calm glittering sea 500 yards from Jurien Bay's North Head on Saturday (19 August). He had just seen his companion Bob Bartle "like a baby in the shark's mouth". Warner had shot his heavy spear at point blank range into the top of the shark's head, between the eyes and a little back from the ice-cream-cone shaped nose.

He saw the shark rise from below and come at him "like a 12 foot bull". He had no weapon left except a knife he used for cutting lines, no bigger than a pocketknife, which was stuck in his belt.

His empty speargun had a knob at the end for winding the line around. He thrust it at the shark's eye. "The eye was that big," he said, circling his thumb and forefinger but with an inch gap between them. "The shark brought a white membrane down over its eye. I saw that come down. I had never imagined sharks could do that."

His next impression is of the shark circling him at about 8 feet. I asked him how a shark so big could turn so tightly. He said a shark could turn on its tail.

And then he recalls another precise detail. He saw his companion's loaded speargun floating butt-down a foot or two below the surface.

"Bob had told me his gun always sank. I can't understand why it was floating, unless he'd switched guns lately without telling me."

Warner again faced the shark fully armed with that gun. It was a situation he was used to. Once he and his friends shot so many grey nurse sharks that their 14ft boat sank when they loaded them aboard.

He fired and saw the spear, trailing its long cord, fly over the top of the shark's head. The spear completed almost a cat's cradle of lines tangled around the shark in the clouded water. There was the long 250lb line from the spear embedded in its head, with Warner's gun being towed at the other end. There was the dead man's float line, which had a sinker on one end and a float at the other, with a red diver's flag with white diagonal flying above it. There was Warner's float line and now Bartle's gun-line.

The shark slowed down, still trying to swallow Bartle's legs. Suddenly a 4ft bronze whaler shark began making lightning dashes near Warner, seeming no bigger than a minnow compared with the big shark. When he got closer to the shore he could see the red and white flags on the floats bobbing and fluttering as the shark towed them below the surface.

I took a good look at Warner as we talked in the press car near Scarborough. He seemed short though he was 5ft 10in and the expression on his bearded face was mild. He left teaching about two years ago and has been leading an amphibious existence since, voyaging to the Eastern States, prawning at Exmouth Gulf, and hunting the big jewfish and gropers with fanatic zeal.

Bartle and he had paired off on Saturday morning and decided to head for a reef half a mile to sea, over which big waves were beating in a white ridge. They were looking for good territory for the next day's competition with Dandaragan spear fishermen. They wore their black rubber suits, flippers and web belts weighted with blobs of lead. Facemasks, skullcaps and snorkels converted their features to an angular design.

The water deepened to about 25 feet. It was clear enough for them to see the sandy bottom. They zigzagged seawards for an hour and a half, disappointed at the lack of fish or even irregularities in the seabed that could harbour jewfish.

All they saw was some banded sweep, which are traditionally fish you pick up on your way home if you have speared nothing better.

At last they came on a big cave, more like a sandy hole in the seabed, about 40ft across with a lot of knobbly ledges. Before they dived to investigate, the more cautious Bartle unhooked his float line from his belt and let it drop to the bottom on its sinker. The risk was that in swimming under ledges, the line could snag on the shelf.

They saw nothing in the cave and surfaced for a breath. Bartle had to make another dive to pick up his float line. Warner swam seawards across the cave. As he did so he saw the blurred form of the great shark streaking under him in the opposite direction, about 8ft below him, heading for Bartle.

[The paras below in italics are added from news reports elsewhere in the paper. My feature had no need to include them].

Warner: "It moved so fast that by the time I looked back, it had Bob in its mouth and was shaking him like a leaf. It bit Bob in half and then rose up at me. I put a spear in the top of its head right where its brain should be but the spear didn't seem to affect the shark. It broke Bob in half and rose up with Bob's legs and flippers sticking out of its mouth. Its teeth stuck out past its nose.

"I tried to belt the spear (from Bartle's gun) *into the shark's eye. But its eye is set close to the top of its head and the spear went over its head. I don't know how I could have missed.*

"It was still circling and I could see that its jaw was much wider than Bartle's body - the jaw must have been two and a half feet wide. I was stuck in this big cloud of blood. I could see Bob was dead.

"The shark was black on top and white on the guts. Its body looked about 5ft thick from top to bottom. "I did not get a good idea of its length - I was battling to see the extremities. I don't remember seeing its tail. "

Warner got to shore but had no way to alert another six spearfishermen in his party at sea along a mile of beach. He drove to Sandy Cape and returned by sea in a crayboat Gay-Jan. "Before we picked them up we headed for the floats. The shark was still tangled in them and our two guns. We could see it above the sandy bottom. I fished out my gun, cut the cord off and made it fast to a stanchion. I wanted to put another spear in the shark. We started to tie a three-quarter inch rope to the spear-line to pull him up but by the time we got it ready the shark somehow straightened the coil of welding rod which held the line to our first spear and it swam off.

"We picked up Bob. He was unmarked above where the shark bit him.

Then we picked the other four fellows up (Two more had come to shore). They were only 200 yards from where we found the shark and did not know what had happened. The shark had swum off in their direction with that spear still in its head. "We took Bob's body to the Moora Police Station. The police told his father about 7pm that night."

The attack has not deterred Warner from further spearfishing. He had not been attacked by sharks since he began diving at the age of 9, though sharks have seized fish from his float, his gun and even his hand.

Bartle however had had a narrow escape from a 9ft bronze whaler shark at Dunsborough three years ago. He was spearfishing with his friend Peter Herman of Innaloo when they became separated. Herman said that the shark brushed past him, travelling at high speed. He looked desperately for Bartle but finding nothing and with the shark looking menacing, he swam to shore. Bartle later appeared further along the beach. The shark had forced Bartle into deeper water and Bartle decided to make a stand where the water was clear. The shark rushed him but each time he warded it off with his heavy spear. He did not want to fire the gun as it was his last resort. The shark tailed him to within 20 feet of the beach. The two men returned next day to try to kill the shark but did not see it.

"The incident un-nerved him for a while," Herman said. "Bob told me: 'if anyone asks me if I'm scared of sharks, I won't shrug my shoulders and say, 'I'm not'."

Herman said spearfishing had been Bartle's whole life. They had been weight lifting for six months this year and wanted to keep training till Christmas to compete in the pairs title in the Australian spearfishing championships.

Note: By 2018 standards Lee Warner's account of mass spearings of grey nurse sharks is rather horrifying. This species is harmless to humans and there was no reason for such wholesale destruction.

THE LIVES OF OTHERS

Toiling inside a drain pipe
18 June 1968

Ambling across Kewdale [a south-east industrial suburb], I discovered a big stormwater pipe newly-laid underneath the railway line. Funnily enough the weeds were not disturbed and trains had been shunting up and down all week.

"How did the pipe get under there?" I asked the foreman.

"We shoved it through the embankment with a jack."

"You don't say. How did you stop the dirt from clogging up the pipe?"

"We had a fellow squatting in the end, and as the dirt came in he shovelled it into a trolley and we pulled the trolley out with a rope."

"Why didn't he suffocate?"

"We gave him an air pipe."

"How did he see what he was doing?"

"We gave him an electric light."

"Didn't he get tired?"

"No, we put a different man in every hour."

Only one thing went wrong. A train went over and its weight squashed the pipe end by about 6 inches. This made the whole pipe travel a bit skew-whiff, and the water supply people are not sure whether the water will run down it all right. They may have to pull some of the pipe out.

The usual way to lay pipes is to dig a big trench and put them in the bottom. You can also dig a big tunnel and slide the pipe through. But to whack a three foot pipe through solid earth with a man (called a 'mucker') frantically bailing out dirt inside didn't seem sporting.

The first such pipe job was at Swanbourne Army Barracks 18 months ago. A pipe had to go under a 30-foot high sandhill that has a bitumen car park on top. They pushed the pipe 200 feet. The man in the pipe got claustrophobia.

They passed him down a transistor radio and the Monkees' pop music and commercials kept him in touch with civilization. The sand was dry because the car park surfacing stopped the rain seeping down, and the sand poured into the pipe.

Then the pipe end could not stand the pressure and began to spread like a stick of celery. There was great relief and rejoicing when the pipe end popped out the other side of the hill.

Next job was under Canning Highway near Rome Road, a 200-foot push that saved having to close the highway down. Later the pipes began nipping under Scarborough Beach Road and Kewdale, and a project will start soon to shove sewerage pipes under The Boulevard, Floreat Park.

The firm's mucker-in-chief is Lew Italiano, 44, small and sturdy with a black bushy moustache. He can shovel three tons of dirt in a morning with a shovel only 2 foot long, all done kneeling or squatting.

Fellow-mucker Leo Fucile, 44, was not in sight but Carlo Lipari, 34, was cheerfully digging wet clay in a big pit, wearing a pink handkerchief beret-fashion. Between them they have 11 children.

They can hear buses and trucks bump-bumping over them when they're under a highway, but they burrow too deep under railway lines to hear trains passing. They get $44 a week. [Modern money: $525].

At first they were supplied with rubber knee protectors but they preferred kneeling without them because wet sand got inside the rubber.

The pipe-pushing scheme offers nice prospects. Someone could push an 8ft tunnel under St George's Terrace to save me waiting at the traffic lights. While they were at it, they could put a pedestrian and power-line tunnel under Blackwall Reach [where the Swan River narrows near Fremantle], except the mucker could get a bit soggy.

A diesel driver's diatribe

27 December 1967

Of pigeons, dogs, cats and people, people are the most stupid, according to the diesel driver I talked to between Fremantle and Midland one day.

Take cats. They like to walk along the railway line at night, because it's easy on their paws. When they see the train headlight they sit down and squint. Our driver dims the beam, blows the horn (a sonorous blare like a ship's siren), whizzes the brake dial around half a turn, and then puts his lights on full again. If the cat still sits there, he repeats the procedure.

"Then they usually step off the line," he said.

Dogs are also fairly sensible. He collected one on a bridge once, but that could not be helped. And pigeons do their best, though life on the tracks is innately hazardous.

But people ... he's already killed one chap who ignored the diesel headlight, the continuous horn, and the crossing signals and light and bells.

On Mondays and Tuesdays car drivers are not so bad, but Wednesdays to Saturdays they like to play chicken. The men drivers do it from bravado, and having nipped over the line, turn and give him the sign of the thumb. Women drive over the line in a daze and jump visibly when the diesel thunders up. They see the diesel driver jotting their car number down for prosecution. Then they either turn a cold shoulder or shake their fist and say insulting things. "Women are very bad," said the driver.

From a selfish point of view, he hates collisions. He kicked the front of the cabin. "Thin plywood," he said. The only metal in front of him was soft eighth inch sheet. Cars hit the diesel well below him, he said, but if he hit a truck he'd get squashed.

His most interesting collision was with a kookaburra. It grabbed a 30in snake near the tracks but couldn't get out of the diesel's way. It hit the front window with a bang and ricocheted towards the central door. He had opened the door inwards to get a breeze and the kookaburra tumbled in. It banged its head on a cupboard, got caught in a slipstream, and shot out the side window, dazed but still airworthy. "It never let go of the snake," said the grateful driver.

At that moment we were leaving Cottesloe Station, and he brought his foot down on the horn lever, producing a loud 'Whowww!" Far in the distance a mother was about to wheel a pram over a crossing. She looked up, stopped, and we clickety-clacked past.

"What's your stopping power like?" I asked.

"Lousy," he said, swinging the vacuum brake full on, since we were entering a station anyway. The diesel came to a leisurely, protracted halt.

"They've switched to plastic brake blocks. They're cheaper but they don't stop us like the cast iron ones did. The cast iron would burn out in a few days, but these last months. They don't squeal either. I stop in seven car lengths. The iron brakes would stop me in three. They tried fibre blocks a few years ago. They were very quick but they damaged the wheels."

I noticed the guard gave two clangs on the bell as we took off from the platform. Reluctantly, the driver explained that once some boys sounded the bell and the train took off and left the guard on the platform. The second bell was then instituted as the 'all clear'.

We seemed to be purring along slowly but the speedo read 40mph. The speed limit is 45. The driver said the railways once put recorders on diesels, but the idea didn't work. "If we work strictly to the rules, the whole system's had it," he said meaningfully.

As a boy he had always wanted to be an engine driver. He broke his father's heart over it. His father wanted him to be a salaried officer.

He still loved the smell of smoke from Collie coal. But diesel fumes were horrible, stinking and repulsive. It was much more fun driving steam trains. They had a big wheel and all the time you had to turn it one way or the other to keep the speed up on the least amount of steam. You got plenty of exercise but in the diesel you just sat and did nothing. The only thing that broke the monotony sometimes was when drunks thought his cabin was the lavatory.

Our views outside were mostly depressing though several stations were oases of lawns, flowers and trees. The railways department has given several stretches an acne of tinpot factories. The worst example of leasing railway land to industry was just east of Subiaco where neat gardens gave way to factory sheds and piles of rubble and junk. To make it worse, the eyesore bordered Subiaco Oval and a public park.

Our joint idea is that the railways takes all the money it gets from leasing land to factories and advertisers and spends it on planting trees by the lines. The flame trees at Daglish station and a willow in a drain near Success Hill show how trees can transform the scene.

"It's amazing how things can grow even between the rails," the driver said. "I remember a tomato plant that thrived there. The diesels used to water it with oil. I've never grown such tomatoes in my own garden."

Proud guardian of the dump

January 1968

The old man standing in the heat and dust at the east end of the Causeway wore a soft white hat with a handkerchief pinned behind, legionnaire-fashion.

This was Bill, keeper of the industrial dump; scourge of scavengers; master of repartee; and a loyal servant of the Perth City Council.

Like the fellow who flags in 727s at Perth Airport, he directs hundreds of trucks on the tipping face with pinpoint precision. Let any lazy driver try dumping near the entry and Bill will be after him.

Seven tons of old bricks in the wrong spot make him cross, but let a utility loaded with rotten vegetables approach, and his wrath is Homeric.

Rotten vegetables are not for him; they must go to the other rubbish dump further down the river. He takes only things like rubble, sand and old timber.

"A fellow from a fruit shop comes and shoves bags of veggies off his truck," he said. "After an argument he loaded them back but when I returned to my shed after I'd knocked off, I found he'd dumped rotten spuds all around it. But he slipped up. He'd left some old envelopes in the muck, so I was able to phone his address to the health inspector. The next morning there wasn't a potato near the shed."

His shed had arrived on a big truck, but it almost fell apart when it hit the ground. First, Bill put a nice pipe in it to make a sunshade stand for his car instead of having to seal all the car windows with brown paper. By next day, scroungers had taken the pipe. Then he got a big brass lock from the council, and put inside the shed his shovel, pick and towrope that he used for helping bogged trucks. Next morning he found the lock hacksawed through and the shed empty. Now he just uses it as a lunch shed.

He watches seagulls and blowflies to track down forbidden foodstuffs in his dusty domain. Like vultures on television about the

Serengeti, the seagulls circle over vegetable peelings and fish heads. Once they led him to two reeking sacks. In one he found a drowned cat and four kittens; in the other, a kangaroo.

"Do you get many scroungers?" I asked.

"Don't look but that's one behind you."

I stole a glance behind, and saw a new-looking green truck. The driver, it turned out, would wait all afternoon watching the trucks that arrived, and sneaking over to poke at the rubbish when Bill's back was turned. This gave a flying start on the other scroungers. At 4 p.m. one was waiting at the gate for Bill to knock off at 4.30 p.m.

"But what do they get? Those trucks are worth thousands of dollars."

"Bottles, bits of metal, old tyres, scraps of furniture, rags - there's one woman who's a tiger for the rags, even filthy rags I wouldn't put my hand to," he said. "The only worthwhile things I've seen were two transistor radios in a crate – the firm must have overlooked them."

He remembers once some fellows coming down with a bag of cheques. They could not be bothered burning them and let the bulldozer bury them instead. Next day the bulldozers happened to skim the dirt off. For months, banks were plagued with people trying to cash the cheques.

We mooched across to a great heap of debris. "Someone would try these records," Bill said, pointing to half a dozen 78s, badly scratched. The paint tins would go off – florists bought them for flowerpots. Some stiff kangaroo hides – he didn't know about them. But there was a gasket; someone would strip the copper off the back and sell it. They would take that iron bedstead home and put it in the back yard. They loved old carpets.

Bill's main diversion used to be chasing rats and mice with a piece of pipe and flattening them. When he took over the dump after a spell in the Hollywood Hospital [largely used by veterans] they were everywhere but he has killed only one since Christmas.

He got the bulldozer to bury the rubbish quickly so the scroungers would not spread it around. The bulldozing converted bad land to good land.

"Every night when I go to bed I estimate how much ground I've recovered in the day," he said. "In 50 years I will say, 'I reclaimed that land, that is my pride."

Bill said he also took pride in keeping trucks out of bogs. He knew precisely where a multi-wheel, a dual wheel and a light truck could go safely.

"Do you like working with rubbish every day?"

"It's like everything else, you get used to it. If things stay nice and tidy, good, but if the place gets out of hand I go crook, even to the bosses. This tip is my baby. It was just black mud, once."

Bootmaker, make my boot!

9 February 1968

"Buon giorno, signora," said the Fitzgerald Street bootmaker.

"Buon giorno," said the woman and her mother simultaneously.

The mother passed over a pair of green plastic shoes, showing how the uppers had come away from the downers.

The conversation included laughter, hand circling and angry motions towards east Hay Street. Once, they snatched the shoes back, but only temporarily.

"What was all that about?" I asked, when peace (except for traffic noises) re-descended on the little shop.

"On Saturday they bought the shoes in town. They pay three, four dollars. Now the shoes have come unstuck. They say, 'If it costs too much to fix them, we will chuck them away and buy another pair.' I must charge them only 75c."

The shop, like many other suburban bootmakers, had an air of mild poverty. About the size of a washhouse, it contained the family vehicle (a girl's bike), a be-splintered work bench heaped with old shoes and tins of tacks, a green cupboard with hinges improvised from leather scraps, and a counter with posters showing beautiful teenagers painting their shoes with shoe-paint. An antique machine held a man's shoe threateningly in its iron paw, as if longing to thump it on the counter-top.

Around the walls, the bootmaker had stuck up nine pictures from calendars – two with sun-tanned people drinking a well-known beverage, one of the Queen, four pin-up girls – and two cows, looking apprehensive about their hides.

"One calendar for each year I have been in business," said the shoemaker, curly-headed and blue-jowelled.

"What is your favourite?" I asked.

"That one." (Pointing to a pin-up). "She's a good girl."

"A bad girl, you mean."

"She is good for the young people who come in the shop to look at. I am too old."

If he were younger he would be a bricklayer or a carpenter. Anything but a bootmaker. But at 45 you didn't feel like 25 or 30. He had already worked in a shoe factory. The factory boss said, 'Do this! Do that!' He didn't like it. One time, he started stitching a new shoe and the leather was bad down one side. He told the boss: "See this, in two weeks the shoe will be broken."

"That's good," said the boss. "The customer will buy another pair next month. That's good for me, good for you. Otherwise, you'd get the sack."

That was why he kept on now with the shop. Many people from Europe came in to pick up their old shoes he had fixed, and they would say, "Those could not be mine; mine were just rubbish before, now they are beautiful!"

He showed me a list of 50 bootmakers in the bookmakers' federation. About eight had been crossed out in the past year. Shoes can be bought so cheaply that people throw them away instead of getting them repaired. Nor do bootmakers make boots – it doesn't pay.

Australia was not a shoe country, he said. In Europe, the cold weather was nine months and shoes had to be stout. Here winter was short and everyone wore thongs and scuffs.

Do-it-yourself shoe repairs have also cut into his trade. Any red-blooded male will have a go at sticking on those rubber soleplates, though in my experience the honey-like glue produces nothing but tar-baby situations. Once stuck, according to the bootmaker, the rubber soles create a shoe ailment known as the pong syndrome.

"Leather soles are healthier," he said. "Your feet don't get so hot and don't stink."

Did he charge extra for fixing smelly shoes? - He'd like to. Some were very bad; he even had to put special powder in them. He couldn't refuse to take them.

In the summer he made less than the basic wage, in winter more. But overall he made little more than the basic wage.

He was thankful for the pile of army boots under his bench. Army surplus dealers bought used boots in bulk and sent him some to fix. This gave him something to do in the summer, when he had only 10 or 15 customers a day.

While we talked, he started on a couple of toe-jobs. One was an ultra-pointed shoe looking a bit jagged at the end, the other a child's shoe with fractures and lacerations. (From kicking things, he said).

He patched the small shoe roughly with leather scraps and put the edges to the grinder, which gave a plaintive howl and made a branding-time smell of hot leather. He passed the job through his squeezer, his stitcher, his stretcher and finally his polisher, and brought up a glowing tan in a few seconds.

His boy Michael had just got his junior certificate. Maybe he would try for university to become an engineer. Australia was a good country for the rich people, he said, giving my shoes a farewell and free-of-charge polish on his polisher. It was not so good for the labourer who was getting old.

Six goggles and the pit's banned for sheilas
18 January 1968

The men who ride the motorbikes at the Claremont Speedway are practically unkissable. Their helmets come over their ears; they wear six pairs of goggles, one on top of the other; and a stiff leather facemask that goes past their chin down to their leather collar. Furthermore, the pit enclosure, reeking with fuel-alcohol fumes and shrieking with revving motors, is out of bounds to wives and girlfriends.

I noticed a lass gesturing at the gate. A rider handed his bike to his mechanic and clumped gate-wards, wearing one steel shoe (for skidding on) and one leather boot. He leaned over the fence. She took the bottom of his visor and lifted it daintily to plant a kiss on the lips. He hurried back to his bike, hopped on to the toy-sized seat, and his mechanic pushed him down the slope till the engine fired and he disappeared round the track.

Why the six pairs of goggles? Because during the race, mud from the track flies up at his face. As soon as his goggles fog up, he rips the outermost pair down to his chin, leaving him with five clean pairs. When his last pair gets covered with mud, he gives up the race, as the mud could blind him in a second. The spectators sometimes jeer his departure, not knowing what is behind it.

I spoke to one rider, Bob Leisk 32, as he returned, a mud-brown colour, from a race.

"Who does your washing?"

"I wear black underwear, and peg it on the line and squirt it with a hose."

"Does your wife like you racing?"

"I've always ridden. She knew what she was in for."

The bikes all look as though they need a yellow [dangerous condition] sticker, and only a motorcyclist could love them. They have no gears and no brakes, weigh so little you can lift a wheel with three fingers, and tend to somersault backwards when you open the throttle.

"You take the engine up to full revs and drop the clutch," said Bob. "The front wheel goes up in the air, the back wheel spins violently, and you lean right forward to keep it on the ground. In three seconds you're touching 60 mph with the other riders churning around you, and you're preparing to throw it into the first corner."

By 'throw' he was speaking literally.

"You broadside until the back wheel goes past the front wheel. Then you're round."

"Don't you worry about hitting the fence?"

"No, but we're always scraping it with our footrest. See how mine's bent up?"

"What's your occupation? Mechanic?"

"No. Company director."

The speedway has a noise and atmosphere all its own, as nearby residents have noticed. One minute tiny TQ cars are streaking down the straight like fluorescent cockroaches; then the sidecars roar up with pillion riders scrambling back and forth over the back wheel.

Now the track is jammed with a hundred beat-up Holdens and Vanguards, crashing gears, spinning and climbing over one another. The tow-trucks hustle them away, and the speedcars, snarling aristocrats of this Petit Prix, slither through fowlhouse corner and sprint down the straight. Bright reflections course along their bodies from the overhead lights.

All drivers made the following points: That speedway racing is as safe as can be; it is very easy; and it is relaxing after a hard day's work.

The most exotic vehicles are the 'super-modifieds' that carry a short upside-down wing above the cabin to keep the back wheels pressed down on the ground. Driver Alex Cairnduff, 30, invited me inside where I found a steering wheel like one on a bus, and iron rails all around me as though I was in a telephone booth. In the distance in front I could see two big wheels and a fat, dirty motor.

"It's very noisy when you're racing," said Alex. "You only hear your own motor when you're by yourself. You can hear the big blokes coming up on you - like Alfie Barbagallo - he's got a V8. But mostly you just see someone's front wheel appear when you're sliding round a corner; that means he wants you to move over. You've got to watch the fence too. If you hit the fence the front wheels can dig in and you just hang on because you're going over."

Drivers said there was rarely any foul driving. They feel there is more threat from novice drivers who can do unpredictable things when three cars at 60mph are five inches apart.

"Geez that was hard work," were the first words of speedcar driver Geoff Stanton 27, who had just come second.

He was shaking violently, but said that was only because he had a jolting on the rough track. Sweat was running down his face. White-overalled mechanics began washing the dust off his steaming car. His outside front wheel looked unused; he explained that it spent most of its life in the air above the track.

"Do you take long to unwind after a night's driving?"

"I wouldn't know. I just go over and have a beer and a hamburger and a cup of tea and go home to bed," he said.

Dialogue with a computer
29 December 1966

Computers are only machines of course, but it's still a little eerie to watch one leaping into action like the genie of Aladdin's lamp.

I was talking to WA University psychologist Dr John Ross about his research on thought processes, and noticed a small Teletype in the corner of his study.

This is a remote-control box hooked up to the university's massive DEC-PDP6 computer.

You can type questions to it and get the answers typed back at you without leaving your office chair. These consoles are appearing in laboratories and studies over the university campus and it is even possible to work the computer from Sydney.

"What if two people try to use the computer at the same time?" I asked. Dr Ross explained that even the fastest typist creates a tiny pause between one key striking the paper and the next stroke. In this pause the computer gets busy on the other fellow's work. It can work for scores of people simultaneously, like a waiter rushing soup to Table A while Table B makes up its mind about the entrees.

I thought mistakenly that it would be a fearsome operation for Dr Ross to get the computer dancing to his own tune. But he showed me how easy it was.

"Core 3", he typed on the Teletype, meaning, "Give me three memory systems of 3,000 items each."

Computer (in an immediate burst of keys): "Job 3 initialised" (your code name will be Job 3).

Ross: "DTA 3 Ford 1" (find and memorise my program of work, which is coded Ford 1).

The computer paused a second. Over at the physics building, it was spinning through reels of magnetic tape, looking for Dr Ross's how-to-do-it instructions.

Computer: "Job set up (I'm ready to go)."

Dr Ross then got into trouble through a bit of clumsy typing.

"Accep X," he ordered but left off the 't'.

"Syntax error," barked the computer, which won't recognize any word unless it is spelt correctly.

Dr Ross fixed that up and began giving the computer a series of values standing for X.

The computer instantly typed back its solutions to the equation, to eight decimal places. Any one of these problems could take a mathematician hours.

"What does it do if you give it a meaningless instruction?" I asked.

"I'll type X=Y/Z," he said. "I've never told it what X and Y equal."

Computer (triumphantly): "0.16736401."

Dr Ross took a while to work out how the computer had made sense out of nonsense. "It must have looked through my program for Ys and Zs, and not found any. Then it must have gone looking for the last time someone else used Y and Z, and used those values," he said.

"You'd better think of something more far-fetched," I suggested.

He typed, "X equals ZZ/GG."

Computer: "Syntax error."

Dr Ross tried again. "X equals ZZ/GG."

Computer: "Syntax error."

Dr Ross: "X equals Go to Hell."

Computer: "What?"

"What?" is the computer's standard reply to cheek or any other instruction that it can't make sense of. It always gets the last word, and "What?" is rather effective.

If you forget any of the simple rules of computer work you can type "Help" and the computer will give you a sheetful of helpful hints.

Later we met the man behind the computer, Dennis Moore, one of a handful of people in WA who knows in detail how to make it tick. He and his fellow consultants write the language that enables non-specialist users to talk to it. Words typed by researchers are made to work like door-keys, each word opening a different lock that sets different operations going in the computer's insides.

The computer sprawled across the floor in ranks of tall blue cabinets. At one end, reels of magnetic tape twitched nervously back and forth as the computer hunted for programs. Long rows of little orange lights fluttered and pulsed. I thought those lights were just a science-fiction touch but it turned out that each light represented "on" or "off" – a one or zero in the computer's two-unit number system. The figure 111 would represent seven, and 1,000,000,001 would equal 513.

The air was cool and fresh, a convenience meant for the machine rather than its operators.

The reels of magnetic tape are the slowest parts. They will be replaced soon by magnetic disks like big gramophone records. Their surface is made up of microscopic magnets, and the computer detects whether each is coded north-south or south-north. That gives it the equivalent of one or zero – the only numbers it needs to know. These disks will pop in and out like jukebox records.

The big development now is making computers small. Trays of transistors and other electronic components – now as big as cigar boxes – can be replaced by capsules the size of paper clips. The tall cabinets could be shrunk to the size of suitcases and work just as well.

The computer's memory is in a box the size of a grocery carton. It can remember 16,000 tasks, each involving 36 steps. "We're going to double its memory next week," Mr Moore remarked. "We just put in another box."

"How much is a box?" I asked.

"Eighty thousand dollars [today $1,030,000]."

Though a modern computer will outlive its operators, every advance in design makes it obsolete.

"Surely it's still useful," I said.

"So are T-Model Fords," Mr Moore replied. "But if you've got one, you don't drive it to work. There's a glut of second-hand computers around."

"Won't people begin leaning too heavily on computers if it's made easy for them?"

"You don't worry about people leaning too heavily on the motor car," he said. "Computers will get abused. There are always some joy-riders."

Computers may one day be used on the week's shopping. Mrs Smith would dial her order on her console. The master computer would find the right shops, check Mrs Smith's credit standing, and place the order. If her bank balance was a bit low, it could even arrange an overdraft for her. All for a small charge, of course.

"The human memory is about a billion billion times as good as the computer's," Mr Moore said. Even the best computer's memory began to get filled up and clogged after a while. A human in that plight would have to forget how to dance to make room for learning shorthand.

"No-one knows how the human memory works and what systems the brain uses. If someone cracks that, they will make a million," he said.

Note: This article could generate a yawn and a 'So what?' from the reader, but in 1966 it was so amazing it won me a prize from The West Australian as its Feature of the Year. Its prediction that housewives would one day do their week's shopping from home by computer with a bank credit check (forget the sexism for a moment) has come true in spades, though they aren't using "consoles" to a remote "master" computer (whoops, more sexism). The arrival of personal computers was a bridge too far for my interviewees' imagination in 1966.

PDP-6 expert Mr Moore seems to have been fidgeting for an upgrade, which with my hindsight was not surprising as that model was an over-complex clunker generating cascades of electrical faults. Only 23 were sold worldwide (some buyer boobed at UWA). For the record, the machine had a 144 kilobyte memory. My laptop typing this sentence is a squillion times more powerful.

Kicking up heels at the horse hospital

5 January 1968

When I met the vet, he was scouring his backyard, looking for a bit of hoop iron to use in some surgery on a horse's leg.

"Have a look in there," he said to the stable-hand, and pointed to a pile of pickets.

"That's a lot of junk," said the stable-hand.

"Junk's what I'm after," said the vet.

The stable-hand emerged with a circular iron band.

"That's perfect. It's not only iron, it's a hoop."

We all walked over to the horse. "We've got the only horse hospital around," said the vet, climbing into his operating garb, a pair of overalls with one bloody knee.

"Do you have a matron?" I asked.

"No, but we have a triple-certificate sister."

He wasn't joking. She told me later that she'd gone as far as she could with human nursing.

The mare had a gaping cut at the bottom of a hind leg. The vet had put a plaster on it that morning, but the mare had gone berserk subsequently and all that was left of the plaster were some white smears on a stable door.

Near the outdoor theatre rested a trolley with a few instruments - scalpel, snippers, hacksaw, a big pot of ointment and rolls of plaster and gauze bandages. A round table nearby supported some buckets.

The horse arrived reluctantly in the pen, propelled from the tail end. It made occasional whooshing noises – like a jet engine. They manoeuvred it around with soothing murmurs of "C'mon love, up you come, half a pace back now, tch tch tch."

The cut had been caused by barbed wire. The vet bent the splint of hoop iron to match the curve of the horse's ankle, and began wrapping wet plaster above and below the cut.

"We vets have to practice in groups or we'd never get a rest or a day off," he said over his shoulder. "We're even a little intellectual stimulation for each other, heh heh. Would you like to become a vet's assistant? Hold this hoop iron on the leg."

"What if the horse kicks?"

"All horses don't kick all the time. If it starts up, drop everything and go like a hare."

He went to work. The horse was full of antibiotics, he said. He then got a bucket of disinfectant and swabbed industriously.

The former trotter began to fret. It gave an almighty kick.

"Weedup! Wee my lover!"

Then the horse was out of the pen, its leg thumping like a battering ram, and I was sprinting a hundred yards backwards and almost colliding with another horse that had its head out of a stable door.

"Don't let her kick that wall!" shouted the vet, fearful for his plaster. People began swarming like ants around the yard trying to head off the horse.

Kick! Kick! Kick! Clang! The hoof caught the little table and plastic buckets of red slosh flew through the air. Finally, the horse hopped on three legs on to a grass patch and began to graze as if nothing had happened.

"I'd let her potter round there for a while," said the vet.

Over morning coffee, he told me Perth was now pretty well served with vets. Before, people whose dog got sick used to diagnose constipation, mostly, and feed it two tablespoons of castor oil. Now they were likely to get it treated for distemper or flu.

Vets had to know all about six animals - horse, cow, pig, sheep, dog and cat. Of those, the pig's innards were most like ours. With other animals, like budgerigars and white mice, they had to improvise.

With commercial animals like sheep and cows, the question was whether the animal warranted the work. When sheep were down to $4 at Midland, it was hardly worth asking one to say, "Aaah". Cockies usually did nothing unless 20 died, whereupon they took a dead one to him for post-mortem.

The vet said the other value was the sentimental and emotional value people placed on pets. In the dog hospital he had a big black dog that had been hit by a car and crawled on to someone's veranda. The people had brought it in their car, and were going to pay for the operation.

"Animals often take the place of children," he said. "The kids grow up and go away, and Mum gets a cat or a pup. If it dies, it's like a child dying on her."

With three vets working together, they could expect 60 to 70 hours work or on call (the same thing, he said) each week, and a solo vet commonly worked 100 hours.

Many people used vets as a free telephone advice bureau. One woman so exasperated them, always calling, never bringing in the animal, that they sent her a bill for telephone consultation, $1.50 - and she'd never rung since [Today, $20].

The free advice I got was not to kill my pet with kindness - over-feeding and lack of exercise killed dogs just as it killed people. Cat's meat shouldn't be cut up.

If vets' charges seemed dear, it was because they had big overheads - land, $20,000 hospital, staff, and bad debts - and particularly because vets had to stock a chemist's shop of drugs.

My next visit was to the small-animal hospital, featuring among the patients a Siamese kitten that had fallen down and broken its pelvis, an old tom cat with lacerations, exhaustion and malnutrition (during some weeks of *cherchez la femme*); a miniature fox terrier described as an F-B, which means swallowed a foreign body; a kitten with a ruptured navel; a black dog hit by a car, still trembling and glassy-eyed from shock; a poodle with the flu, lying on cushions; and a country dog with an F-B, to wit, a bullet, in the leg.

The vets' house cat, which they described as the best mouser in the world, was recuperating from a caesarean - two of three kittens alive and peeping. They said no vet would last ten minutes unless he liked animals, and remembered that even the mangiest mongrel was a thing of great beauty and charm to its owner. Of their group, vet A had a dog and a cat, vet B had three dogs and two cats, and vet C had a dog, a cat, a galah and two horses.

A bonus for Rover's scalp?

16 June 1967

Country shire representatives talked tough about "knocking off dogs" but were not sure who should pull the trigger.

Even the law dithers about who should shoot them, giving the job jointly to the shire council officer and the local policeman.

Three pastoralists turned up at the shires' executive meeting last week to urge a tougher policy.

Pastoralist Association Secretary N.O. Munns asked if shires would support amendments to give only police the job.

"Dual control means there's a good deal of duck-shoving on who actually destroys the dogs," said pastoralist E.P. Lacey.

The trio complained that dogs were over-running the outback. There were all the dogs abandoned when people left mining towns. Natives accumulated vast retinues of dogs on the reserves. ("They can't bear to kill a pup," said Mr Lacey.)

People let domestic dogs loose and they teamed up with wild dogs. Jekyll and Hyde dogs from the towns killed sheep and came home with innocent expressions.

Mr R. Herbert (Great Eastern Shire) was expressing a great truth when he said, "The trouble is that people get a lovely pup for the kids but it grows up into a big horrible mong."

His local policeman would not shoot dogs because he didn't like doing it.

Pastoralists meanwhile are having a bad time. After the meeting Mr Lacey told how he once lost 300 sheep in three weeks to dogs.

"Did they have dingo blood in them?" I asked.

"It's a wise dog that knows its own father," Mr Lacey said.

Several delegates viewed the pastoralists' proposal with suspicion.

"Pastoralists have shotguns. They should knock the dogs off themselves," said Mr C.P. Daws (Kalgoorlie). "If pastoralists cannot handle them, how can the local authority? Even town dogs take some catching. And we would get as much action from the police as we would from Moses."

Other delegates were sensitive about local authorities losing any powers, even dog-shooting powers. One argued that once the power went to the police, shires could never get it back. Another said the problem would be getting the police to accept the role.

Chairman V. Stephens mentioned that NSW police had the dog-shooting power and shires were trying to get it off them.

Pastoralist Maxwell said dogcatchers would not catch their friends' dogs. And if a country shire officer told people to keep their dogs chained up, people would laugh at him. "But a police officer could afford to antagonise anyone," he said.

One delegate suggested a bonus on dog scalps, to get people interested in dog-shooting.

Eventually the executive decided to let shires think it over and consider a joint deputation to the government.

Kibbles and concrete 9 floors high

6 March 1968

The crane driver swung the kibble of concrete over our heads, and it disgorged a grey lump of concrete on to a tracery of iron bars. We were standing on the 9th floor being built for a ten-storey city hotel.

While this floor was still soggy underfoot, the kibble had already poured its concrete into tall hollow boxes – future columns to support the tenth floor.

When the roof goes on there will be a party for the tradesmen after knock-off time; for the clean-up men, whose shovels play an unending tune on the rubble; for the bricklayers, reputedly the best swearers on the job; for the electricians whose bright orange conduits lighten the uniform greyness; for the scaffold men, walking the planks above trucks the size of matchboxes (from our dizzy height); for the plumbers, the carpenters and the other tireless labourers.

However the 9th floor was no place for daydreaming. There were pieces of iron waiting to trip the unwary. Rough projections were targets for the head. The kibble, an iron basket with flapping jaws, was zooming in like a dive-bomber, and holes gaped in the floor.

A young plumber was welding pipes in a duct while bricklayers were laying bricks four floors above him. A bricklayer stood back with a brick in his hand and slashed at it with his trowel. The unwanted half brick bounced towards the duct and fell in. "Look out below!"

While Italians were heaving and scraping to level the concrete, the foreman electrician was lounging in clean clothes against some scaffolding. "He's not working hard," I said,

"He's watching to make sure they don't cover any of his piping with concrete," my guide explained. "He has to put his wires through the piping later."

"How does he thread them through? They're bent at all angles."

"He's got a snake. It's a piece of spring steel that worms through the piping and drags the wire after it. On the Exmouth job they used to tie the wire to a powder puff, put the powder puff at one end of the pipe, and suck it through with a vacuum cleaner. Another way is to tie the wire to a cork, and squirt it through the pipe with water. But none of these methods works if a small blob of concrete sets in the pipe."

"This is a very happy project," said my escort, who I had found in the senior executives' humpy among the plans and charts. "Jobs are either like this or seething with discontent - mainly when something goes wrong."

The workers did seem contented. There was the scaffold man who used to look after the slate roofs in Scotland, had worked in a steel foundry in Australia and hated it, and now led a life of tranquillity and ease on the outermost scaffolds of the ninth floor.

One of the pleasures of high living was at once apparent - there was hardly a building in sight without young women sunbathing on the roof. If closer study was warranted, a theodolite served as a good telescope.

My guide was envious of the tradesmen. In the middle of the night, he said, he would be wondering about the next day's paperwork, but when a tradesman knocked off he stopped thinking about the job.

There was indeed something of the noble savage in the tradesmen, clambering round their iron jungle with nothing on but black shorts and boots. The boots were the more functional; they were protective.

On the case of Mr X, adulterer
28 June 1968

It was a surprise to discover that the small ageing man in the red cardigan was one of Perth's old-established private investigators.

"How do you get on in your punch-ups?" I asked.

"I leave them to my partner, he's a judo expert," he replied.[10]

His office was the desk-and-two-chairs sort. The contents of one drawer would turn white the hair of a thousand errant husbands and wives. For when it boils down, nearly all of a private investigator's work is finding out for Mrs X where Mr X is (or vice versa) at 1 a.m. and proving it to the satisfaction of our divorce courts.

He said that if a wife came to him complaining that her husband was often out late, his first question was, "Does he play cards?" If not, there was a woman involved.

The private investigator, a former law clerk, nonchalantly pulled out a sheaf of briefs tied with pink ribbons and bows. There was evidence here designed to kill 14 marriages, and the drawer was full of such bundles. Not all would get to court, he said. Some people would find the lawyers' fees too high, others - not many - would return to their repentant spouses. "By the time anyone sees me, their marriage is pretty far on the rocks," he said.

His own fees? He wouldn't say, but said he was making money hand over fist - the only reason he would ever stay in the job. Someone would come to him and explain the position, and he would say, "$x, a tenth now and the rest when the divorce comes through. You can walk out now if you like."

About one client in five walked out, the rest stayed and hoped to get some of the cost back through a court order.

Why did he not like the work? – Long hours. He had to be in the office all day talking over briefs, and up half the night snooping on

---

[10] Crime fiction writer Michael Collins made his detective one-armed so there wouldn't be any fistfights. He sometimes forgot and had his detective folding his hands behind his head [cited by Michael Wilding, *Quadrant* March 2018].

couples. It was no joke to have a husband ring at 12.30 a.m. saying, "Quick! To Innaloo! I know she's with him there!" And then he had to decide whether someone would be waiting for him with a blunt instrument. On each job he might make a friend but he was sure to make an enemy.

He did not carry a gun: adulterers did not carry guns either. But one time an investigator went up to someone's door and the chap inside fired through it and hit him in the thigh.

"OK," I said. "You've gone to the house at Innaloo. Then what?"

"If the house is owned by your client, you can break a window and jump in. I don't like breaking windows; you can get into trouble that way. But I will put the brick into my client's hand.

"The easier way is to knock on the door and say, 'Mrs X, I am an investigator and I have your husband with me.' Then you jump inside and go on: 'We understand you are living with a man. May we come in?' By that time the husband is usually hunting the rooms for evidence."

The spouse nearly always knew that the partner was involved in an affair and with whom. If not, it was a simple matter to follow a husband or boyfriend's car. There was so much traffic on the road that no one would know. At night he was just another pair of headlights. In an empty street he sometimes followed without lights but if hit anyone he could be charged with manslaughter.

What happened if he was asked to investigate a friend? "I'm in a yacht club but members know I'd never act against them. I don't take the case. On the other hand, I don't tell a member that his wife is looking for an investigator."

His other work was mainly to trace missing people, he said. If a mother wanted to find her adult daughter and the daughter did not want to be found, the police would tell the mother, 'Your daughter is alive and well but she doesn't want you to know where she is.' Mother's only hope then was the private investigator.

How does the private investigator find people? This man's method set the skin crawling on the back of my neck. He knows people who work for certain organisations that have huge numbers of people on their files. All it takes is, "Hello Fred, have you got an Anthony Paul Thomas on your records?" The arrangement is highly unofficial.

He said the North-West was a haven for people who wanted to fade away - singly or in pairs. They were 1000 miles or more from the city and got good jobs too.

Another of his jobs was to sneak up on people who wanted damages from the Motor Vehicle Insurance Trust, claiming that since their accident they were unable to stoop, run or ride a horse. He takes movies of them stooping, running and riding horses. "It must be embarrassing for the claimant when the judge sees the films," I said.

"We have a word with his solicitor beforehand," he said. "He knows when he's licked."

His anecdotes, though fascinating, were mostly borderliners. There was the wife in a two-storey block of flats who was sure her husband was having an affair with the girl upstairs. "Better make a point of going out," said the investigator, and then they both kept watch. The husband came out but instead of going up the stairs, he climbed up the drainpipe and swung like Tarzan along the gutter from where he could look through the upper bathroom window. It turned out he did this every time he heard the bathwater gurgling upstairs.

The investigator shone his torch, crying, "What are you doing up there?" The husband, who was wearing a black mask, clattered down the drainpipe with great velocity. "I still love him!" said the wife. He spent some time with a psychiatrist and the couple lived happily ever after.

Another case involved a Perth businessman who kept a mistress in his launch. One night the investigator borrowed one of the old river ferries, the Valhalla, as he recalled, and chuff-chuffed over to where the launch was moored. The famous last words of the businessman were, "It's all right darling. It's only the Valhalla."

Thank heavens, 'No fault' divorces arrived via Labor's Senator Murphy in

1975, seven years after I wrote this piece. The reform probably put the private eye out of business. The official indifference in the 1960s to breaches of privacy is shown by my interviewee's brazen boast that he could access databases (insurers, financiers, police, traffic or social security?) to hunt down addresses and other personal data. I recall no fuss about that claim after my piece was published. Maybe I should have followed up that angle. Today a copper can be fired just for looking up any personal data without having a good lawful reason. Disseminating such information to third parties outside the force would be a criminal matter.

Pouring oil on troubled watches

28 March 1968

If you ever see a watch repairer crying at his bench, it's because someone has been oiling their watch at home. In a watch shop the other day, the watchman showed me how he oiled watches.

He had a blue plastic rod, with a small bent wire stuck in the end. The wire was as hefty as an ant's antenna. He dunked the hair in a bottle of oil the size of a baby's little toe. Then he carried a drop on the end to show me on his thumbnail, where it left a mark smaller than a flyspeck.

So when you squeeze a few drops of sewing machine oil into your watch, remember that this is like pouring a four-gallon drum of sump oil on it.

There were two watch men in the little shop. The father had been fixing watches for 51 years; the son was somewhat younger.

The son's side of the bench was immaculate. He was squinting at watch innards on a sheet of glass, and whenever he put a bit aside, he put it under an upside down liqueur glass with the stem broken off.

"See that dust?" he asked, indicating the motes in a beam of light through the window. "I don't want all that falling into a watch I've just cleaned."

The father had a different system. His side of the bench was covered with a yellow mass of little cogwheels, pins, springs, face glasses and Lilliputian machinery.

"The only fellows with clean benches are those who don't work," he said, though not in his son's hearing. "Also those who've just lost something." He led me to the back of the bench and pulled out two cardboard boxes, each an inch deep in watch innards. "I had a wheel in a pair of tweezers and it shot away somewhere. I collected all that rubbish in the boxes from a square foot of my bench."

I'd often wondered how watch makers know they'd fixed a watch. I thought they kept an eagle eye on the second hand as it went around, but they have a machine.

They put the nearly fixed watch on a little cradle, which is hooked up to one of those sleek Japanese boxes of electronics. The box listens to the tick of the watch and with a loud arrogant tick of its own, puts out a tongue of paper like a bus ticket. On the ticket it stamps rows of short strokes, like iiiiiii. If the watch is two minutes a day slow, the row slopes two paces to the left, and if one minute fast, a pace to the right *iiiiii*. Dead centre means the watch is OK.

A stethoscope also came with the machine. I put it in my ear, and heard a muffled thunder like the ferry pulling out of South Perth jetty. Background noises included a pressure cooker blowing off steam and a far-off pneumatic drill. "Bit of big-end knock, that," said the son after a quick listen, and making a little joke.

He resents people who say: "What! A bill of $5 just for cleaning it?" People thought the shop just ran a vacuum cleaner over a watch or dunked it in soapy water, he said. In fact, they dismantled the watch to the last screw and carried the pile to a bottle of ammonia, acetone and meths. This went on a machine that spun it around. Then the bits went into two rinsing bottles, and finally were spun dry in an oven. Next was oiling and finally, reassembling.

"What about the bits left over?" I asked, and got a cold look.

The watch-fixing trade falls off about now [March]. People stop going in swimming with their waterproof watches, and bronzed teenagers no longer dose their watches through the winding hole with beach sand and sweat.

Waterproof watches, incidentally, are not waterproof unless you get the seals checked twice a year. But shockproof watches are. The pin that spins around turns in a red jewel, with another jewel as backstop. When you drop your watch on the bathroom floor, the two jewels twitch, and this absorbs the shock. Then they flick back where they started from.

Till the Great War, no one wore wrist watches. Men wore pocket watches and women wore them on necklaces and in their belts. People started giving the troops wrist watches as presents, and when the men came home, the women wanted a wrist watch too.

Later, women's watches started shrinking in size until they could hardly be seen. Only a change in fashion saved them from extinction, and now they are penny size and thriving.

Nearly everyone's watch is a present from someone. The watch man fixes watches that should have been melted down years ago, but have been kept for sentimental reasons. The watch father said, "I say to them: 'If your mother gave you a car in 1919, would you still want to ride around in it?'"

Lately the trend had changed, he said. Every time the cruise boat came back from Singapore about 10,000 watches came on the market.

Clocks should not be mentioned to watch repairers. They showed me with some pride a clock for which they had kept the owner waiting for three weeks. They could not explain why they hated clocks so much, but said, "It's like going to an artist and saying, 'I've got a job for you. I'd like you to paint my front fence.'"

"You chaps would make good surgeons," I said. "It's the same thing, getting everything back right and all that."

They shrugged modestly and the father said, "You know, it's a six year apprenticeship for doctors and also for watch repairers."

Note: I dropped in on a posh Swiss-watch shop in Melbourne the other day to see if any really expensive watches in 2018 use electronics rather than intricate spring-wheels. Answer: They're all still mechanical.

Firewatcher 200ft up in a tree

October 1968

WA has a select band of men and women whose work is to sit alone on top of a tower and look at the forests, hills and valleys below. They spot bushfires and because there might be only one on a month, it's a dull job.

Frank Campbell, in charge of fire control in the State forests, said that only a certain sort of person could stick at the job. A cheerful towerman – as they are called – was once interviewed on television.

"How do you fill in the days?" he was asked.

"I read comics," he said, to the consternation of his superiors. A devoted towerman does not feel the need for such distraction. His tower-top cabin, equipped with a map table, a sighting instrument and a chair is world enough for him. There is always the fun of spotting a fire more quickly than his neighbouring towerman 40 miles across the valley.

"But surely in this age you don't need a human for such dreary work?" I asked a table-full of fire control officers who are here for a three-yearly conference. "Can't you invent a fire-detecting machine and put it in the tower instead?"

They said the Russians have television scanners that rotate all day on 200ft poles. One said, "But the cameras can't match a man. Their range is much less and they only see a fire when the smoke is a big black cloud."

Said another: "Infrared heat sensors have a range of only a few miles."

Infrared gear is proving of some use. After an electric storm an aircraft flies to spot any smouldering lightning strikes. Infrared can show the outlines of a fire through smoke, or pinpoint invisible hotspots.

Australian military scientists are said to have developed infrared sensors to detect a difference of only a tenth of a degree Fahrenheit. The aircraft could fly overhead and then tell you that your temperature was 98.3deg instead of normal (98.4). It could spot a rabbit in a field because the rabbit would be warmer than the ground. Sensors could make normal military camouflage futile.

Even without sensors, the 35 people in WA towers can watch the entire forests of the South-West. The only qualification is the ability to shin up 50ft or 200ft to the top, and then patience.

There is a veteran, Albert Calnins, who sits in a tower near Dwellingup daily from November to March. His last real excitement was in 1961 when the tower burnt down not long after he vacated it.

Another two towers were burnt down in the Tasmanian fires last year (1967).

A woman in solitary splendour looks after a tower named Solus Tower north of Dwellingup. Women mind Mowan Tower, near Nannup, and Garven Tower nearby. All are married.

Etiquette dictates that whenever a forest officer and the towerwoman ascend together, he climbs the tower first.

The most famed towerwoman is one who starred in a Disney film called "A Fire Called Jeremiah". She was crowned Miss Montana, being attractive.

The only awkward moment with the fire control people was when I asked which State had the highest tower. Queensland delegates proffered their 130ft steel tower; West Australians capped it with the 200ft Gloucester Tower at Pemberton. Queenslanders claimed a foul because that was a tree with a cabin in the branches, "not a real tower".

Pianos, pots, pans and a lost tea chest

4 January 1968

When those *Whom God Hath Joined* split up, it is often the removal van man who gets caught in the crossfire. A van driver named George went to a house at 1 p.m. the other Saturday, and the woman said, 'that's the stuff, it all must go." As the job progressed, she got rather nervous, saying, "Could you hurry it along? I'm clearing out and my husband will be home soon."

George and his co-worker, who like a quiet life, had the furniture flying out of the house and into the van like an old movie sequence.

Scene 3: The husband arrives.

The foreman of the Perth moving business was telling the tale in a storage shed as big as Council House, and filled with wardrobes, kitchen tables and tea chests.

"Well," he said, "there was a nice old row. 'Give us that bit of rope!' shouts the husband. He grabs her and ties her to a street tree, and then begins carting the stuff back into the house. The neighbours - we call them 'treacle-beakers' – thought it was terrific. I forget how it all ended. The cops arrived, and made him untie her, I think."

The moving people were a happy-go-lucky crowd, though they could muster enough trailers to transport Perth to Ballarat. For my benefit, the manager called the accountant, the accountant called the foreman, the foreman called a few of his cronies and they all told their best stories.

Another woman called a driver out in July for a quote, and then gave him a tearful history of their marital troubles. Out went the van for the furniture. Meanwhile, the husband decided to have a yarn with his wife's father during his lunch-hour.

"The father broke the news that she was off to Queensland. He was incredulous; he'd thought he had a model marriage. 'You'd better go and see,' said the father. He tore home, and we'd just loaded everything on. Then the complications started. She's already paid us from a fat handful of notes. 'It's all going,' we told the chap. 'Like hell!' he said. 'It's all my stuff.' So she, he and us all went off to ring up our lawyers. When we got back, he had discovered where she got that bankroll. She'd asked him the day before for a blank cheque to pay the newsagent. She raided his account for her air fares, and left him $7."

Some of the bust-ups don't have a funny side. The firm had a pile of furniture in storage and a hire-purchase company gave a repossession order on some of it. The manager went to the owner's address to break the news, and found a very young, pregnant mother in a bare house, a two-year-old daughter sniffling around her skirts. She burst into tears, said her husband had walked out on her and she didn't have the money even to pay the storage bill. "I'm a pretty easy case," said the manager. "I told her we'd send the furniture round free next time an empty van was going that way. We'd only be landed with her stuff for a year and then have to auction it." Fly-by-nighters worry the moving people. They run up bills with the butcher, baker, milkman and the hire purchase firms, and then when things get difficult, ring up a van and move somewhere else. They order a different van each time which then joins the creditors. "You'd be surprised who some of them are," said the manager.

Huge spaces under the firm's tin roofs are packed with furniture, some stored since 1940. Often a widow moves in with her mother, and cannot bear to sell the household furniture. "Finally she dies and leaves it to her children and they sell it," he said.

A wealthy woman in Darwin is driving the firm mad over her pile of furniture in storage. Every week or so, she directs that Chair X be auctioned, Stool Y be sent to her nephew and Umbrella Z be burnt. Each mysterious operation she refers to under a code name. 'Nimrod' was one.

Piano removal is an art in itself. When the occupants of a big Mt Lawley home sold out this year, the removal men carted out a grand piano once owned by Queen Victoria, and insured for $20,000, as well as another $35,000 of period furniture pieces. The manager, when he helped to shift his first grand piano, put the strap around his neck instead of his shoulder, with painful results.

In Townsville, removalists were just getting a piano on to a house ramp when a tropical downpour started. They were pounding down the ramp when the leading man, who was fat, crashed through the ramp to his waist and bled profusely while the rest of the team tried to work out what to do with the piano.

Then there was the piano of the crown prosecutor in Melbourne that was to go up flight after flight of terraced lawn. The men, of the bluff, practical sort, whizzed a rope around a tall tree at the top, and swung the piano through the air on their makeshift crane.

The North-West is keeping removalists busy. One of the firm's big trailers lost a wheel between Port Hedland and Broome. The driver couldn't leave the trailer because any vehicle left unguarded up there is instantly stripped by phantoms. The relief trailer got half way, hit a hole and ran the fan into the radiator. A four-wheel-drive vehicle was then sent from Perth with the spare wheel but a Port Hedland stone holed his petrol tank. The wheel travelled the final 230 miles in a taxi.

The trailer driver, bored by the ten day wait, had kept a billy on the boil and was entertaining the occupants of four cars and two trucks when the taxi pulled up. To occupy himself between guests, he had made a catapult from an inner tube and used it to shoot goannas with rocks as they crossed the road.

"Do you ever lose things?" I asked the manager. He paled. He had a whole continent in which to lose things, he said. Once he lost a vicar's tea chest and the vicar said it was full of rare and costly things. There was the heirloom necklace, a rare Bible, an old Madonna... he'd need at least $700 compensation. With much grumbling, the firm paid. Then the chest turned up. "You know what was in it?" the manager said. "Pots and pans."

Films on a rubbish tip
25 October 1967

Once a year a solemn band of film distributors drives out to the Perth rubbish dump. The pyres are lit; the waiting bulldozer's engine throbs. From the back of the utility they feed to the flames all those films that they can no longer sell even to country theatres. In the trade they call them 'stinkers'. Then the bulldozer buries the ashes.

Each film has its death certificate ready: it is signed and witnessed on the spot. These last rites prevent any film falling into the wrong hands and being screened without a rake-off to the distributor.

This is not the only precaution against naughtiness. Every few months another party of distributors heads for the State Library and checks through the country newspapers' film adverts to make sure each film has yielded a payment to the distributor. Offenders are 'dealt with' – I couldn't find out how but it's something to do with the contract.

I found out some other things while talking to distributors the other day (what follows may not be true of every firm).

Where do films disappear after they've been shown in Perth? What causes that mysterious hiatus before they begin appearing in the suburban theatres?

"It's designed to bamboozle you," I was told. "If a person knows that, say, 'The Filthy Five' is going straight from town to Osborne Park, you may prefer to wait for it there. So we give the city theatres a four-week protection period, shoving the film round the countryside instead."

Low men on the totem pole are the hardy citizens of Broome and Kununurra. Films sent up to the northern ports are away six months, so nothing is sent up less than 12 months old already.

There is a lot of haggling and horse-trading between the theatre-owners (exhibitors) and the distributors. "Go on, chuck us an old cartoon," says the exhibitor after browsing among the racks of films stored in the vault in six-sided tin cans. "Go jump on yourself!" replies the distributor.

Fiesta time is when the distributor hires a movie theatre and invites 200 exhibitors, critics and relations to see what's coming up in the next season. However much they enjoy the show, the exhibitors keep a sour face.

"How'd you like it?" asks the distributor.

The only reply he ever gets is "So-so" or "It's worth two bob". As Wally remarked in our back-page comic strip, "How much is it if I hate all of it?"

When it comes to a dud film, distributors put on a bold face and swear it will be a hit. But exhibitors are assiduous readers of trade papers, which let them know which films have been nose-diving in Sydney.

On good films the distributors ask for a percentage of the take; for trash they may charge a flat $X.

Films are scarce because long-run films gum up the works. Distributors can mostly dictate terms. They even have a say on how much exhibitors charge for admission [Note: In 2018 that would be illegal].

Contrary to my expectations, exhibitors have to pay for even the trashiest short. They are not paid to screen it. Many shorts these days are made by advertising firms. Television killed the market for shorts. Perth's two theatres that used to screen only shorts have switched to full-length films.

"Who wants newsreels now?" I asked.

"Every country theatre takes one, and most drive-ins."

What do country audiences like? – Give 'em a Western, you can't go wrong.

Do they like romances? – They can't stand them.

What do people like generally? – Family films like '*Born Free*'.

What don't they like? – Gory films like *The Beast from 1000 Fathoms* and all that. Theatres show those to the blood and guts fans on Sunday nights.

Religious films are unpopular; they've been done to death. The public abhors arty films, except for *The Collector* and *Mondo Cane*.

I also got a neat definition of Westerns. "A Western is a Western, but an Adult Western has a bit of sex in it."

Incidentally I was told WA has more drive-ins than any other State. Perth alone has 13 while Sydney has only half a dozen. I don't know why.

How to do the Coup de Pique

16 April 1968

Perth dance studios dwell on a monthly circular from Britain's high priest of the ballroom, Alex Moore. It keeps them in touch with the variations in the standard dances.

Samba fans will want to know how to do the shadow botafogo; in the paso doble, a dance based on bull fighting, a variation called the *Coup de Pique* has just been introduced. (One studio manager claimed to have invented the Pique in his youth. He told a girl who had just refused to dance with him, 'You're not pretty enough to be a wallflower').

Variations have been added to another old-time dance called the jive. These include the flick into break; the mooch; chugging; and the ending to stop-and-go.

In the cha cha cha (sometimes incorrectly called the cha cha) there is now a fall-over step, easy to learn, and quickstep fans can revel in the fishtail ending with open drag. In detail, the English newsletter resembles a knitting book with instructions like, "RF forward, diag, to wall, outside cross LF behind RF, Lady."

The august circular records that "there are two pop records with vocals that are danceable: *'Gotta Little Girl'* is a good foxtrot."

The studios have been taking hard knocks ever since the stomp came in, followed by a rag tag and bobtail of frugs, shakes, watusis, hitch-hikers and go-go.

His studio would be sunk without the lessons for schools. The adults wanting to learn were usually couples who didn't know how to do the bridal waltz.

He asked one couple, "When are you getting married?"

"Tomorrow," they replied.

"I taught them three turns and a ricochet. They probably wound up in the wedding cake."

Did he still enjoy dancing? He would rather pick up a black snake.

But it was dance or starve.

Things were never better than the era of *"Mack the Knife"* and that song "Leah" that was on the back. Then they started stomping in the boat sheds at Crawley and the crowds moved off to stomp at the old picture theatre at Maylands. His studio started to fade - he would not let stompers wreck his floor, and stompers always attracted the larrikins. Ever since, kids had been wanting more noise and less dancing.

Every film that came out had a dance to go with it. The Zorba dance from Zorba the Greek was just catching on (he demonstrated it perfunctorily, arms held out like an old clothes hoist), there was a *Thoroughly Modern Millie* dance called the *Tap Tap Tapioca*, and a puppet dance and a *March of the Mods* dance that had been invented just to go with new hit parade songs. Now he heard there was a *Bonnie & Clyde* dance in which you pretended to shoot your partner with a sub-machine gun.

Dances weren't things of beauty any more. What was the good of a girl getting a nice frock when she was just going to frug to an amplified racket from a crowd of longhairs who could not play Pride of Erin to save their lives?

Jiving however was now a serious dance in the studios' catalogue. It started in England during the World War, when the Americans used to jitterbug and throw their girls over their shoulders and through their legs. The English developed a more staid version called American Swing, which became jive. All dance lore came from England - even the Japanese dancers had to make pilgrimages there, he said.

The efforts of Perth's seven studios to engineer a comeback to dancing have been hampered by their own lack of unity. They are split into no fewer than three associations.

In the course of the decline, the sex ratio has shifted and males, who used to line the walls in disgruntled throngs, are now in mute demand.

Dancing's other worry is the competition from squash courts, bowling alleys, skating and roller skating, and the Speedway races, which introduce the sexes as quickly as 'May I have this dance?'

Note: This story got me into a lot of personal doo-doo. It happened that our neighbours in Gooseberry Hill were a couple running one of the dance studios, whom I hadn't interviewed. On the evening of the day my article appeared, about 9.30 p.m., my wife was summoned by a pounding on the front door. There stood the dance-woman from next door, utterly enraged by my piece. She gave my wife (I was working night shift in the city) a piece of her mind, and my wife did likewise to me when I got home. I guess the neighbour felt dance studios, her bread and butter, should not be mocked. There followed a witch-hunt in the Perth dance world to identify who had given me these subversive interviews. Sad to say, one dance studio owner was misidentified as my source and given a hard time. One of the real and covert sources was Winnie Wright, a much-loved mature lady in the local dance world. She obviously kept her head below the parapet and escaped censure.

When a teenaged cadet, I was myself enamoured of old-style ballroom dancing. I was assigned to the "night police rounds" in the Fremantle office, and as nothing much ever happened, I spent a lot of the night prancing round the office with dance-recipe book in one hand, trying to learn extra steps in the waltz and quickstep. I got my come-uppance when an old drunk fell off Fremantle wharf and drowned. Predictably I was scooped on that story by the Daily News next afternoon, and got a rocket from my Chief of Staff.

Check the dipstick, and a gallon please

15 January 1968

They aren't 'garages' any more, they're 'service stations', though I haven't noticed any rush to clean my windscreen lately.

"Fair go!" said my garage man. "If you asked us to clean it, we would."

Some women customers liked to come in regularly three times a week for 50c of petrol, he said. Each time, they wanted the tyres checked, the battery water topped up and the dipstick examined.

"Just to keep them happy, we pump up the tyres too hard on Monday, so we can let some air out on Wednesday. They like us to fuss over them."

Normally, garage people's talk contains 50% motor parts. For example:

"Got a needle and seat for an FE [Holden]?"

"Yeh, what else?"

"Sump gasket."

"Want a plunger and spring for an oil pump?"

"Nah, had a new one when it was done up."

I followed the proprietor around as he greased up a car on the hoist, dodging the occasional drips from the sump.

"I don't own this place, I only lease it from the oil companies. They only own about 99% of the garages round here. They can afford to buy the sites. This block would cost $100,000 [today $1.2m] to buy and build on.

"They've got to have marketing channels. What if Brand X petrol didn't grab a few sites round here? Brand Y would get them and X would have nowhere to sell its stuff from."

He thought the companies had put their heads together about new sites, on a "you take this, I'll take the next" basis.

[My interviewee was doubtless correct, exposing another of the myriad of then-legal collusive deals among professed competitors. This deal was at the expense of site sellers].

I said impertinently, "Of course no motorist really cares what brand goes in his tank."

"Look," he said, "a bloke who runs on X runs on X. It wouldn't matter if I dropped my price 25%, he wouldn't switch."

Customers developed a real loyalty. One had shifted from nearby to Wembley but he kept coming out of his way back here for juice.

Did his company ever run its own garages? No, because company staff would not be allowed to give credit, and without credit garages couldn't keep customers. He ran on 50% credit sales. It was murder trying to keep up with the accounting, but he had no choice.

That was how he had survived eight years. Most garages changed hands every 18 months. Blokes could not keep up with the hours - 7 a.m. to 7 p.m. and bookwork every second night. You'd never make your fortune, either; the earnings wouldn't compare with wages and overtime.

His profit on petrol was 10% but he had to hand over about half his profits as rent to the petrol company. If he sold twice as much petrol, the company took twice as much rent. He was paying $160 a month [today $2000].

He was irked by his electricity bill. "The company comes and puts up a dirty big Brand X sign outside. That one's got 20 globes in it. I have to keep it lit from 7 p.m. to 11 p.m. The company says it brings me business. But would you go out and leave 20 lights on at home?"

Was his repair shop more profitable than the petrol? - He couldn't say. He had to pay the mechanic but some jobs weren't worth it. People were always wanting things free - like fitting a fan belt. They wouldn't like to be charged $3.70 if it took his mechanic an hour.

Wouldn't you make it up on the lubes? – Lube work was on the way out. Tune-ups were getting popular instead.

Long oil-change intervals were often costly to the owner, despite what the makers said. Infrequent oil changes helped to burn out the motor. And when the car finally came in for its 36,000-mile grease-up, he might find dozens of things had gone wrong.

"Take automatic brake adjustments. The owner never worries about the brakes. By the time he thinks of them, they're making a lot of noise and they'll cost him plenty."

The key to a profitable garage was a good mechanic. The mechanic had to be able to drive a car around the block and diagnose every noise right: "That's wheel bearings"; "that's universal joint". It was no good guessing and pulling the wrong thing to pieces.

He does good business repairing repairs done by hopeful owners. Those repair-repairs were tricky, he said, as he never knew which parts had been left in the grass or put on back to front.

Modern cars were much harder to fix. You used to be able to fix anything on a car with a spanner and screwdriver.

He viewed cheerfully the trend to faster, more powerful cars. "They're petrol consumption is getting higher every year," he said.

The government lays down strict rules about what garages can sell. Most carry a host of gimcrack lines like plastic aeroplanes and popcorn. Garages are certainly not allowed to sell used cars.

However, I sometimes wondered about those rows of cars in garages' parks, and my confidant was keen to let a visitor have an FC - "for ninety quid".

Piano punch-ups and propaganda
15 November 1968

Piano selling is not as genteel as I thought. Perth has just been invaded by eight makers of famed British pianos in what they describe as a hard-selling visit. By this they mean getting sweet with dealers and agents.

After some research I found that the hard-sell is traditional. In 1878 there was a battle between the representatives of the Steinway and Weber piano firms, fought with unscrewed piano legs in the corridors of a Philadelphia hotel. The Weber firm won on a body count.

It happened like this. Steinways liked to get testimonials from opera stars and put a Steinway in the hotel room of each singer. While the singers were at tea, the Weber men arrived with their own grand and shoved the Steinway out. The rival squads of piano movers met in the lobby.

A similar battle took place at a Cleveland song festival in 1893, when the festival committee and the Board of Education ordered a Chickering & Sons piano and a Knabe piano respectively. The police had to be called to restore the peace, and the local music critic discreetly recorded: "The accompaniments were played on a . . ."

The same year, Chicago piano makers put pressure on the Chicago World Fair committee to exclude Steinways. The committee resolved, "If any Steinway pianos are announced for concerts at the Exhibition grounds, the director-general is authorized to send teams and dump the pianos outside the gates."

The visiting pianist Paderewski sneaked his pet Steinway in labelled 'Hardware' and played on it unmolested, though the Chicago Herald slated him and the conductor for "unscrupulous resistance to reasonable appeals."

The British piano representatives at a Perth hotel were relatively mild. Their hard-sell was limited to stray remarks like "Some American piano firms survive because a lot of Americans are tone deaf." For their archrivals the Japanese, a kind word might even be heard. "Some of their grands are rather good, even if the uprights are not brilliant."

I talked with Mr Douglas E. Brasted, a director of Britain's biggest piano makers. Rhythm players and fussy housewives were a piano's worst enemy, he said. The rhythmist beat time on the loud pedal and for some reason attacked the pedal sideways with his toe. This got everything out of alignment.

The housewife killed the piano with kindness, polishing it every week until its stout timbers were almost polished away. This inspired him to make a plastic piano. Its weight was massive, it sounded plastic and no one would buy it. He recouped his losses by hiring it out and it proved indestructible.

Development of the piano, alas, mostly finished 50 years ago. Before that, development soared to such heights as a combined bed and piano that played when you reclined on it. For another piano-bed made in 1868, the piano stool alone contained a workbox, a looking glass, a writing desk and a small set of drawers.

Mr Brasted's firm has almost perfected an electronic piano designed for apartments and homes where one faction wants to watch television and another wants to practice scales. The player puts on a pair of earphones and hears his own music but no one else does. It is also transportable. When asked to play after dinner you can say, "As a matter of fact I do have my piano with me."

Modern pianos are triumphs of mechanical engineering, their frames supporting up to 30 tons of pressure from the strings. Iron frames have made those loads possible.

The early virtuosos tended to smash up wooden-framed pianos during concertos. This is a contemporary description of Beethoven playing Mozart, by someone turning the pages for him:

But I was mostly occupied in wrenching snapped strings out of the piano, while the hammers stuck among the broken strings. Beethoven insisted on finishing the concerto, so back and forth I leapt, jerking out a string, disentangling a hammer, turning a page, and I worked harder than Beethoven.

I asked Mr Brasted if television was ousting pianos. He said, "Only while people pay their TV sets off. Television's been marvellous propaganda for all sorts of things. Who used to go to watch horse jumping? No one. And now television has created a horse-jumping boom. It's the same with music and pianos."

Few people bought pianos these days for prestige, he said. The only ones were the new rich who went to the furniture shop and said, "Do our house and don't forget the grand pianner."

The piano trade would be wonderful if only everyone would use granny's old piano for kindling. People had the idea that pianos were like violins – the older the better. But even violins deteriorated if they were not lovingly stripped and overhauled. With pianos, labour was so dear that it was mostly cheaper to buy one than overhaul one.

A clanking through the forests

August 1967

Once upon a time when Yarloop near Bunbury was a great industrial centre, Miss May Usher used to scramble aboard a steam machine and sit up on it with her uncle Barry Stephens. About the same time she fell for a strapping young feller, a tree-feller called Norm Smith, who now exercises his 79-year-old biceps on tea and crackers at their cottage in Victoria Park.

The machine, called a whim, was as tall as a double-decker bus and with a brace of logs between the wheels, weighed as much as a DC6 airliner.

Driving the monster was both an art and a science and the Smiths know of only five men who succeeded. They were Harry Stephens Senior, who shipped in the first one, less its wheels, from Victoria; his son Harry, blown up at Bullecourt in 1917; another son Jim, burnt to death in a tent fire about the same time; and George Fish and George Scott, who drove it thereafter till about 1918.

The Stephens dynasty would steam into the bush at dawn, at about 7mph. Pregnant with logs the machine would labour out of the trees at 4mph to drop its burden by the railway line for the trains to collect. Its day's work might be 12 logs, some 50ft long.

The great wheels were 10ft high and bound with 15in wide iron tyres. The back ones were studded with knobs as big as a fist.

The driver steered by steam, worked the winches by steam, and drove it along by steam. His mate would feed firewood into the boiler, rather like stoking up a chip bath-heater.

The whim made its own route through the bush, like an elephant's pad, butting down scrub and small trees as it went. Fellows called swampers went ahead, cutting wood and stacking it by the track for him to collect as he went along. The main problem with the machine was water – it would boil away about 150 gallons on a three-mile trip. When it could, the machine would stop by a creek to refuel.

The logs would be sawn up in Millar's thriving mills at Yarloop.

From here went millions of railway sleepers to South Africa, India and China, where the trains ran on our jarrah for decades. Yarloop beams, 16in thick and as long as a cricket pitch, helped build Belgium's sea walls and were driven into Thames mud to support London docks.

The business went well and the drivers decided, on a whim, on another whim, a more streamlined, or should we say, steamlined version. This second whim was too big for the Midland workshops, where no one was able to forge the 8ft arched axles.

But at Yarloop dwelt a Hercules among blacksmiths who did the job with his steam hammers. Even so the axles still had a tendency to snap when 26 tons of whim hit a rut. I had visions of the wounded machine being horse-freighted city-wards, but Mr Smith pooh-poohed that. He said they just draped their blocks and tackle over a tree, manhandled the machine clear of the ground, unbolted the axle and carted it off to the Yarloop blacksmith.

It took 12 months to make it at Yarloop and it would cost about $20,000 in modern currency [in 2016, $250,000]. But there was big money to be earned in the timber country. Mr Smith was once paid 73 gold sovereigns for a month's work cutting beams and piles from logs – seven times the pay of a mill hand and equal to $200 a week [2016: $2500].

I asked how he managed to spend it all. One way, it appeared, was the annual trip to Melbourne for the Cup, staying till the money ran out about March. The depression ended all that.

Mr Smith had started in the timber industry at 14, earning $3 a week for 56 hours of sleeper cutting and log-hauling. Later he became a champion axe-man. Mrs Smith, over his objections, brought out the gold medal the Prince of Wales gave him in 1920.

Another time General Birdwood of Gallipoli fame visited Pemberton and offered a bottle of champagne for a log-cutting exhibition. Quick as Norm was at cutting the log, his mates were quicker and he returned to find them smiling foolishly around the empty bottle.

Of his alarming number of stories about the Prince of Wales visit, the best concerned one Tom Caldwell, said to be the first Australian soldier into the Hindenburg line. The Prince used to visit them in the trenches and once came across the men playing two-up.

"Mind if I bite you for ten bob?" asked Tom the opportunist.

On the Pemberton visit Tom was one of those standing by ready to fell a tree for the prince.

"Do you remember me, Prince?" he asked. "I borrowed ten bob off you at Ypres."

"I think I do," said the Prince.

"Well, I'm not going to bite you today," said Tom.

I published other detail about the whims a month earlier (20/7/1967). Two sons of founder Harry Stephens went to war, Harry Stephens Jnr was killed and only one came back. He was so unhappy that he gave up his business and left the steam machine standing by the railway between Cookernup and Hoffman's Mill, where it long astounded passers-by. The old railway was made into a road. The Forests Department built a special firebreak round the machine to protect it.

Bunbury Tourist Bureau secretary A.G. Baxter, who told me this story, went to see it recently. He found nothing left but a pile of junk. Somebody had decided the bronze bushes in the wheel hubs must be worth a few dollars as scrap, and chain-sawed through all the spokes to get at the hubs. Such was the violent end of an historic icon.

GARDENS AS A WORK OF HEART

Kangaroo Paws – with a difference
30 January 1969

For the overseas tourist, Perth Airport features kangaroo paw plants outside and chopped off paws of kangaroos inside.

The souvenir shop's paws are about 10in long and the fur ranges from white through fawn to brown. At one end the five claws and palm are lacquered black and, at the other, the amputation is concealed by a steel circlet. Fixed into the circlet is a bottle-opener, paper knife, can opener or shoehorn.

One model in this novelty line has a thermometer fixed midway down the paw. The thermometer fluid seems to be red ink, and from a distance it looks as though the poor paw is still bleeding.

"Greetings from Perth, WA," is inscribed on the metal fittings. Prices are $5 to $7 [$60-80 in today's money].

"Where do you get the paws from?" I asked Miss Andrea Lee-Steere behind the counter, wondering if they were a local industry.

"Kangaroos," she said.

"Do you like them?"

"We've got a bottle-opener paw at home. It looks tremendous on the cocktail cabinet."

"Do they sell well?"

"Four or five a week. Some people think they are gruesome but most people off the planes are really impressed."

My arrival at the importers, in Perth, caused some consternation and steely-eyed glances, particularly when I wanted to know who produced the paws.

"We don't say where we get any of our stuff from," said a

representative. "Once we told someone and people started ordering stuff through him direct instead of through our agency."

He agreed the paws were horrible, but said they sold well. They were made by a struggling migrant in a garage in an outer Melbourne suburb. He had been looking for something original to make, and the paws combined the attractiveness of kangaroo fur with absolutely unshakable authenticity.

Where did the struggling migrant get his raw material from? No one knew.

I suggested the paws could be a by-product from the pet food industry, but they didn't think so. I eventually decided that a truck must materialise once a month and tip a load of kangaroo paws on his driveway - an interesting subject for Salvador Dali to paint.

Was anyone here [Perth] thinking of setting up a rival factory? We were, after all, the Kangaroo Paw State.

No, they said, there was nothing brewing in that direction.

Maybe it's time to pause on the poor paws.

How Mr Munns runs the University's grounds

24 December 1965

"How do you keep the university grounds so nice?" I asked Mr George Munns as he fled around the toolshed. "Brute force and ignorance," he flung back, disappearing.

Gardens curator Mr Munns is a familiar sight to everyone at W.A. University, usually leading his horse-and-dray loaded with soil, manure, plants, tools or compost.

He's a retiring person, blending with the stipple of his shrubs, greenery and trees much as the university itself blends with its garden setting. Because Mr Munns has nursed and watered these grounds for 34 years, every student must be in his debt. The all-encompassing greenery is to students as a cup of tea is to housewives or a sleeping pill to insomniacs; it is balm for book-worn eyes and incense for nostrils that for too long have consorted with fumes and chemicals in the science blocks.

Cornered in his office after protestations, Mr Munns weakened. "In 1932 when the depression was on, I got a fortnight's work here," he began.

"What were you then?" I asked.

"I was a thing. I was out of work," he said, summing up an era. "I cleared some of the bush here to make a site for the old tin huts from Irwin Street. There was a hue and cry about putting unsightly buildings on the university grounds. The university authorities said they were to be only temporary. They are still here. There is nothing so permanent as temporary buildings. I clung on here on sustenance work, breaking up the ground with a horse and Tumbling Tommy."

"What's that?"

"Come and see."

I followed him through some undergrowth and there it was, an iron scoop the size of a baby's bath with wooden shafts broken off short.

"I keep it here," he said. "Put in new shafts and it may come in handy one day. It is not eating anything."

I doubted privately that the campus would ever again be scratched by Tumbling Tommy.

His boss in those days was Dr Somerville, he said, a staunch upholder of keeping trees, even sometimes to the ridiculous.

"What do you mean by that?"

"He was very dogmatic," Mr Munns said, guardedly. "So time went on. I got married, I got a university rental house, the war came on, I went in the war. I stayed on here because it developed that way, that's all." Now he is in charge of 23 gardeners. His hair has greyed and his short moustache is white. He looks younger than his 59 years, though his gardener's arms and hands, leathery and scarred, seem to have done more than a lifetime's work.

"I live on the campus here 24 hours a day. After the years, you get attached to everything. You see dozers for car parks coming in, you want to rear up and do something about it. Someone spits on the ground and you want to say, 'Clean it up!'"

The phone rang. "You've got three rams just near the Perry Lakes stadium," he acknowledged to the caller. "I'll tell the men to look out for a truck." He explained that the university had gone in for sheep again - 72 ewes, ex-York, were grazing at Shenton Park. He wanted to build up a flock again. The original university flock had to go when campus development broke up the enclosures.

"One of the best things we ever had was sheep. One time when the Yanks were here, they befriended one young ram. They even used to take it on parade with them. Then it disappeared and we found out much later that some Yanks had put it in their Catalina and taken it up north with them as a mascot. It probably wound up in the pot though." He bore the aviators no grudge. "Some of the chaps in the Catalinas got beheaded," he said.

Dogs were the sheep's worst enemy. Packs of them would savage the flock and even when he traced dogs back to their homes, their owners would resolutely deny that their dogs had killed the sheep.

"The dogs disappeared in the end. The sheep must have eaten them," he concluded.

He had many other stories from days long past - of the first residential summer school held in tents under the trees, with billiard tables used as beds; how money was so tight when Winthrop Hall pond was being built that they surfaced it with sweepings off the floor of a cement works; how Bob Hawke, now the razor sharp trade union advocate, drove a horse and dray for the gardeners to earn money for his student days; how the university's parking worry used to be to provide enough bike sheds. "People were just as happy in those days," he commented.

The Sunken Gardens, I learnt from Mr Munns, was the hole the university emerged from - the sandpit used for the building of Winthrop Hall.

Mr Munns cherishes three events. The first was 25 years ago when he successfully transplanted a Christmas Tree near the old physics building. That was a feat that had not been done often, he said.

The second was transplanting some 60ft high poplars growing at Rosalie to the rear of Winthrop Hall.

"But the biggest moment of my life here was when I met the Queen. She planted some trees here. She just turned the spade actually; the hole was there already. She talked to me for quite a while. She was very decent."

Note: Forester Roger Underwood, a friend of mine, comments:

"When I was a botany student in 1960 our dear old lecturer Miss Alison Baird (known to us all as "Jungle Jill") once took the forestry students on a walking tour of the campus and Matilda Bay, identifying all the trees with their scientific and common names and giving a potted silvicultural history of each. I was amazed at her botanical expertise, but also at the number and variety of the species - presumably, many had been planted by old George over the years. It was my first exposure to the science of dendrology and was a revelation.

"I still visit the campus occasionally and wander around the gardens or sit for a

few minutes in the Sunken Garden. There is a stand of African mahogany (Khaya senegalensis) at one spot near the student gym which has the finest specimens of this species I have seen anywhere in Australia. Just out of curiosity one day, and thinking it might make a nice little article for the Foresters' Newsletter, I measured their heights and diameters, and then wrote to the University Grounds Manager to find out when they were planted and how old they were. Nobody knew, and there were no records. I could tell the place was being run by gardeners, not foresters!"

Why pigs feast on market gardeners' leftovers
17 December 1967

When the auctions are finished at the Metropolitan Markets, a truck comes around collecting unsold vegetables - lettuce, carrot, parsnip and cabbage by the boxes. Then they are fed to the pigs.

"Why don't you pick up your unsold stuff?" I asked an Italian market gardener whom I pass on the way to work.

"Cost too much time and petrol," he said.

We walked over to what had been an acre of cabbages. He had run over them with tractor and plough, and the churned white sand was speckled with pale green shreds of cabbage leaves. "Good manure," he said.

My new acquaintance was about 5ft tall, with a young wife on her knees nearby pulling weeds, wearing a straw hat. In the summer he starts work before 5 a.m. and works till 7 p.m. In winter the light is poor and he works from 8 to 4.30. He pays $16 a week [today, $200] to rent the 19 acres from a friend. "I have the house, the garden and the job," he said.

"Are people complaining about market gardens?" his wife asked nervously. I re-assured her.

"It's a bad life. Too much work, no money, no fun," she said. "You can't go for a picnic, you must work the garden. Saturday, you still have to work in the garden. On Sunday you must do the market for Monday."

"Don't you ever get a holiday?" I asked.

"Christmas Day," she said.

Her husband, in an incongruous pork-pie hat, had gone off to his little grey tractor.

"I'd rather he get a job in a factory," she said, sotto voce. "In the garden you can make some money but in the factory there is cash money."

I walked through forests of tall tomatoes tied to grids of bamboos;

sprawling cucumbers, their star shaped leaves bordered with yellow and white; the patterned green whorls of the lettuce; olive-leaved capsicums like dahlia bushes; and sea-green cabbages with tall weeds bursting up between the rows. White cabbage moths were having a field day.

A market gardener runs two risks - that the crop won't come good and that the prices won't come good. He took a chance by planting tomatoes early, and had to cover the 3000 young plants with palm fronds to protect them from frost. He was counting on a good price for first-of-the-season fruit. "Market gardens - they're like Donald Campbell, go for risk." [Campbell broke eight world speed records on land and sea in the 1950-60s].

"This is the first year I got a good crop of tomatoes," he said. "Sometimes when the canker starts, it goes right through."

When the tomatoes are ready, the couple will be working round the clock, picking, packing and taking them to market. Through the rows we could see clusters of reddening fruit straining towards the ground. "Three plants makes two flats (cases) of tomatoes," he said.

The easiest crops were carrots and parsnips. You just spray with kerosene to kill the grass, and they are ready to pull in three or four months. He reached down and yanked up a few rosy carrots. The idea that food came from under the ground stunned me.

He twisted a young lettuce that shrieked like a mandrake as it came off, and we ate half each. It was very fresh. But a cabbage was cracked and unappetizing. "I should have picked months ago but the price was down. Now it's no good for the market, I'll make a loss. There was the blood and bone and poison, $30 or $40, and about a day's work altogether. But this patch would have been worth $500 [$6100 today] on a top-price day."

The parsnips could stay in the ground, he said, waving at what looked like a field of mint. Maybe he'd pick them after Christmas. With parsnips it didn't hurt to keep them waiting. All you could do was keep planting and sending to market, and some time you would get the good price where you picked up what you'd lost.

"Blood and bone's very dear; poison spray's very dear; if you don't work very hard and take a lot of stuff to market you won't make expenses."

His best crop had been five beds of cauliflower, which sold for $500 [$6100] one enchanted morning at the markets.

The worst weed? He pointed to some grass - he didn't know its name. "Another one is 'Never-die', that is a true name," he said, pointing to a weed like a miniature pigface. "You pull it up and turn it upside down but even a small plant goes on and makes its seeds."

He was mildly bitter about the vegetable shops. He sold them lettuce at $2.50 a box, and they sold each lettuce for 25c each. They could make $3.50 profit on a box, while he had all the expenses of growing. But when lettuce was dear, shopkeepers had to buy at $7 a box and lost money in order to keep customers.

The bureaucrats leave him alone. He never had officials "on the back", as he put it, except once when he used some chicken manure and it had worms in it. "You don't get into trouble if you respect the government," he said. "If you don't respect the Tax Department you get into trouble. I know a few people, they made $10,000 profit each year but don't tell; after four or five years they catch you."

His last word was on people who ran spare-time market gardens. "We have to live with this job. People who work in the factory, why should they take stuff to the market? They have their 30 pounds in the pocket every Friday. They should pay double tax, they make double profit."

Wildflowers commercially plundered

4 August 1966

Perth's 60-odd florists are divided into two camps - those who sell wildflowers and those who don't.

I rang ten florists at random. Five offered to get me all the wildflowers I wanted. Five pointed out that it was illegal to pick wildflowers and said they had none to sell. Nevertheless I could have ordered two pounds worth yesterday with no trouble at all - kangaroo paws 5d and 6d each; banksias 2/6 each; dryandra 1/- a piece; yellow boronia 2/- a bunch; hakea, berdette - if it was flowering I could have bought it.

At the peak wildflower season it is a wonder that interstate aircraft can take off from Perth Airport at all, so laden are they with consignments of WA wildflowers for the lucrative Eastern States market (kangaroo paws, 1/- each). TAA takes about 50 consignments per flight; Ansett ANA, up to 150.

Like a bottle of Boronia perfume? You can buy one for a guinea. It's manufactured in West Perth and the manufacturer buys the flowers from professional pickers. The perfume trade is interesting from a wildflower conservation point of view. The manufacturer pays a royalty to the government to pick Boronia down Mt Barker way, and the royalty is so much per pound of blossom. The firm uses several thousand pounds of blossom a year. It does not think the land is about to be bulldozed - it is just swampy government land, it said.

Presumably the vast wildflower trade is legally innocent. Perhaps the wildflowers have been picked from private property with the written consent of the landowners. Or perhaps they have been taken from particular tracts of Crown land about to be bulldozed, and with a permit from the Forests Department, ridiculously cheap at 5 pounds.

But there is not a single full-time paid official to police the Native Flora Protection Act. In any case, the Act is full of loopholes - a child could exploit them.

And even if, owing to calamitous bad luck, an illegal picker got caught by the Forests Department, he could take comfort that there has never been a single offender brought to court, let alone suffering the slight inconvenience of a fine of 'not more than 30 pounds' - even after three or 30 convictions.

To be caught may even be a blessing in disguise. A permit-less Boronia picker near Albany was caught red-handed with a vehicle load of this sacred plant. He was subsequently presented by the Forests Department with a permit to pick some more.

Botanists now say our Boronia reserves have just about run out of Boronia, and one predicted that soon there would be more Boronia under cultivation in Melbourne than in the whole of WA.

Theoretically one can pick wildflowers only from private land with the written consent of the owner, or from Crown land with a Forests Department 5 pounds permit to pick in that particular tract. However, once a sharp operator has either of those permits, he might break the law and pick holus-bolus on roadsides, national parks and private land, and if caught, defy the Forests Department to prove that his flowers did not come from the permitted area.

Way back in 1962 a wildflower preservation conference chaired by the Premier's Department then under-secretary R H Doig, was so concerned about commercial exploitation of wildflowers that a big part of its report was aimed at closing the loopholes in the Act. The onus of proof should be on the possessor of picked wildflowers to prove he got them from permitted pastures, it said. Wildflower exporters should be licensed, and traders at each stage should need statutory declarations saying where the wildflowers came from.

After a stormy passage through the Assembly, the government's watered down version of the recommendations was thrown out by the Council, some government members seeing in it the makings of a police state.

The government, rather pained at this, fulfilled part of the recommendations by proclamation, legally protecting wildflowers over the southern sixth of the state, but the measures were but a shadow of a shadow of what had originally been proposed.

South Africa, our greatest rival for wildflower beauty, stamped out the casual traffic in wildflower picking and made it possible for wildflower cultivation to be a commercial success. WA has no hope for wildflower orchards while pickers can sell bush wildflowers by the truckload.

The Forests Department has enrolled 350 voluntary wildflower wardens, and issued hundreds of 'Don't Pick' signs. It is quite possible that picnickers do now exercise less pluck. However law enforcement on the cheap would hardly deter a picker-for-profit.

The 1962 conference also had some recommendations about the question of creating reserves. This conflicts with WA's farming expansion. The conference wanted more reserves created and the reserves placed under the control of a single authority with a program of research and a permanent qualified staff.

WA's Gilbertian plight is that we have no less than 5.5 million acres of fauna and flora reserves, cared for to the best of their ability by two full-time paid fauna officers. No wildflower reserves exist in our most prolific wildflower areas, Lake Grace, Coorow and Carnamah, for example.

Separated by ocean and desert from the rest of the world for countless ages, South-West plants have followed their own evolutionary road. But every year bulldozers level WA land equivalent to a strip ten miles wide stretching from Perth to Albany. When they knock down trees and scrub in the South-West, the bulldozers are hewing flora in some of the world's most unusual habitats. Only Brazil and Cape Province (South Africa) can boast as high a proportion of plants not found elsewhere.

Mr C.A. Gardner, who was Government Botanist from 1927 to 1960, is spending his retirement documenting the flora of Western Australia – about 5,500 species. He knows of six species that have become extinct and fears that up to 150 other species face the same fate – or have met it. For example, *Darwinia carnea*, a sort of mountain bell, now exists only on a small patch of land on a farm near Gingin.

One reserve in Rhodesia – purely for lions - was much bigger than the total area of reserves in WA. But North and South Rhodesia combined was only half the area of WA.

Small reserves of 500 to 800 acres were useless. Weeds and ensuing higher soil temperatures due to cultivation nearby killed off plants.

WA roadside reserves of two or four chains width were usually useless for conservation because the road and bared land raised the soil temperatures, and this killed many of the plant species within 20 years.

In WA's arid areas clearing could upset a delicate balance of nature and turn an ever-increasing amount of country into desert. The evidence was that when trees went, drought came.

Thousands of years ago, in Mesopotamia, China, Ethiopia, Carthage, Mexico and Peru, lush countryside produced wheat to feed big populations. But much of them turned into waterless desert, probably through grazing and clearing. "We are fools," said Mr Gardner. "We look weeks ahead when we should look centuries ahead."

WA's sand-plain areas near the coast were fast disappearing under the plough. The only sand-plain reserves of any consequence were near the Murchison River and Cape Arid, east of Esperance - and these were not permanent reserves. These poor sandy soils supported much more splendid plant life than did better soil.

Till yesterday's announcement of a new fauna/flora committee to study reserves, the government had 'no set policy' on setting aside wildflower reserves. This could explain why, in the carving up of 100,000 acres near Badgingarra this year for farms, the patches that nurtured near-extinct kangaroo paws were nearly all alienated from the Crown. No government wildflower experts were consulted during the subdivision. The 120,000 acres left in the region as reserves was the poorest, unfarmable land.

The botanists disagree on which policy would best look after our wildflowers. Phrases like 'the reserves must be as big as possible' are not much help – wildflowers are not the State's only need. We have some huge reserves but they are in the remotest parts of WA while plant and animal species are threatened close to home.

Indeed a 3,000-acre reserve for marsupials near Pingelly, under the close supervision of WA University zoologist Dr A R Main, has increased its stock of refugee possums and what-have-you. The key word is supervision.

So let us see what WA could do.

First, spend some money on wildflower conservation for a change.

Secondly, if creation of a special body to look after all reserves is too hair-raising a step, reserves should be made A-class and vested in a strengthened National Parks Board. This body has experience in reserve management and is not subject to political or vested interest control. Its board includes the government botanist and the government entomologist although it currently lacks a strong field staff and full-time scientific direction.

The reserves policy would then have to be decided on. One suggested program (with authoritative backing) is that the government should aim to provide a scattering of reserves of about 5,000 acres throughout all the land being opened up for farming. If 20 farms are to be allocated, natural scientists should pick an area offering the best prospect as a fauna and flora reserve, of the size of about one farm. Admittedly, the jealous system of territorial rights among animals, insects and birds would limit its effectiveness; however as a flora reserve and carefully controlled by roving, caravan-equipped wardens, it could suffice. At present all that can be done is tenderly lift out the choicest pair of wildflowers and transplant them in Kings Park. The animals, birds and insects die.

Farmers, we hope, would not begrudge this one bite from their big slice.

Lands Minister Bovell said yesterday that this suggestion was no good because it would litter fire-hazardous and vermin-infested reserves throughout the farming landscape. It would cost too much to pay salaries of extra reserve wardens, he said.

Reserve management boils down to a careful study of what is on the reserve and a program of fire control that makes sure that burning off occurs at the best time for plants and animals. Two fires at the wrong time are all that is needed to wipe out a species; no fires leads to a hazardous build-up of inflammable brush.

Reserves should be A-class so they can be tampered with only with Parliamentary sanction. B and C-class reserves can disappear with the stroke of a minister's pen.

It was less than 20 years ago (1946) that government-sponsored wildflower tours offered prizes to whoever picked the most Boronia. Wildflower trains chuffed home oozing wildflowers at every pore. We have much to atone for.

Chasing the honey flow

20 May 1968

The worker bee works hard for six weeks and then its wings wear out. Gritting its teeth, it goes home on foot. Its thighs are laden with pollen, its insides with nectar, and it has to fight off ants.

When it gets home it climbs into the hive and the other bees tell it to buzz off. If it won't, they sting it.

WA beekeepers know how it feels. They load their trucks with hives and chase the flowering gums from Geraldton to Esperance, moving their bees to the cool south in summer and the flowery coasts of Dongara in winter. They carry home their honeycombs, wring out the honey, offer it at less than cost price – and the public prefers sugar.

When I visited a bee-keeper's shed last week, I found a cosy reek of honey, a thing like a giant milk separator and a big truck, sunk to its tray in a loading hole in the floor. Ian the bee-keeper has been chasing the honey flow (as the trees in blossom are called) for 15 years, but still needed to refer to his son's Wonder Book of Bees and Ants before answering some questions. However his language about those who control the Australian export of honey would never be found in a Wonder Book.

Most honey has been exported but Communist China has undercut Australian prices. The hope now is to sell more honey locally by persuading people of the deliciousness of honey in tea, honey on cereals and honey over ice-cream.

Ian said most people hardly knew when gums were in flower and a few were not even sure that honey came from bees.

"Honey's an easily digestible food because the bees have already eaten it," he said. "They suck up the nectar and spit it out in the hive. Sometimes dragonflies beat us to it. They bite the bee's backside as he flies home and suck his insides out."

"Is there much nectar and pollen in gum flowers?" I asked.

The question set the family leaping at a nearby red gum which was covered in pale white blossom. Ian got a switch of flowers and smacked his hand with it. His hand showed some yellow pollen and a sticky spatter. Those flowers were pretty dry, he said, but a good bunch would leave your hand wet with nectar.

The idea is to keep the bees near the flowers all year round. In winter, banksia and scrub near Jurien Bay are in flower. Before Christmas there are flowers on white gum, jarrah, York gums and in the Mallee country near Coolgardie. After Christmas the red gums, white gums or karri are in flower.

If it gets too cold the bees huddle in the hive and won't go out. If it's too hot the beekeeper may have to drive back and forth, giving them drinks of water.

The hives are just three boxes, one on top of the other. The queen and drones live in the bottom box but the workers, being smaller, can get through a mesh into the top boxes with their honey, thinking it will be good food for the hive later. But the beekeeper arrives, robs the top two boxes and puts new boxes in their place.

The boxes are fitted with things like empty picture frames. The bees fill up each frame with perfect hexagon combs made out of wax. It took me quite a while to appreciate that this mesh was not factory made.

Ian checks his hives at 10 or 11 a.m. when the morning air is moist and the bees can stick a lot of pollen to their legs. He lifts the lid and if the bees are 'whitening up' - that means making new comb out of wax - the hive is prospering. If not, the bees need the honey more than he does.

"I suppose the stings don't worry you," I said.

"My oath they do! You can't avoid them. You wear a face veil and they wait till the veil blows against your face and stings you through it. They sting your armpits where your shirt sticks to your skin. They get inside your clothes and sting where it hurts most."

His best weapon is a thing like an oilcan. He fills it with pine needles, lights it and pumps smoke out of the spout.

According to Ian the bee cycle starts on a hot day when a lot of bees can't stand the over-crowding and fly off with a queen. They usually wind up hanging in a mass from a tree. The lump of bees tells the scouts to find a new hive, such as a hole in a tree or a chimney or an old drum.

In the home they build the comb so that the queen can get busy laying 3,000 eggs a day and the drones can earn their keep by fertilizing her. But the worker bees are getting worn out and there are no new bees yet to take over. The bees get weaker and weaker while the eggs slowly hatch, become larvae, are sealed away and turn into young bees.

The last of the original bees will drop dead just as the new bees are ready to carry on the work. But if honey is scarce the hive comes to grief because the workers die before the new bees are ready.

"What makes a queen bee?" I asked.

"Royal jelly. The bees get an ordinary larva and feed it with this royal jelly instead of honey. I don't know why women use royal jelly. They don't want to spend their life laying eggs."

When the karri really flowers it can make a fortune for every beekeeper who can get his bees on the spot. The big year was 1948 when two Eastern States fellows even loaded their bees on a train and joined the karri-blossom rush. That honey flow lasted six months.

There was a small one a couple of years ago, but it was intermittent and Ian was always putting his bees just where the honey flow had stopped.

"Honey is the best food in the world, there's nothing like it," he said. "I used to eat two pounds of honey a week."

Rather crestfallen, he told me his allergist had recently put him off honey for two years.

The last Chinese market gardener

20 March 1968

Behind Chesterton Lodge in South Perth and between the rushes of the foreshore and a horse paddock, you can find a little patch of odd-looking vegetables. There are bean-like things curling from creepers, water weeds growing in a puddle in a wooden box, armour plated gourds and orange cucumbers lying in the grey sand.

This is – or was – the vegetable plot of Wong Chew, to my knowledge the last of all the Chinese market gardens in Perth and country towns.

Wong Chew's hands on the coverlet of his bed at Gairdner Hospital were spindly as a bird's claws. He was sitting in blue-striped hospital pyjamas, begging us to tell the doctor he was well enough to go home to Hong Kong. He did not look very well. Malnutrition and age had hollowed his cheeks and below his short grey hair we could see every vein in his face.

My interpreter was second year economics student Lai Chik Peng who could speak Canton Chinese. Wong's speech was hard even for Mr Lai to understand, as it spluttered indistinctly through Wong's last two bottom teeth.

He could not remember how long he had been gardening in South Perth. He said he had used a horse and plough; lately he dug by hand and carried water in a can made from a four-gallon tin. He lived in a government building, which I found later to be a dark wooden shack with holes patched with hessian. His best possessions, after a lifetime's labouring, were some antique chopsticks and some Chinese plates.

"Find out what he likes doing," I asked Mr Lai. "Does he like to pray or watch the sunset or what?" Mr Lai translated and they both laughed. "He says he has no religion, he likes to go to a friend's place and watch television."

He had never had any trouble with anyone. He did not count the children, who used to run after his horse and cart shouting 'Ching Chong Chinaman!" and steal his vegetables. He still remembered a raid by six schoolboys. Three kept watch and three took his parsnips and cauliflowers. He told the headmaster and the head paid for the vegetables.

"Did you forgive the children who gave you cheek?"

"No, I told their parents."

His saddest times were when the river rose and drowned his vegetables. There was nothing to do but plant some more.

Our oldest surviving gardener is See Quing, who is well over 90 and lives at Sunset Home. He used to garden on the South Perth foreshore and at Bibra Lake, near Jandakot, and like Wong Chew, he sold his vegetables from a horse and cart. He said he used to work 16 hours a day sometimes, tending his tomatoes and carting swamp water in pails. All his friends had gone home to China and all his family were dead.

"Why didn't you save up and go home?"

"Playing fan-tan, drink, racehorses. I was a silly fool. I spent all my money."

Fred Farrell, second in charge of a firm of vegetable marketers, remembers how kind the Chinese used to be to their horses. He had seen one Chinese wait an hour in a laneway for his horse to start moving, swearing in vernacular but too gentle to hit it. The horse finally took him home, three-quarters asleep in the cart.

Among the last gardeners was Li Li Chun, whose garden at York folded up about five years ago, and John Gooey, who worked his garden at Leederville till he was more than 80.

Treatment of local Chinese has been nasty, especially when seen through the eyes of a Chinese Kuo Min-tang historian, writing in 1935.

In the middle of last century, traders in Singapore and Hong Kong lured Chinese labourers here with stories of hills of silver and gold. They used to hold parties in teahouses to spread the message.

"Indeed," our historian writes, "the poor Chinese slaves' lives were as worthless as a feather. Come to think of it now, one can't help feeling sad."

The labourers often died of thirst or ill treatment, and also had to contend with Aborigines "armed with bows and arrows" [he got that wrong]. Their sole ambition was to save enough to get back to China. This is why they were not an influential group despite their hard work and frugal habits. They got a grip on the vegetable, carpentry and laundry trades but when jobs became scarce in the 1880s, there began a long series of restrictions and boycotts on them.

In Geraldton, for example, the general store called Kwang Li Chang was one of the biggest in town. The Labor Party campaigned to destroy the shop "to satisfy its whim", our historian records. Whenever party people saw the name of the store on any goods, "they would either kick it or throw it about with hands". The owner, Kung Liang, sold his shop at an auction.

In 1910 Fremantle's Chinese shops were closed and the Chinese were allowed to deal only in vegetables, which were scarce, and curios. Soon West Australian growers were agitating against them and seeking a ban even on door-to-door veggie sales.

In the 1920s the hounding took the form of hunts for illegal immigrants. Rewards were offered and many people found it profitable to cause much harm to innocent Chinese people, the historian says.

By 1928 the Chinese gardeners were so depleted that a vegetable shortage hit Perth. The government imported Italians to take over the gardens. By the mid-30s, only 300-400 Chinese were left here, a remnant of the original thousands.

A pocket of Chinese gardeners held out on the swampy parts of the South Perth foreshore, but the South Perth Road Board evicted them in 1952, to the indignation of residents who enjoyed buying cabbages straight from the soil. The board said it wanted the area for playing fields; the Chinese retaliated by laying an ancient Chinese curse on the area.

The neat gardens became a wasteland. Bullrushes took over and covered the district with objectionable pollen. Rats bred and mosquitos hummed. The board's first playing field turned back into swamp. The Key West adult playground scheme failed. The latest plans for selling some of the land fell through.

The curse did not apply to Wong Chew's vegetable garden, which kept him going another 15 years, nor to Wong Chew himself, who is about to fly home to Hong Kong. A fund has been opened to give him a few hundred dollars for his needs there.

PLANS FOR THE DISTANT FUTURE (NOW ARRIVED)

Perth planning: corridors or clusters?

23 August 1968

Add 20 or 30 years to your age and then try to imagine what Perth would be like.

Dr David Carr, chief planner, Town Planning Department, has tried the exercise and come up with two notions - Perth as a starfish shape (corridor development) or buckshot shape (cluster development).

With the starfish, Perth city would dominate the future 1.5 million people settled between Mandurah and Yanchep. With the buckshot idea Perth city would stop growing and half a dozen mini-Perths would spring up on an arc about 15 miles away.

Either way, Dr Carr says, Perth would remain a liveable region. But without tough government planning from now on, we might get a Perth that is mess-shaped and pure hell to live in.

With corridor development, Perth city would remain the heart and brain, and people would speed into town along four narrow transport arms, in super-buses or super-trains.

One arm would reach north to Hamersley, one to Midland, one to Armadale and one to Kwinana. Development would snake out along the arms, but not in the gaps between them. Here would be rural land, like the market gardens at Spearwood, land actually used to grow things, with the help of sensible taxes and a bit of irrigation.

The cluster idea involves giving up the notion that Perth city can maintain its dominance over the region. If we can't afford A-grade freeways, buses and trains, there'll come a time when the city must put up a House Full sign and turn extra workers away.

These workers would spend their days working at such centres as Fremantle, Rockingham, Armadale, Midland and Hamersley.

The roads wouldn't get clogged because everyone wouldn't be heading into the city.

But the government would still have to spend a lot of money. It would have to tempt people to start factories at the sub-centres. Unless it did so the sub-centres wouldn't catch on. The government might have to buy land there for development and even sponsor private building on the land.

Dr Carr feels that present development in Perth is conforming more to the corridor idea.

The cluster scheme could react against Perth if public transport did not catch on, as had happened in the US. It was hard to predict when such a decline could start, he said, but it could be when the city's workforce exceeded 80,000 people.

In both case, open space (the beaches, hills or foreshores) would stay as in the 1963 scheme, and so would the industrial land zones. But the big new suburbs of 10,000 people grouped in sub-centres of 40,000 to 60,000 people, are further in the future than the 1963 scheme goes.

There is a third possibility - repeating the great urban sprawl that has overtaken Melbourne, for example, turning it into a morass of housing, factories, tawdry shops and choked, infuriating highways.

Dr Carr said that to get the orderliness of cluster or corridor development, the government would have to organize things a lot more than it has so far.

For the corridors, for example, we would get dense-living strips three miles wide, bordered by high-speed highways. Down the middle would go the spine, in the form of exclusive bus or train routes. The spine would make it easy for people to get into Perth to work when die-hard car drivers were thwarted by the lack of parking space.

For corridors, the government would have to invest massively in public transport and pay for extra miles of freeways when the present scheme is already running out of funds.

If it is the people's will that the government should keep its strong arm out of regional development, what then?

Dr Carr has already started looking at compromises. He sees that an axis across Perth is forming, north to Hamersley and south to Rockingham. This would make for a cheap freeway scheme, since such a corridor would team up with the Kwinana Freeway, Narrows Interchange, Mitchell Freeway and northward towards Leederville.

This one spine alone would bring a deal of order to the giant region of the future. It would connect seven industrial areas (Hamersley, Osborne Park, West Perth, North Lake, O'Connor, Bibra Lake and Kwinana), the Perth city, the suburbs of Hamersley (to be 50,000 people), Medina-Calista (60,000) and Rockingham (50,000). It would go through such suburbs as Osborne Park, Doubleview, Leederville, Brentwood and Coolbellup, which could become high-density areas.

There would still be scope for corridor growth to the east and south-east. But most of the public effort would go into the north-south axis. The axis would miss out on the corridor ideal of separate public-transport highways.

Dr Carr stresses the need in all of these schemes to keep the rural-land zones intact for farming. Otherwise scattered growth everywhere would weaken public transport, boost the bill for water, power and sewerage, and create an excess economic demand for schools and hospitals.

Perth 1969: you can keep those sprinklers whizzing
22 January 1969

Perth hasn't had water restrictions for nearly a decade, and the government's ban on sprinklers for a day or two this month took our lawns by surprise.

But those were mild restrictions compared with the annual troubles late in the 1950s, when severe restrictions went on from October to March.

Thanks to the Water Supply Board's activities, lawn-growers need fear no serious restrictions in the next few years and housewives can continue to surfeit lawns day and night from front and back hoses.

In 1961 Works Minister Wild said restrictions "should not be needed" until 1970. His successor Mr Ross Hutchinson told me last week that "should not" did not mean "would not". Restrictions were always possible in hard times. To build a water supply big enough to avert any restrictions whatsoever would be stupid - it would cost a fortune and prejudice other aspects of water supply.

When could we expect restrictions? - If we got a run of low-rainfall years or drought that lowered reservoirs, followed by a hot summer. There was plenty of water in hills dams for normal years. The other cause would be bottlenecks in the pipelines from the dams to the tap in our front yards.

The water was sent to half a dozen small reservoirs in the suburbs, which were a sort of liquid nest-egg for the scorching days when people kept their taps on. If householders were sensible and did their watering at night, the level would stay up, but when no one used restraint it would drop too low for comfort.

The national picture shows how well off we are in Perth. [I omit details here about other capitals' water restrictions].

Perth's total water reserves are not big, but our population is still in the tiddlywinks category [about 400,000]. If we had a million people now, we'd be a scarce-water city even if all hills water were used.

Perth's use of water has been increasing almost recklessly. In 1963 the biggest draw on one day was 121m gallons. In five years the peak has risen to 186m gallons. *[2018 usage: daily average in week to January 18 was 868m litres or 186m gallons. With 2.2m people, about five times the 1969 population, we're using a similar amount of water to 1969]*.

Some of this is due to population increase. A lot is due to rising affluence – the sweet life. And some is due, curiously, to replacement of half-blocked iron pipes in many homes with copper piping that gives better water pressure.

The high usage in Perth has two excuses - our soil is sandier than that of other capitals, and our summers are rather rainless.

On a hot day, consumption may reach 180m gallons. The next day it goes back to 120m. Because there is about the same amount of water drunk and used for domestic purposes, the extra usage is caused by sprinklers.

Mr G. Samuel, head of the Water Board, said the restrictions were our own fault. The day before, you needed only to drive around to see house after house with sprinklers whirling in the heat of the day – when water barely had time to hit the ground before it evaporated.

Mr Hutchinson agreed. For example, he thought people didn't move sprinklers often enough.

The government is not sure what to do about our great water waste. A drastic measure would be to increase excess water charges and lose friends [politically]. Less painful would be public education on wise watering. A board committee has been thinking about lawn watering but hasn't finished its report yet.

The board and the government are between two fires on this issue of reducing consumption. The board has to be self-supporting and lives partly on our excess water bills. Half its income ($3m out of $6m) is used to pay back loans, and that expense goes on even if no one uses excess water. Its other worry is that it has few financial reserves - it has accumulated only $500,000 in 60 years. To cover itself for emergencies it would need to raise charges, and put the profit aside – a practice that ratepayers would dislike.

Letting things drift is bad policy too. The board is having to spend more and sooner on water works because of the public's extravagant usage.

The new Serpentine Dam vanquished Perth's water bogey in 1961. Since then the water people's main job has been a second big pipe from Serpentine: you could almost drive a small car through it. The department has built fair-sized suburban reservoirs near City Beach and Hamilton Hill and put in a few water tanks and water towers – one at Hamilton Hill is even bigger than the colossus at Tuart Hill.

The next big scheme is a $10.7m hills project on the Dandalup Rivers, a few miles past Serpentine. In 1970-71 they will put a wall across the North Dandalup and run the stream into pipes. About 1975 they will build a bigger storage than Serpentine on the South Dandalup. That will cost only $3m – it will be made from earth gouged nearby. But the steel piping will cost $7.5m. It will connect with the main pipe from Serpentine to Perth.

Within a year or so, new mains will go to Rockingham-Medina and Hamilton Hill to benefit Fremantle suburbs, and the extra reservoir will improve supply to the Yokine and newer areas.

If you think water has a different taste in some suburbs, you're right. Since 1967 the water people have sunk two 2,400ft bores near Mt Yokine. In all there are 14 deep bores that supply up to 8% of Perth's daily consumption. The board is now going to drill shallow bores at Gnangara, nearly Hamersley.

The deep bores can make your tap water warmish. The shallow bore water will taste all right and be cool.

After Dandalup, the Canning River (a second storage) and Wungong River south of Armadale could be dammed, followed by the Murray late this century.

In the 1990s our natural supplies will run out. In the 21st Century, the water people expect that Perth will be drinking treated seawater. Every big city in the world will have to find the way before Perth has to.

ARTY-FARTY STUFF

Come-uppance for cruel Cynthia at St Kits

3 January 1968

Waiting for a loaf of bread at a comatose smallgoods shop, I plucked two 'School Friends' from the shelf and began to read. The casual gesture introduced me to a fabulous and seductive world. Noble English schoolgirls are eternally putted against smugglers, class sneaks and tyrants of the upper form.

The precede reads, *"Tyrannical head prefect! Fourth formers unhappy under her harsh rule! That was the position at St Kits at the start of the new term."*

The opening panel shows a roomful of seven young girls in shin-length checked tunics with 1920s collars, playing table tennis and draughts and reading books. In the doorway looms the horrid Cynthia, in blouse and black skirt and wearing a tie. "You can take 100 lines each for making too much noise!" she orders.

"But - but we weren't making any noise!" says a table tennis player (overlooking the normal din of bat, ping-pong ball and table).

"That's unfair, Cynthia," says another.

On Drawing No 4 the caption reads, "An intriguing message!" On the note, held by two fingers, is printed, *"If you would fight Cynthia Drew's tyranny come secretly to the crypt at 6 o'clock."* It is signed by someone wearing a black Ku Klux Klan-style hat.

"Gosh! How jolly strange," comments Joan Derwent. Her chum Peggy West, also below the threshold of nubility, says: "Who on earth wrote it? But I vote we go - even though the crypt is out of bounds!"

Events move on winged feet. As the chums creep to the crypt,

Mildred Briggs, the form sneak, is watching. In bubbles, Mildred thinks, "Two girls going towards the crypt! I'll tell Cynthia about this!"

Mildred wears glasses which alone would brand her as a pimp. [1960s slang for tell-tale, I hasten to add today].

In the crypt is a girl dressed up in a pioneer Batman-style outfit. "Who are you?" exclaim the chums, ink lines radiating from their heads like a sunset.

"I'm sorry, I must remain unknown," replies the masked girl crushingly. "Call me No 1. Will you join me to form the SILENT THREE in the battle against Cynthia's tyranny?"

Cynthia, I must explain, frames girls, gives them 100 lines, tells lies, crawls to the head and to cap all that off, she helps her father smuggle gold bullion from a sunken ship.

"Don't worry, we'll take any risk to bowl out Cynthia," says the plucky Peggy.

I won't reveal any more of the plot, in case I spoil it for you, but I was interested in the sociological and moral aspects.

First, the end seems to justify the means. Our heroines are always sneaking into Cynthia's study and rifling her drawers for evidence.

In my companion volume, 'Mystery Hotel', young Elaine Jackson is great stuff at spying on guests through their bedroom keyholes - voyeurism in a good cause. The swearing is continual: Jolly, gosh, my goodness, whizzo, what the blazes! (Used by crooks), golly and phew - these are just a few of the crimson oaths.

It turns out well for the good girls in the end, especially when the police inspector says, "Thanks to these three girls, ma-am, I have proof that Cynthia and her father…"

But virtue suffers gruelling trials for most of the book. One of the Silent Three is framed and expelled for theft. The other two are drummed out of the school (almost) as members of a banned secret society.

They are always being locked up in, and escaping from, the detention room, seemingly a standard feature of English school architecture. The escapes are always on narrow ledges 200ft above jagged rocks.

Technically the comics are advanced, with dizzying shifts of focus or arrested motion tricks. Loud speech in School Friend is indicated cleverly by jagged speech balloons.

The publication specializes in the neat punchline, not only wrapping up the plot but inviting us to fork out 15c (1/3d to West Africans) for our next issue:

Peggy: "Well, we can put our robes away now that Cynthia's tyranny is finished and Betty's name is cleared."

Betty: "Yes, perhaps one day we may need them again, who knows?"

Who knows, indeed, eh chums?

School Paper – more of a Pick-Me-Up
26 August 1967

In Parliament Place is an old cottage with generous verandas and a top-heavy second storey. From its warrens emerges *The West Australian School Paper* - a million free copies a year. Like its headquarters, the paper is friendly but not swinging. Bundles began lobbing on my desk lately and I began to wonder about them. Were they still warning, as I recalled from my school days, about 'The Boy who Double-Dinked' or had they moved on to 'I was a Third-grade Shoplifter'? Which departmental officer is the author of 'I, Chacma the Baboon'?

For 16 years the papers have been run by Mr R. Grace. I found him small and greying in a purple cardigan, with his eyebrows constantly raised over his spectacles. He has a bad limp from polio at three months.

He told me that children got sick of their textbooks, especially when they were hand-me-downs. The School Papers were a monthly pick-me-up.

In the pioneer issue in 1952, fat greedy Sam scoffed 40 sausage rolls. He had a fit of the sausage-roll Delirium Tremens, which cured him of the vice.

"No thanks, Mother," he would reply when offered sausage rolls after a meal. "I have had plenty to eat." Then he would get up from the table and help his sisters dry the dishes.

Six questions followed in the text, such as 'How many sausage rolls did Sam eat?' and 'In how many minutes did Sam eat the lunch his Mother made him?'

No. 2 issue idolizes the Royal Family:

"Our king and queen are very kind, friendly people who work just as hard as your father and mother. Their two daughters have been brought up to love their father and mother and be good and kind also. So, you see, princes and princesses are not very different from you."

God help them then, one might add. Mr Grace confesses, "In

those days perhaps we were a little anxious to teach. The pill was a bit more evident."

Current issues are lavishly illustrated and much less ethereal. They have cartoon covers, adventure serials and meaty stuff on Egyptian slave drivers:

"Poor devils," muttered the officer. "I would not like to be working under you, Raschid."

"I just do my job, sir," Raschid replied with a laugh. "I drive them just as you use a whip to speed up a horse when it gets lazy. A slave or a horse - what's the difference?"

I found three young ladies, all ex-teachers, inventing stories in a back room. One produced a brown notebook marked 'Plots - ¼ acre' (the '1/4 acre' having been added by a waggish artist) in which she jotted ideas as they came to her, night or day. Sample: 'Willy Wagtail taking bath in horse's trough: horse comes to drink at it, what happens?'

They told me that girls liked stories about boys but boys didn't like stories about girls – and that both liked stories about animals.

In the art room a middle-aged artist was working on a joke cover. His battling Viking in a winged helmet was about to speared by his foe. In the next sequence the Viking was doing a vertical take-off, powered by his helmet wings. "The children must detect the movement of the wings," the artist said with a frown. "The point will hinge on that."

However children sometimes arrive at a super-subtle analysis of the jokes. One joke showed competitors in a bag-race looking askance at the boy on the end of the row. He is to race in a blood-and-bone bag. But one reader, after long study, declared that the boy was being frowned at because his bag was a shade wider and he would be able to take bigger steps in the race.

"We make sure there is nothing anyone could take exception to," Mr Grace said. "We keep right off anything of a religious nature, except some stories in December with a Christmas flavour."

"That must cramp your style," I suggested.

"That is quite true. There is not much that is not controversial," he said.

Thus no Chinese child appears in the series 'Children of other Lands', though staff have been so bold as to mention the geography of Russia to high school children.

Aboriginal legends are OK but stories about half-castes might cause reactions in country districts. The poetry is a little cissy but the plays abound with such lines as 'Bind the rascal!' and 'Police here! Open the door!' The line below caused me some concern:

Elsie (nodding weakly): Yes, I'm all right, thanks to Penfold.

It was with some relief that I found in the cast list that Penfold was a dog....

You would think I had written myself out on this minor 'School Paper' topic but ten months later, on 10 June 1968, I splashed over three columns about how a new issue was mired in controversy bordering on scandal. The paper's editor must have died a thousand deaths to read my piece attributing superstition, heresy and rubbishy content to his literary offspring.

At a half-century remove in time, I can't say today whether this 'High School Magazine for First-Years' was the same, or from the same stable, as the purple-cardiganed Mr Grace's 'School Paper' of yore but I'd say it was, based on some internal clues.

My piece was headlined, intriguingly, 'Moving Cof.ns of Barbados'. It began:

Of course the Education Department doesn't believe in ghosts, whatever you might think after reading the latest High School Magazine for First Years.

I had a ring from Mrs F. Fitzpatrick of Scarborough, whose offspring came home from school with knees knocking on the day that the June magazine came out.

"Do you believe in ghosts?" was Mrs Fitzpatrick's first question to me.

"Not usually," I said cautiously.

"Well, the department can believe in ghosts if it wants to but there's no need for it to convert schoolchildren."

She referred me to an article called 'The Moving Coffins', part of a series in the magazine on mysterious events. She said that authors' conclusion was that only "supernatural forces" could have moved the coffins, and "she objected to this kind of rubbish being put into the hands of children as fact". Furthermore, it was heresy to dabble in the occult. And moreover, instead of getting children to adopt a critical attitude to supernatural hocus-pocus, the questions at the end of the article encouraged the supernatural thesis, she said.

I set off at a run for the magazine's headquarters and soon had a copy from the bewildered staff. The story was about an 18th century vault in the Barbados, in which coffins were prone to go leaping around – five times between 1812-20 – though the opening to the vault had been sealed.

"Whatever produced the disturbances must have been either human, natural or supernatural," says the author, a female, spreading the net a little wider than is usual in scientific circles.

She disposes of human and natural causes, and concludes by quoting Conan Doyle, "The disturbances were the work of forces desiring the more speedy decomposition of the bodies". She continues, "What it was that caused the disturbances is a mystery which remains to excite the imagination."

She follows through with questions for the kids to answer about the difficulty of attributing the coffin movements to human agencies or earthquakes or floods.

In my article I offered some alternative questions, about whether Conan Doyle was a fantasist and whether the Barbados natives had managed to stitch up their British colonial overlords. I concluded with a third question: "If you get a flat tyre, is the cause likely to be human, natural or supernatural?"

The school paper's editor, who I didn't name, explained how he had tasked his underling with writing a series about unexplained mysteries to get the kids intrigued.

"What do we mean by the supernatural?" he asked. *"It is a general term to cover anything that is left that can't be explained by natural laws or human interference."*

On that note, I spirited myself away.

Hits and misses at His Majesty's – why "Mame" is spelt "Maim"

December 1968

A few years ago, show business had no business in Perth. His Majesty's Theatre was non-functioning for nine months out of 12; the few big musicals that crossed the Nullarbor returned eastwards $10,000 or $20,000 poorer. They included *Bye Bye Birdie* and *How To Succeed In Business Without Really Trying*.

Entrepreneurs made a fearful resolution: no more shows for Perth. But TVW7 came to the rescue, offering to share the risks three ways with the Edgleys and the JC Williamson Co.

The first such import, *Oliver*, broke the hoodoo two years ago. Within six months *Funny Girl* was another hit, followed by *Fiddler on the Roof*, which looks like breaking the records in Australia set by *My Fair Lady*.

However *Mame*, which finished about a week ago has sent a chill wind through theatrical circles. It was one of the most lavish shows to come to Perth, cost nearly six figures and lost a five-figure sum. Wags have christened it *Maim*. To break even it needed at least 80% full houses. The night I went, it looked rather like a 70% house. Too many people were saving for Christmas or had Christmas do's on.

At His Majesty's last week teeth were set in fixed smiles, on the assumption that one downpour doesn't make a winter.

Speaking generally, JCW representative David Petersen said that Perth was now in the running for any big show on the Eastern States circuit, and other things being equal we were likely to see shows even before Sydney.

Michael Edgley put it even more strongly. "Whatever musical is successful over there, you will see in Perth," he said.

It was the success of *Oliver, Funny Girl* and *Fiddler* that induced Edgley and Dawe to buy the theatre this year and that in turn will lead to its air-conditioning and renovating early in the 1970s.

His Majesty's will have its lights up nearly all the year in 1969.

The present roster is: January–Matt Monroe, an English pop singer; February–Eartha Kitt; March–the English Black and White Minstrel Show; May–*Snow White Panto*; June-Gilbert and Sullivan Society's *Pirates of Penzance*; July–Russian classical ballet; also July–Joyce Grenfell return season; August–WA Opera Company; October – Australian Ballet and Elizabethan Opera Trust Opera.

The musicals *I Do, I Do* and *She Loves Me* are possibles for Perth next year – though *Mame* has not enhanced our chances of getting them.

JC Williamson and the Edgleys are a Siamese twin ensemble. The Williamson chain of theatres stretches from Adelaide to New Zealand, and they need to stay busy. The Edgleys have a gift for recruiting exotic shows, which they run through Williamson theatres.

Theatre in Australia has seldom had it so good; many of the Williamson theatres are running ten months of the year, with hardly a week between productions.

To most of us, Joan Sutherland is Our Joan. To JCW's, she's Our Two Hundred Thousand Dollars, which is the loss they made on her in 1965-66. They made $100,000 the next year, and in the 1967-68 financial year their profits trebled to $300,000, thanks to *Fiddler on the Roof, Man of La Mancha, Oliver, Half a Sixpence*, The Spanish Dancers, *Spring & Port Wine*, the Moscow Circus and *Mame*.

What did a musical need? I asked Mr Petersen of JCW's. Sheer entertainment, he said. If the audience had to listen too hard and follow a complicated turn of plot, it lost interest and the show went flat. So musicals lived by the minute, with scene changes every second minute and a new frock for the leading lady each 30 seconds. The motto: Please Everyone. The cost: Hair-Raising. And pull the wrong rope backstage and the whole glorious illusion collapses about your ears.

Musicals were much the same as ever. The standard fare was still the period piece – the Twenties or The Great Waltz or what have you. Then there were the sentimental ones like *Oliver. Fiddler on the Roof* had everything – period, sentimentality, good music and a sane story. It was already having a return season in Sydney and might run a second time here.

Was it hard to get chorus girls and boys? "To get into a chorus is an honour. Australia's full of graduates from singing and dancing schools. Their greatest achievement is usually to tour Australia in a chorus. It's only two steps from the chorus row to a bit part and stardom.

"Audiences are discriminating and when they judge a musical they don't just say it's great but talk at length about the merits or de-merits of the principals, the chorus and the choreography."

The story of a musical starts when directors take a trip to Britain and the US looking for shows. They buy the rights and royalties to the ones they like – the people who get the money are the authors and composers.

The show is usually bought as an abstract proposition. The firm recruits its own directors – mostly from the US – and designers and cast. The stars are mostly imported. Australia has some stars but somewhere in America there's always a star of the right sort immediately available. Thus for *Mame* they got Gayle Byrne, an American; but for *Funny Girl* they went for Jill Perryman, an Australian, because she was good box office.

"I suppose there's a lot of lobbying from leading ladies as soon as they know a show is brewing?" I suggested.

"Yes," said Mr Christensen (with no need to elaborate).

The casting directors are the angels that every chorus girl dreams about. When the casters see a show, they remember any talented player, and when - maybe years later – it's time to grab their own star, they backtrack and make an offer.

Entrepreneurs in other States have the English and American stage circuits sewn up, while the Edgleys have gone for the East European and now the Asian circuit.

Michael Edgley has spent only six weeks this year stationary in Perth. He flies to Moscow like we fly to Rottnest.

Did he still think of Perth as his home? – "My oath!"

The Playhouse falls on hard times
May 1967

Edgar Metcalfe as Lady Macbeth was an aesthetic failure, but he and Playhouse electrician Malcolm Hoff made their point.

They were out to show me that they really needed expensive new stage lighting.

Mr Hoff wormed himself into the control box and prepared to light up Lady (Edgar) Macbeth as she/he toured the stage with a candle. He crouched like a sprinter before dim ranks of L-shaped levers. Lady Macbeth moved off.

Mr Hoff tore at the levers, flicking a dozen upside down and pushing a dozen more into gear. He made them rattle like a cash register. With Lady Macbeth almost round the corner, he put in a frantic finishing burst with his right knee.

"Edgar sometimes expects me to use both knees," he panted.

He switched off all stage lights by pulling down a handle the size of a railway signal. "You hear the clunk ten rows back in the stalls," he said.

He wastes several days a month laboriously rigging and unrigging the control box, and the gear uses $240 worth of power a month.

Next, Playhouse Director Metcalfe took me on a tour backstage. Paint was peeling and the dirty ceiling sprouted naked bulbs. The mud-brown lino was worn through in strips. "We don't want anything fancy, just something that doesn't trip you up," he said.

In the makeshift costume room, women were making trimmings for Henry IV's robes by cannibalising a fur coat.

"If we had bigger storerooms we wouldn't need to ruin costumes after the play," said Mrs Betty Pearson.

A crate of black and brown rags – looking like shoe-cleaners - turned out to be the costumes from the production of *Macbeth*. Made from hessian and spray-painted, they could have survived if properly hung.

"Some theatres I know have bought warehouses and old churches just for storage," Mr Metcalfe said. "We've no chance."

It was also hard for an actor to live glamorously on Playhouse pay – $40 to $44 minimum equity rates. "We've only got six full-timers: me, Rosemary Barr, Alfred Hurstfield, Alan Harvey, James Beattie and Peter Morris. It's not enough. They have to take big parts all the time, when they should play a lead once and then recuperate in the next play with a minor part. They get tired and the audience gets fed up with seeing them all the time."

Disgustedly he shook curtains of the set for *Present Laughter* by Noel Coward: "This is supposed to be a posh flat but the curtains are just red cotton. They should be velvet."

Everywhere, I found penny pinching, with the resulting inefficiency increasing costs. Caught in this vicious circle the Playhouse hopes the businesses and people of WA will meet its appeal for $20,000.

Chairman of Committees H. Smith said they had tried everything to make the theatre pay its way – except watering down the program with worthless but profitable comedies.

"Our audiences per play dropped from 7,000 to 3,500 when television came in," he said. "They are still 1,000 behind the pre-television mark."

I suggested: "Maybe you could drop free tickets on Perth from an aeroplane. That would widen your circle."

He said, "We have. At least, we used to post 500 free tickets at random a while back. Even then, only a fifth were used. Not even enough to fill out the seats."

The number of Perth people who had ever gone to a play would not be more than 25,000, he said. About 7,000 people saw several plays a year, and the Playhouse had 3,000 regulars. From 1929 to 1956, virtually no plays were performed here and people grew up watching films. "Even Laurence Olivier ran out of audience here in Perth. About 20,000 came."

Perth audiences were not sophisticated. Many came only if they knew that a play had done well somewhere else; that it had a big stock of accumulated appreciation.

"Take *Loot*," he said. "It was the *Evening Standard's* best play in England last year, and it's still running there. Some film company has paid the highest-ever price for film rights. And we lost money on it. Perth hadn't heard of it."

Mr Smith said Perth audiences were also notoriously slow starters. They didn't like to come at the beginning of a play's run; they waited till the last days. First nights had to be filled by issuing big blocks of seats to charities, which raised funds by selling them. The Playhouse charged them only 20c to 25c a seat. Unless first nights were crowded, the actors couldn't get confidence.

Mr Smith sighed when I asked him why people went in their thousands to films but not to plays.

"I get more pleasure watching second-rate actors than first-rate films," he said. "They spend millions on one film and they can get the best talent in the world, and they put on a ham show. Before the depression we had no money and we made our own entertainment – amateur theatres, concerts, debating clubs. Now people buy their entertainment ready-made."

The Playhouse is pinning its distant hopes on the young generations – it has 1,000 high school members. But it's immediate hopes rest on that $20,000 appeal.

Playhouse's survival: hanging by a thread
2 January 1968

The Playhouse has had another lean year – its sixth in a row – with small hope of any fat years to come.

Survival is the big issue for the Playhouse now.

It has survived so far only by going ever deeper into debt. Its choice is to try to bring back the crowds, or to cut costs and service so that it loses less money. If both fail the Playhouse will have to fold up or throw itself on the government's mercy for a permanent subsidy. It got $10,000 this year as a special grant.

It was easy to find a scapegoat for the losses last year. If the Playhouse wanted to put on sexy, horrible modern plays like the Marat-Sade effort, serve it right if people stayed away. What the Playhouse should do, people argued, was to put on nice wholesome plays that gave you a good laugh and a tear or two in the sad bits. Then they'd make some money.

The Playhouse more or less did this in 1967. It ran the gamut from *Goldilocks* to *The Boyfriend*, with *Henry IV* thrown in for duty's sake. Certainly no one could accuse it of being highbrow.

But to the dismay of the Playhouse board, the new policy didn't do much better. Chairman of Committees Howard Smith told me that the year had been more successful, but by this he only meant that the losses had slowed from a gallop to a canter. He needed houses 60% full but houses averaged 50%.

The first and most popular play, *Goldilocks and the Three Bears at the Circus*, got a total audience of nearly 16,000 small fry. The box office collected $9614 and the profit was $500.

Then came the crunches. *Oh What a Lovely War* (audience 5,100) lost $1,000; *Semi-Detached* (5,900) lost $1500; *Loot* (4,500) failed to produce any and lost $2,000. Then the Playhouse tried Coward's *Present Laughter*, half-hoping to make a pile. The play was a hit, the audience was 8,800 but costs were high and the profit ended up as a meagre $350.

The figures illustrate a grim law for the Playhouse: that a not-too-successful play loses thousands of dollars but a brilliantly successful one will only clear a few hundred profit. The popular plays are mostly musicals, which need big casts, orchestra and lavish costumes. And since only one play in six does well, the Playhouse is on the skids.

Here is a run-through of plays this year:

Henry IV (audience 5,232), loss $400; *Luv* (5,100), broke even, as it was cheap to put on; *The Boyfriend* (14,000), profit $1,500; *Mary Mary* (6,000), broke even; *Wizard of Oz* (9,046), profit $650; *Captain Carvallo* (a grim 2,775), loss $2,500 - the biggest loss of 1967; *When We Are Married* (6,350), loss $1,200 despite the good turn-up; *And So To Bed*, which has done fairly well.

As a matter of interest, its most avoided play ever was *Blood Wedding* in 1958 which drew 68 people on the opening night. The theatre seats about 750.

Late in the year the Playhouse was counting on *The Devil's Advocate*, which had saved a Sydney theatre from bankruptcy. But Perth held its nose and stayed away in greater numbers than usual, and the play lost $1,500.

What's in store for next year? Nothing's decided yet but Mr Smith's predictions were ominous. He said the board was "hoping to put on a better type of play" and when pressed, cited *Pygmalion* and a French farce called *A Flea in her Ear*, as likelies. "Keeping solvent is the main thing," he said.

The only regular subsidy for the Playhouse is that the Elizabethan Theatre Trust pays the director's salary of $5,000.

This year the Playhouse hired an M.T.T. bus and seven actors went barnstorming the countryside. Despite special subsidies from the WA University and the Education Department, the venture lost $4,000.

Bunbury and Albany went wild with apathy. Carnamah showed more interest than Bunbury; Mt Barker more interest than Albany;

Northam is traditionally hostile to the arts. However, travelling 100 miles to put on a play for 16 children at Woop Woop State School, who pay 20c each, is inherently a losing proposition.

Even the Playhouse's 1967 appeal for $20,000 flopped. Business houses kept their hands in their pockets and the appeal raised only $6,000.

We began talking about how the Playhouse could make more money.

The market for subscribers is pretty saturated. About 2,500 people are members, but only half turn up at any show.

To put on meatier shows would be unlikely to boost profits. The 1,500 to 2,000 who would turn up are only a third of the minimum needed. They are probably the same audience who patronise the Hole in the Wall.

Could your troubles with directors have contributed to the losses? - "What troubles?"

Could you hire out the Playhouse during the day for lectures? - "That wouldn't pay the cleaners."

Cheaper prices? – "No, the people who go to plays are not the people who worry about prices. Anyway we charge no more than many cinemas."

How about reducing overheads? – "It's hard. We've got a big theatre. If we had realised what television would do to our audiences when we started in 1956, we'd never have built so big, or in the central city.

"We're a union shop. We've got nine actors on full-time annual contracts. We have to pay them whether there's a play on or not.

"Backstage we've a stage manager and assistant stage manager, a mechanist to lift the scenery and a property man to shift the odds and ends. There's an electrician and a fireman."

What's the fireman do? – "Puts out fires. Under union rules, he's also allowed to raise the curtain.

"We have to have someone to design and paint the sets. And a wardrobe mistress. The union bans voluntary help with plays."

Why don't you bulldoze the theatre, put a block of offices on the site and start again with a little suburban theatre? – "We can't. We don't own the land in Pier Street. We lease it from the Anglican Church. If we lost the building, we'd lose our main asset."

Mr Smith finally revealed that the board is thinking of turning the Playhouse into a repertory show opening for three three-monthly seasons a year. This would save three months' salaries. It would also make things more flexible.

The Playhouse would work on a repertoire of four plays for each season. Then, if the first play flopped, it could be replaced instantly by the second, or the best play could be run twice during the season. Now, the Playhouse is stuck with any play for a fixed number of weeks because of the money it's invested in pre-advertising and because it can't afford to have dark (play-less) times between shows.

The snag may be recruiting actors. There are not enough locals (because our television and radio are negligible employers of actors). Eastern Staters may rather not come here for a mere three-month contract. If they did, the Playhouse would have to pay airfares and living allowances, which would offset savings.

"The (repertory) scheme's just a fish in the pond," he said. "We wouldn't decide anything until our new director is appointed for 1968-69."

I said, "Looking at the balance sheet, can you see a point at which the Playhouse will expire?"

"Not for a few years," he said. "We'd hope the State government would rescue us."

Perth's Carmen – sexiest girl in Opera
June 1968

The world's worst disaster in opera befell a performance of Wagner's *Tannhauser*, when Austrian baritone Emil Scaria stopped during his aria, turned to his leading lady and asked, "What opera is it that we are singing?" The second-worst was when someone threw a bouquet of carrots and onions at Maria Callas, a prima donna without much sense of humour.

The WA Opera Company hopes that no such events will mar its *Carmen* at His Majesty's next month.

The opera company is manned by hordes of strongmen from Perth's civic, cultural and financial fields. As director James Penberthy put it, "Even if we fail, it'll be spectacular, like the Titanic." At best, he has visions of Perth as the home city of Australian opera, La Scala on the Swan.

There has never been a more popular opera than *Carmen*, which contains a factory girls' song in praise of cigarettes and the sexiest heroine in show business. She is required in one scene to dance a habanera, "which even in its most classic form is bound to be indecent, recalling the dance du ventre (belly dance) of the Algerian café", in the words of one reference book.

Carmen was once produced with a real bullfight. Last week two young ballet dancers were ordered to the Midland abattoirs to pose for photographs. But few bulls had the strength of mind to look handsome there: most looked crestfallen.

Finally the abattoirs phoned to announce the arrival of a super-bull, lean and defiant. He was too defiant for the ballet girls, who would not go within photographic range. They consented to sit on a fence with the bull tied up nearby. "The pong was awful," one of the three told me.

The Perth production features such things as genuine Spanish drinking skins – animal hide filled with sherry and squirted into singers' mouths bagpipe fashion.

One scene requires little boys to play soldiers, composer Bizet instructing that they be as tiny as possible. Choirs from Trinity College and Mt Lawley School will alternate.

Two schools' music masters are alternating in the smuggler's role of Dancairo, precipitating a miniature crisis when Hale and Wesley schoolboys refused to buy tickets unless it was their own music master's turn on stage. They were booked for separate matinees.

Dancairo has another job besides smuggling. There are several choruses that sing backstage, and unless they sing off-key and off-beat they won't harmonise with the fore-stage music. Dancairo has to race backstage and blow an off-key tuning note on a pitch pipe.

The need for a strong band of men singers was solved when someone discovered the resplendent choir at the WA Italian Club. "They're not all bel canto but they sure can belto," someone remarked.

Organisers gathered 40 socially prominent people at a restaurant and exhorted them to come in their diamonds and mink. "We're just poverty-stricken ignorant artists," the women were told. "We make the occasion, but you must make the glitter."

Socialites who want the best box at the opera will have to share it with a percussion team and some double-bass players. The orchestra pit is over-crowded.

The opera caused a furore when Bizet wrote it in 1875 for the Paris Opéra Comique, a bourgeoise establishment where weddings were often arranged and celebrated. The director thought it was bad enough for the heroine to die, let alone get a knife in her back. "Such a thing has never been seen! Never! Don't make her die, I beg you, don't!" he cried to Bizet, and resigned not long after, reputedly because he lost the argument.

Over-enthusiastic Carmens can be a nightmare for the leading man. US soprano Geraldine Farrar, fortified by an afternoon at the movies, once played Carmen in bar-room brawl style, so Caruso had to hold her off like a struggling eel while he finished his aria.

Part of the WA company's worries is that it hasn't a building. Huge wooden sets are travelling from warehouse to warehouse, and the stage architect, Dr A. Comar, didn't even know last week where they were.

He begged me not to reveal the trickeries by which he could convert a mountain to an arena in five minutes. "People will be pointing and saying, 'Aha!' when they should be under a spell," he said. Some of his effects are simple. For example, by projecting intense light outwards through a window of the arena wall, he can conjure the sweat, dust and excitement of the bullring.

When Carmen is in the mountains the stage needs to present a foreboding of death. This is usually done with dead trees. Dr Comar is arranging what he calls a "broken Christ" - the hands still nailed to the cross but the body fallen to the ground.

After some duelling, the organisers have agreed to put on the Carmen in English. This will offend the purists because English with its diphthongs (fee-ur not fere = fear) is less musical than French and translations get awkward when long notes turn 'people' into 'peeep-pull'. But the idea is for the audience to have a good time and they need to know what's going on.

Every part has two or more alternating singers, so in effect there will be several versions of the opera during the season. There are two men to play Escamillo the bullfighter. One is Ed Holding, who was motoring around the world but wouldn't travel further than lovely Perth. His bullfighter is stern and dignified. The other is Allan Pearson, more flamboyant.

The toreador's song: "Tor-e-ador tum tumpty tumpty tum" is so good that few producers can bear the chorus to join in "fatuously" as Bizet directed.

Micaela the good girl is often played as a milksop, with blue pinafore and yellow plaits. Our opening night Micaela, played by noted soprano Glenys Fowles, intends to show a more noble and less jilt-worthy Micaela.

The characters are drawn partly from their music. Carmen gets violins in low register, plus flutes showing her country origin. Micaela the good girl gets violins sweet and high, with French horns; the bullfighter thrives on drums, horns and trombones; and the hero Don Jose is treated to the full orchestra, though the orchestra only draws a trombone when Don Jose is having a row with the bullfighter. The little boys' chorus is scored for flutes.

Good luck, cast and crew! You're going to be Bizet peeep-pull.

Devilish doings in Faust

22 July 1969

In view of modern trends in the theatre, I was disappointed to learn that Marguerite will not give birth on the stage of His Majesty's during the opera *Faust* next month. Faust will not even seduce her on-stage.

In all, the opera is going to be pretty tame, compared with '*O Calcutta*'. I did discover that the Papal Government banned *Faust* from Rome in the 1860s, because the Pope's people would not allow the devil to be presented on stage.

"Whether this was due to excessive respect for the great personage in question was not explained," commented my (likely) Protestant source, a Mr Henry Tolhurst, writing in 1905.

Gounod's opera also fared badly at the hands of Bolshevik censors in 1925. The Commissar of Public Art, Moscow, authorized a revised version, as follows:

Faust becomes Harry, an American millionaire who, in his luxurious Berlin apartment, tells Mr Mephistopheles – the evil spirit of capitalism - that he desires Marguerite, a poor but pretty movie actress. Marguerite, her brother Val and friend Siebel are all left-wing.

Marguerite is won over by a bundle of thousand-dollar bills left on her window-sill. She breaks into the Money Waltz (formerly the Jewel Song) and allows Harry to lead her from the path of Marxian orthodoxy. She is condemned to death for murdering her child, and kills Harry when he visits her remorsefully in her cell. She is saved by the timely arrival of the Red Army's troops.

Marguerite, whether left wing or bourgeoise, captivated Europe from the first performance.

Gounod was at first unable to find any theatre manager willing to put on his opera. Finally a M. Carvalho, who ran the Théâtre-Lyrique, agreed, suggesting innocently that perhaps his wife could take the role of the heroine. Gounod received this badly – the wife was a notoriously shrill soprano, "a regular bird-pipe" as one of her best friends put it.

Mme Carvalho sang her best, but her husband the manager went bankrupt after 57 performances. As it happened, *Faust* became France's most popular opera, and the man who merely published the music made 3 million francs.

Queen Victoria on her deathbed asked for some scenes to be played in her chamber. "The ailing sovereign's face lighted up and her lips parted in a transient smile of recognition whenever some well-known melody occurred," wrote a commentator.

An American soprano spoilt the euphoria when offered the part for the first New York performance.

"Stupidity is the keynote of Marguerite's character," she said. "She was a well brought up but uneducated young person of an ignorant age and of a stupid class, and innocent to the verge of idiocy."

Gounod was musically gifted from childhood, and as a toddler would remark that a dog was barking in A-flat.

Faust was his most successful opera. His first try was called *The Bloody Nun* by 'Monk' Lewis, an 18th Century writer of horror fiction. It was a bold choice by Gounod, who didn't foresee the effect of 'Monk' Lewis on genteel audiences. This is a description of Covent Garden when *The Captive*, by Lewis, was performed on March 22, 1803:

> *It threw a portion of the audience, whose nerves were unable to withstand the dreadful truth of the language and script, into hysterics, and the whole theatre into confusion and horror. Never had Covent Garden presented such a picture of agitation and dismay. Ladies were bathed in tears, others fainting, and some shrieking with terror, while such of the audience who were able to avoid demonstrating like this, sat aghast with pale horror painted on their countenances. It is said that the very door-keepers took flight.*

Gounod's *Bloody Nun* was a failure. "I am inclined to think that the subject is too uniformly gloomy," he commented after the premiere.

What the devil! I'm sure our *Faust* won't be that bad.

PROFILES SWEET AND SOUR

Shipwrecked with Captain Clink
4 April 1968

There would be few people still around who have rounded Cape Horn seven times in sailing ships or been wrecked off San Salvador with Captain Clink, alias the Liverpool Bulldog.

One of them is Mr J. L. Rycroft, 74, of Mt Lawley.

His parents paid 80 pounds to the owners of the Caithness-shire, a three masted barque, to get their 16 year old on a sailing ship. Captain Clink paid him a shilling a month wages, just because the lad was a Briton and Britons never never could be slaves.

Carrying nothing but sand as ballast, the ship of 3,000 tons was on its way to Tampico, Texas, to load four-gallon tins of kerosene for Australia. The tail end of a hurricane caught the ship in the West Indies. Rycroft and the other seven midshipmen were shaken awake at 2 a.m. when the ship lurched on to a reef. With crunches and groans, masts fell like big trees, while Captain Clink's bellows could be heard above the uproar. Six men drowned.

"I suppose there was a mad scramble for the boats," I put in.

"No, you don't do that at sea, boy. We all helped lower the sails."

The captain ordered the midshipmen to stay and sent the others off in the boats. Soon they heard a rifle shot, which meant they had made the four miles to land.

At first light, the captain decided the ship could not be saved. So they set off for the island in the captain's gig. There they made tents out of the sails (each sail was as big as the front of a house), ate turtles and turtles' eggs, and gave Rycroft the job of diving to the ship's pantry ("Not 'pantry', lazarette, boy!") for tins of rabbit, herring, bully beef and ghastly tasting dried spinach and cabbage.

They were marooned on the Rottnest-sized Island for six weeks, to the delight of the midshipmen. Mr Rycroft found the island's natives poor and emaciated, and they were always trying to steal things Captain Clink caught one woman and raised his rifle at her.

"You shoot me, you hang, I am British subject like you," she said in English. The captain lowered his gun, rather ashamed. In those days, Britain ran the world.

Another facet of the British eminence was seen when Mr Rycroft's next ship furled sails off Iquique, Chile, with a cargo of South Wales coal for the silver nitrate plants.

The jolly tars had the normal stimulus of native brandy (called pisco) and dusky maids, plus a mardi gras in the town. "It was customary for people to throw paper bombs full of scented water at each other," he said. "Everyone was wearing old clothes. But there was a police chief, a vigilante, there on horseback with beautiful white uniform, knee boots, lasso and sword on the saddle, and tall peaked cap. "The fellows let fly with the water bombs. The police whistles brought every soldier, policeman and fireman running. The tars were fighting mad. We got them away in the gig, just in time.

"Next day the vigilante rowed out with an escort. The sailors got up in the rigging. 'Arrest them if you can catch them,' shouted Captain Clink." But when the nervous troops were half way up, the tars put their sheath knives in their teeth, swearing fiercely. The vigilante called down his men and they drew their pistols. "Get off the ship!" shouted Captain Clink. They wavered but when he pointed at the red duster (Red Ensign) and said, "None of that on this ship", the Chileans left with everyone booing.

In 1912 Mr Rycroft was on the Kinross-shire, which was taking 5,000 tons of pig iron, furnace bricks and coke on a 20,000-mile trip to Seattle. The journey took 268 days, including 18 weeks off Cape Horn.

Mr Rycroft and the sailors stayed on deck to haul the lines that pulled the sails up and down, and as each wave crashed over, they would hang on to safety lines to stop being smashed across the deck.

They lost five or six men overboard and returned to the Falkland Islands for repairs.

In the harbour at Port Stanley were another five sailing ships the Horn had smashed up - a German five-masted barque called the R.C. Rickmers, a four-masted Russian barque, the last of the British windjammers called the Claverdon, an American barque called the Nuanu, and a British ship the Albion.

"That cork will sail safely around the world," he said, pointing to our sherry bottle. "That's because it doesn't resist the waves. But we had to beat through them. It's like when you smack the bathwater with your hand. You could break your fingers that way."

Mr Rycroft's best stories were about the shanghai-ing of crew. They put out from Melbourne once with a parson, a boxer and his manager, a Russian prince called Nikitenko and his servant Kuropatkin.

Sailors would come to port after two years at sea and spend their pay in one big bust-up. Then they would be forced to run up debts at boarding houses. The boarding-house runners would meet new ships and offer to sell their debtors to the captain for five pounds or so each. The captain deducted the cost from the conscripts' pay. It was called 'working the dead horse'.

The worst boarding house runner in the world was Cockney Jack in Vancouver. Cockney Jack enticed a man called Paddy on a ship in the port to see off a friend called Mick. Paddy had a steady job ashore in a timber mill and did not want to go to sea again. Paddy swore, as Vancouver receded in the distance, to return and find Cockney Jack. Years later Cockney Jack was clubbed to death one night among the stacks of timber on Vancouver wharf.

The legacy of Sister Kate

August 1969

I met an elderly woman hanging out clothes at Sister Kate's Home at Queens Park the other day. She was nearly deaf and bent-backed.

Miss V. Bennett has been looking after the part-Aboriginal children at the home for 35 years, since the day that Sister Kate arrived on June 1, 1934. Before that, she worked at the Parkerville children's home; before that, she was herself a child there.

Sister Kate's consists mainly of tumbledown shacks that would be condemned instantly by a dozen authorities if used as private housing. Doors swing drunkenly on one hinge, floors and ceilings warp and sag, ragged blinds grey with age flap in the wind and interiors reek of poverty and neglect. True, many of the 80 children there used to sleep in the dirt; a derelict cottage is at least an improvement. The two new brick cottages on the site are a promising contrast.

People bring their junk to Sister Kate's – some with good motives, some simply wanting to get rid of it. Staff pick through it all and give the best old clothes and furniture to the children. Some junk gets sold and some just lies around.[11]

Sister Kate is just a name to most of us. She sounds like a kindly old dear handing out boiled lollies on Sundays.

Certainly there is a mystique lingering, though Sister Kate died at 85 in 1946. In the chapel and in the original cottage, people get what they call "a special feeling." Quarter-caste mothers will drop in on their old friend Miss Bennett, ask to be taken to the chapel, step inside and say, "I'm home".

The story of Harry is typical. When Sister Kate was in the Tresillian Hospital, about a day before she died, she asked for the little dark boy Harry. She gave him a cake and some lollies and promised him a new bicycle by which to remember "Gran".

---

[11] The above two paragraphs I've interpolated from two other West articles of mine, June 26 and 27, 1969.

For his whole life Harry had slept in a small bed by Sister Kate's side. Who was Harry? The child of a young Aboriginal woman herself dying who knew of no person except Sister Kate who could look after her baby, already weak and emaciated.

The woman caught a train to Kenwick station and trudged through the hot sand and scrub to Queens Park to beg Sister Kate to take yet another waif in the crowded cottage.

Sister Kate, the daughter of Captain Clutterbuck of Wiltshire, came to Perth in 1901 when no one troubled much about waifs. She arrived with four other Anglican sisters and 22 London waifs, all of whom had travelled in one third-class cabin.

Her first problem: how to locate Perth waifs. She opened a crèche in William St where the Metro Theatre now stands, then re-opened in an old school in Fremantle. This quickly attracted eight destitute mothers only too glad to get rid of their half-starved, sickly babies.

The Sisters bought an uncleared block at Parkerville containing only a shed that would have been disdained by any self-respecting cow. The first night, rain poured through the roof. They made a day's train trip to Perth for supplies and returned to find that a neighbouring woodcutter had re-timbered the roof.

Any mother who has raised three children may appreciate the effort of a few Sisters in raising 870 children during 1903-33, each child with a history of rejection, neglect or sickness – often all three.

Sister Kate was no bureaucrat. She ran Parkerville but did her share of cooking, washing and comforting too. The sickest children were put in her room at night.

At the age of 72, she had the ordeal of nursing a dearly-loved Sister and workmate through a long, fatal illness. Afterwards she went away for a rest, intending to return to her job. But someone decided she was too old and she was eased out with an OBE as her only compensation.

One can hardly credit the next action of that 72-year-old woman who for 50 years – from the 19th Century slums of London to the backwoods of Parkerville – had done nothing but look after the poor and unwanted.

Sister Kate, with Miss Bennett as one of her right-hand women, started a new project: to scour the native camps of Western Australia for quarter-castes, then raise them and educate them into white society.

Some of those she found could speak nothing but tribal language and did not know what a comb was. They were undernourished and susceptible to disease.

She started the home in a cottage at Beach St., Cottesloe, but soon felt obliged to move to an outer suburb. Then the war came and she had to evacuate with the children from Queens Park to Roleystone. She returned at the end of the war with more children, of course, than she had started with. But her 85 years were slowing her down and she was getting too weak for the daily chores in caring for a dozen children. She went to hospital, had a rest for four days and died.

In the chapel fitted out by her former waifs, Sister Kate's presence becomes most tangible in a single-framed snapshot of a tall, smooth-faced woman with a big nose and swarms of grinning children clinging to her skirts.

The children used to dash into the chapel every morning, many clutching dolls, and hear her begin: "Adults are welcome but I am speaking to the children". Another photo in the chapel shows six of the 11 boys who came out here with her in that third-class cabin. All six were killed in the Great War. The army sent her their medals as next of kin and she mourned the lads like a mother.

"She was one on her own," said Miss Bennett. "In every way, to my way of thinking."

Machinegun Major at Stalingrad
22 January 1968

Russian ambassador N.Y. Tarakanov, bald and amiable, has a bit of his left ear missing and some scars above it, mementoes of the Battle of Stalingrad.

His English is rather thick, and though he struggled manfully through his speech opening the Summer School, he and I talked in his hotel room through an interpreter.

How did that epic battle appear to one who fought in it? The ambassador said he had been a major commanding a battalion of machine gunners, 56 guns in all, six men to a gun. There were so many casualties that the entire battalion was replaced 10 times. The original troops were young lads from an officer school. With no ceremony they were drafted to the machinegun unit and rushed to Stalingrad.

"Defending our troops, we cost the Germans many losses," he said. "Finally our armies encircled the Germans and began to tighten the ring. My battalion was then in a little bit better position, we just followed behind the troops. But the Germans were watching us carefully from a hill, and when we found ourselves in an open position, it was very great fire from every means they had." A shell exploded near him and fragments hit him in the leg and the head. He spent 14 months in hospital.

His account of the battle was rather dry. For example, when I asked if he was coordinating or actually firing machineguns, he replied: "Mainly, coordinating the actions of different units. Sometimes it was absolutely necessary for me to operate a machinegun."

Not a single building was left standing in the city or the suburbs after the street fighting. Most took place amid ruins. His machine gunners always preferred operating from basements, where it was harder for the Messerschmitts to get at them. Sometimes Russians would be occupying one floor and Germans another.

"He recollected one day," said the interpreter, "if he is not mistaken it was 23 October when his battalion was cut off from the main forces and trapped on one bank of the Volga. It was a very big danger. He had very strict orders not to go away, but in the face of this danger he ordered his battalion to cross the river. It was two miles wide, snow was around, the water was tremendously cold, nearly freezing point, and the current was strong.

"Unfortunately they had no equipment for floating. They just used simple things, they put the machineguns on boards and the men swam. All the time there was heavy firing from the German artillery and machineguns; we had some artillery shooting back, not much." They got across with one third of the machineguns. After one day's rest, they were sent back to fight at another place. It was strange but no one became ill from that long swim. You cannot imagine how cold the water was.

I asked Mr Tarakanov what other days he remembered.

Time is doing its job and he doesn't remember all the details, all the horrors of that time, though the war was a great disaster that is impossible to forget. Because you understand, our people did a great deal to defend their country, but the defence was a matter for the whole world. We were defending practically the whole world from the German invaders.

The interpreter suggested that the ambassador tell how he won the Red Star.

Our division was ordered to go on the offensive. It was all right at first but later on there was strong resistance; the division had to retreat. German tanks moved on us. Behind them came groups of German machine gunners.

Our orders were to let the tanks come through, and cut off the machine gunners. And we did. Then the tanks were without support; our artillery began to crush them. We turned our machineguns on the tanks to stop them retreating. After three hours, some tanks began moving backwards, having decided to destroy our battalion.

He continued, "They began to do it" - another of his dry phrases. "We had good luck. The field was hilly and was not frozen. We could dig little trenches which helped us to remain alive, though we suffered great losses. The tanks encircled us in order to destroy us completely. We sat in the trenches until midnight, then I ordered our guns at one area to open fire and the other guns to retreat in some other quiet direction. We managed to save about 30 machineguns and half the battalion."

Over lemonade, he said he had become deputy mayor of a district of Moscow after the war. He used to give lectures on history at a technological institute. The Foreign Office liked his style and here he was.

"It must be difficult being Russian ambassador to Australia," I said.

"It is difficult, but not as difficult as fighting."

Note: I'm not sure Ambassador Tarakanov was telling the whole story about his lucky appointment to Australia. The post was important enough to go to very high-level Communist Party members, for example Y.M. Samoteykin (1983-90), personal assistant to the General Secretary of the CP's Central Committee; and A.V. Basov (late 1970s), a Full Member of the Central Committee.

In the interview, I find remarkable today his remark that he defied 'very strict orders' against retreat and crossed back over the river. The Soviets normally were merciless against such disobedience. Antony Beevor, in his siege history "Stalingrad", says there were 13,500 executions for desertions, self-inflicted wounds and 'retreating without orders' during the battle (p.166-7).

The discordant life of Paul Robeson
22 November 2016

I'm one of a dwindling band who can say, "I heard Paul Robeson sing." These days most people under sixty would respond, "Paul who?"

To answer that question briefly, Robeson (1898-1976) was the son of a former slave. He took up the cause of Negro liberation from the 1930s (like most of his race in the US at the time, he referred to himself as a Negro) while achieving greatness in sport, acting, and especially singing folk and protest songs in his deep bass – "carpeted magnificence" was one description. He was also a militant Stalinist.

I was twenty when Robeson ended his 1960 tour of Australia at Perth, nearly 60 years ago. The world didn't know it and neither did I, but the free concert I attended at the Perth's Midland Railway Workshops was his second-last performance. The last was a day later in Perth.

My ex-schoolmate from Perth Modern School, Mick Thornber, was a cadet in the chemistry labs at the railway workshops, 18km north-east of Perth. Mick was working with cadet Bruce Laffer, also from my school year. I was a third-year cadet at *The West Australian* and Communist Party member (1958-62) at the time.

Mick says, "Bruce was looking out the window of the lab which overlooked the entrance where Robeson arrived. He recognized Robeson there at the gate and said 'Wow' and was jumping around stirring up everyone in the lab. We hurried out to see what was going on, and my first surprise was to see my friend Tony Thomas in the crowd with his notebook out [actually, I was off-duty that day]. There were only about 20 present initially, mostly management types who'd been forewarned about Robeson's arrival.

"Then Robeson cupped his hand to his right ear to get his pitch right and started to sing, unaccompanied. That's what I won't forget, his voice was so powerful and it carried over the fence right into the workshops. The guys inside heard this singing and downed tools and poured out of the workshops. Some of the Dockers' footie barrackers can let go with the decibels but nothing like the power of Robeson's voice.

"I do seem to remember he started by standing on a wooden box. The move to a truck tray must have followed that. We thought it was funny as hell, Robeson mocking the management, who were actually reasonable fellows." Bruce Laffer adds, "We were too young and immature to get any sense of the workplace politics."

We three all got some of our key memories wrong. Robeson *did* have a loudspeaker set up on the truck and he *did* have a pianist – although his contract specifically forbade accompaniment to ensure concert ticket sales weren't undermined. Robeson told the crowd that they would get for free what wealthier Perth people would be paying high prices for at the concert at the Capitol Theatre on Saturday night. He may have reasoned that the tour was virtually over and the contract restrictions didn't matter.

Why wasn't he let inside the workshops to sing? It was to do with management-worker relations, rather than any political enmity. Key union reps there were Communists, but elected for their professionalism rather than their politics. Despite the odd fracas, management-union relations were not too bad, both sides doing a bit of play-acting.

The order to ban Robeson came from the chief mechanical engineer Bill Britter. He was within his rights, as the government had laid down that visitors could only speak inside if they were candidates for an imminent election. The unions had recently been taking liberties by inviting *ad hoc* Communist speakers, and Britter seems to have banned Robeson to re-assert his authority.[12]

The workshops' floor conditions were Dickensian. Safety gear, for example, was rudimentary and men worked amid the noise, smoke and dirt. My ex-schoolmate Mick, however, says there was an

---

[12] The visit is outlined in a 2006 history of the workshops. The history drew in turn on Fremantle Labor MLA Simone McGurk's radio interviews of the key participants when she was a media student at Murdoch University in 2002.

attractive culture of good fun mingled with a can-do approach to difficult tasks - the tradies could make a split pin or recondition a Crossley diesel loco's 10-metre crankshaft. "When the engine drivers marched through 100-strong to a stop-work meeting, we in the lab would go outside and cheer," Mick says.

A senior design clerk roasted his troops for unauthorized use of the photocopier to print sheet music. He blamed an accordion player because the paper that had jammed the machine emerged in concertina pleats. Similarly, a turner called Ron filled out a form to borrow a two-wheel trolley, reason "Moving house on weekend". He got a rejection back: "A two-wheeled trolley would not be large enough for such a task."

The key organizer of the Robeson show was union rep Colin Hollett. I don't know what his politics were, but he was a long-time Robeson fan. He knew of Robeson's penchant for worksite concerts and for a fortnight before Robeson's arrival was angling for management approval.

Hollett went to the Robeson's hotel the day they arrived, but Paul was out and Hollett asked his wife Essie, whose formal name was Eslanda, if Paul could sing for the Midland workers. She said, "He's busy now, but I'll mention it to him later." Colin went home, and at 2 a.m. Robeson rang Colin and said he'd love to sing that day.

In a splendid feat of organization, Hollett immediately got a telephone ring-around under way, expecting management cooperation. But Britter maintained his ban, so Hollett had to launch a second ring-around at 9 a.m. for the noon event outdoors.

They lined up a truck, public address system and facilities for the massive turnout, and the Mayor of Midland, Wal Doney, agreed to join Robeson on the truck and take him to a civic reception afterwards, a rare example on the tour of official endorsement. Robeson, in turn, must have organized his illicit piano and pianist, Larry Brown. "Half of Midland came and there were thousands there," Hollett said.

Perth was still a sleepy city – the Pilbara boom was five years into the future. Visitors of Robeson's global stature were not frequent, and it seemed newsworthy that he gave his Midland concert from the back of a truck to an audience of about 2,000. Maybe half were the workshop workers. (The whole population of Midland was then 9,000, now 4,000 – the Workshops shut in 1994). However, my employer *The West Australian*, chose to give red-ragger Robeson only a pic and five bland paragraphs on page 14 next day. Sixteen years later, *The West* ran a respectful US-sourced, 25-paragraph Robeson obituary across three columns, saying his career "was virtually destroyed in anti-communist witch-hunts of the 1940s and 1950s."

My only other Robeson involvement was last year when I found in Perth's Battye Library a tape of Robeson giving a long private talk to the Perth branch of the Australian Peace Council.[13] I spent a few hours transcribing it for other researchers.

Listening, I got a real feel for his personality and philosophies, especially as he wasn't self-censoring. Even in prose, his voice was full of music and he had an actor's ability to make anecdotes about his punch-ups on the football field come alive. Sometimes, to illustrate a point, he'd break into snatches of song. These qualities disappeared as I reduced his performance to mere text on a page.

He told the Peace Council, "I was asked to go out at lunchtime to see the railway workers, sing to them, I said I would, it would be pretty rough to be in WA and not go to the workers. I came from toiling labouring people. On the backs of my forebears was built the primary wealth of America, from which everything else had to flow."

The chair of the Peace Council reception seemed to be a church minister, judging by his Biblical allusions. At least three ASIO agents were present to file reports. One table comprised Communist stalwarts, such as author Katharine Susannah Prichard, CPA (WA) secretary Sam Aarons and wharf leader Paddy Troy. Robeson joined

---

[13] The Australian Peace Council had invited Robeson to Australia in 1950 but the passport ban made it impossible. The parent World Peace Council, of which Robeson was a member, was outed in the Mitrokhin archives in 1999 as an anti-Western disinformation vehicle 90% financed by the Soviet Union.

their table briefly to chat with Aarons, whom he first met in pre-war Spain during the civil war.

Robeson's tour was not a high point of his career. He didn't want to come – he preferred Ghana. He came only because concert promoters promised him $US100,000-plus for about 15 concerts over two months in Australia and New Zealand, equivalent to about $A1.3 million today. His wife, Essie, wrote that they could "clean up some fast money, and then he can retire, and do only what he wants to do."

Robeson's finances had been wrecked when the US government withdrew his passport from 1950-58, confining him to the US and blacklisting him as a performer. Before the ban he'd been earning a princely $US100,000 a year; after the ban he was lucky to make $US5,000.

Former Tasmanian Labor Senator Bill Morrow (1888-1980) had invited Robeson to Australia when they met in 1959 at a top-level soiree in Moscow of the World Peace Council. At least one of the two – Robeson – was a secret Communist Party member. Morrow, originally a railways worker, faithfully followed the Communist line, but membership was never proved. A clue is that a 1951 speech of Senator Morrow against Western intervention in the Korean War was re-broadcast by Radio Moscow. As with Robeson, the government withdrew his passport. A bio-essay for the Senate by Audrey Johnson says Morrow met "outstanding figures in the peace movement" including Zhou Enlai (peace-loving Mao's offsider) and in 1961 Morrow won the Lenin Peace Prize.

Morrow also helped organize Robeson's concert for construction workers at the Sydney Opera House construction site, where "huge, burly men on the working site were reduced to tears by his presence and his inspiration". A high-quality ABC film of the event is available on YouTube.

Robeson came to Australia fresh from being lionized in East Berlin. He told the press there, "The very basic thing to consider is what forces want peace and who the people are that say, 'Get your bases out of here, you folks from the Pentagon... Let's sit down with Khrushchev, we know that he is honest when he says, 'We want disarmament in the world.'" Two years later, Khrushchev was deploying nuclear missiles to Cuba.

The GDR gave him the German Peace Medal, an honorary doctorate, honorary membership of the Academy of Arts, and the Robeson-only Order of the Star of International Friendship. When the GDR's top man, Walter Ulbricht, pinned it on his chest, "a mighty storm of applause broke out" and the 5,000 in the hall joined in singing, "One great vision unites us."[14]

Robeson's Australian tour, in contrast, started badly when he got into verbal stoushes with Eastern States reporters who queried his support for the Soviet crushing of the 1956 Hungarian revolt. He countered that the revolt was by 'fascists'.

The Russians would 'hammer out the brains' of any country, including America, which took arms against them, he said. In such a conflict, he would side with Russia. Wife Essie lamented that Paul "is angrier than ever and it makes me shudder, because he is so often angry at the wrong people, and so often unnecessarily angry." He told an Australian friend that he was afraid to walk the streets in Australia - "He didn't believe that the people here loved him". Essie gave her own interviews, taking pains to be gracious and friendly. But she wrote, "He resents everything I do, no matter what. So, I'm up to here. Period."

A concert in Hobart was cancelled by sponsors. His promoters were in a panic that his interviews could alienate wealthy concertgoers and jeopardise returns. However, the NZ leg of the tour went smoothly after promoters asked the NZ press to avoid politics. The rest of the Australian tour also went well.

Sadly, by the tour's end in Perth he was exhausted, though he pledged to return to Australia to take up the cause of his black brothers, the Aborigines who were subjected to discrimination 'in

---

[14] *"Days with Paul Robeson"* - GDR booklet, 1960, in Battye Library's Robeson box.

its most loathsome form' and even 'extermination'. Arriving back in London from Perth he was so depressed that he took to lying on the bed in a darkened room with the curtains drawn. At one point the phone rang, with Fidel Castro on the line, and Robeson said he couldn't come to the phone. A few weeks later Kennedy launched the Bay of Pigs invasion.

In March 1961, Robeson abruptly departed London for Moscow – and slashed his wrists about 3 a.m. after a rowdy party in his hotel room. There were indications that some young people at the party had begged him to intercede for loved ones in the Lubyanka Prison, requests which could have put him into insoluble conflict. Other accounts reject that he was disillusioned with the Soviets. His son, Paul Jnr (1927-2014), rushed to his bedside. But after 12 days in Moscow, Paul Jnr had a nervous breakdown of his own, hurling a big chair through the hotel window and nearly throwing himself after it. Paul Jnr blamed CIA poisoners for the father-and-son breakdowns.

It was just coincidence, but my mother Joan in 1961 was with an Australian Communist delegation to China and Russia, and in Moscow she was lodged at a dacha for the elite outside the city. She discovered that Robeson was secreted away in the same dacha complex. She got an unlikely explanation that he was being hidden from potential CIA evildoers; he was actually hidden to conceal from the world the mental breakdown.

Robeson returned to London, where psychiatrists subjected him - inexplicably - to no fewer than 54 electric-shock treatments. Alarmed friends moved him to East Berlin, where he improved under a more humane treatment regime – rather the reverse of UK/East German stereotypes. He died of a stroke in his US home in 1976.

(The non-public-record intimacies are drawn from Martin Duberman's excellent but somewhat uncritical 1995 biography.)[15]

My favourite CD is Paul Robeson, *The Legendary Moscow Concert*. It was 'legendary' in half a dozen different ways, some to Robeson's

---

[15] Martin Duberman, *Paul Robeson*. The New Press, New York, 1995.

credit, some not. That Moscow concert evening encapsulates many of the paradoxes of Robeson as a great man, a great talent, a great fighter, and a great hypocrite.

Angered by the toxic racism of the pre- and post-war US, Robeson made himself a champion for Stalin's thousand times more toxic regime. Robeson's lifelong principle was always to laud and never to criticise the Soviets. This was not the self-delusion of other 'political pilgrims'; Robeson knew first-hand of the reality and lied through his teeth about it for the good of the cause.

The story of that concert in Moscow on 14 June 1949 is dramatic enough, but the back-story twists and turns like an over-plotted work of spy fiction.

Robeson was invited to perform at the Tchaikovsky Hall, Moscow, as part of celebrations for the 150th anniversary of the birth of Pushkin. Meanwhile Stalin, in his final spasm of butchery, was working up the 'doctors' plot' as a presage to a holocaust of Russia's remaining Jews. The 'plot' was that Jewish doctors were poisoning high-ranking party patients. The doctors were confessing under torture, unsurprisingly. When a couple of them held out, Stalin commanded the interrogators to "Beat, beat, and again beat!" – a rare instance of the Lubyanka's torturers being criticised for half-measures.

Robeson was friends with the Moscow theatre director Solomon Mikhoels and the poet Itzik Feffer, both Jews. He met them, in company with Albert Einstein, when they were fund-raising in the US in 1943 for the Soviet war effort.

In Moscow he was troubled by evidence of anti-Semitic purges, and asked his Soviet minders to arrange for him to meet Mikhoels. Robeson in fact knew Mikhoels had mysteriously died - he had taken part in a memorial service for Mikhoels in New York 18 months previously. His minder said that Mikhoels, sadly, had died of a heart attack. The reality was that the MGB in Minsk had set up Mikhoels one evening via an agent, jabbed him with a poisoned needle, then bashed his temple in, shot him, and ran over him with a truck, leaving his body in the snow by the road, along with the body of their own unlucky and potentially tell-tale agent. Stalin's daughter Svetlana overheard Stalin on the phone directing that 'car accident' be cited as the cause of death, although Robeson's minders cited heart attack.

Robeson then insisted on meeting poet Feffer, who in fact was in the Lubyanka awaiting execution. Feffer was roused from his cell bed, tidied up, sent home to be dressed, then brought to Robeson's hotel room. The room was bugged and, in any case, Feffer's family were hostages for his good behaviour.

Feffer alerted Robeson – who spoke fluent Russian – to the facts by gestures and notes on scraps of paper, while conversing about innocuous matters. On one scrap of paper Feffer wrote, "Mikhoels murdered on Stalin's order". As for his own future, he drew his hand across his throat.

Robeson had to work out a discreet way to save his friend's life. He had a powerful position – his farewell concert the next night was being broadcast live throughout the Soviet Union, and he had untouchable stature as a US friend of the regime.

His solution was to use the concert to send a coded message to Stalin himself, endorsing Mikhoels and Feffer by name, and the Jewish community in general. He could get away with it because the purge had not yet become explicitly anti-Semitic and he couldn't be expected to know all the secret rules governing public behaviour.

The capacity audience included party bigwigs and Jewish intellectuals, both groups now living in fear of the midnight arrival of MGB vans. (The point of Stalin's terror was its arbitrariness).

Late in his concert, Robeson, in Russian, said he would dedicate a special encore, the Song of the Vilna Jewish Partisans, to his dear friend Solomon Mikhoels, "whose tragic and premature death has saddened me deeply". He added to the shock by speaking of his pleasure at meeting Feffer, who he said was well and hard at work on his memoirs. There were gasps of astonishment – many there would have known Feffer was on death row. Robeson then said he would sing in Yiddish the song of the partisans, first translating into

Russian a verse, "When leaden skies a bitter future may portend" and its ending, "We survive!"

The audience was in an unbearable emotional state. Their very lives were on the line and here was Robeson fearlessly albeit indirectly deploring the purge.

After his unexpected encore, one brave woman stood up and applauded; the whole hall then erupted in waves of frantic applause. People broke down, weeping, or flung themselves tearfully into the arms of strangers.

Stalin waited three years, then executed Feffer anyway. The censors locked away the tape of the concert for half a century. It was released only in 1995, after the demise of the Soviet Union, minus Robeson's provocative comments. The tape generated the CD, and with the CD I can now read the cover notes about Mikhoels and Feffer written by Paul's son Paul Jnr (1927-2014), and hear Robeson's Yiddish song. I can also hear the first seconds of the fifteen-minute storm of applause, the rest of it snipped by the original censors.

But this rounded story, which so impressed me initially, unravels. First, Feffer had in fact been an NKVD/MGB informer since 1943, but got caught in the meat-grinder himself. Under interrogation, he falsely accused a hundred other Jews, but at his trial he had the courage to express pride in his Jewish identity.

Second, how was Robeson going to handle his knowledge of Stalin's murderous ways, while remaining an advocate for the socialist paradise? He chose to lie about it, to deny the undeniable. On his return to the US, he told a reporter from *Soviet Russia Today* that allegations of Soviet anti-Semitism were wrong: "I met Jewish people all over the place … I heard no word about it." He said the Soviets "had done everything" for their national minorities. "Everything" in reality included genocides of Cossacks, Ukrainian peasants, Crimean Tatars, Kalmyks, Volga Germans, Mongolians and other minorities.

In his book published in 1950, a year after his Moscow concert, Robeson wrote:

The Soviet Union's very existence, its example before the world of abolishing all discrimination based on colour or nationality, its fight in every arena of world con.ict for genuine democracy and for peace, this has given us Negroes the chance of achieving our complete liberation within our own time, within this generation.

He never again publicly mentioned Mikhoels and Feffer, nor criticised Stalin, whom he saw as safeguarding the interests of the downtrodden, especially Robeson's 'own people'.

Shortly after his Moscow concert, Robeson told Paul Jnr the truth, but swore him to secrecy about it during his (Paul Snr's) lifetime. An account of the Moscow hotel meeting with Feffer leaked, via the widow of film director Sergei Eisenstein. Paul Jnr vehemently denied the account as "wholly false according to my father's personal recounting of these events to me". Paul Jnr was also lying, but he recanted and told the truth in 1981.

Robeson viewed the Soviet Union as his 'second motherland', and even thought 'first' might be more accurate. He began his visits to Russia in 1934, getting dizzying veneration and opportunities, contrasting with the America of Jim Crow. He was even inspired to place Paul Jnr in a Moscow school.

Paul Jnr admitted that his father knew of the Ukrainian famine during his visit, but told the son in 1937 that he couldn't undermine the anti-fascist Soviet Union. Paul Robeson didn't just ignore the Stalin-created Ukrainian famine, he lied his head off, telling the *Daily Worker*:

"I was not prepared for the happiness I see on every face in Moscow. I was aware that there was no starvation here, but I was not prepared for the bounding life; the feeling of safety and abundance and freedom that I find here, wherever I turn".

Robeson backed Stalin's purges of the late 1930s. At the height of the terror he sided against the victims:

"I can only say that anybody who lifts his hand against it ought to be shot! It is the government's duty to put down any opposition to this really free society with a firm hand and I hope they will always do it … It is obvious that there is no terror here …"

The nadir of Robeson's career was his April 1949 speech at the 'Congress of the World Partisans of Peace' in Paris, involving 2000 delegates, Picasso and luminaries such as Nobel-winner Frederic Joliot-Curie. The repercussions included the US government withdrawing his passport, trapping him in America from 1950 to 1958 and encouraging his blacklisting as a concert performer, which impoverished him.

So what did Robeson say in Paris? Immediately after the speech Associated Press reporter Joseph Dynan filed his report, which was picked up throughout the US press. It had Robeson purporting to speak on behalf of the 14 million US Negroes to the effect that they wouldn't fight for the US against Russia in the event of a war. Mainstream Negro organisations disowned Robeson and protested their loyalty to the US. Robeson found himself isolated from both black and white America. Dynan's report quoted Robeson thus:

"I bring you a message from the Negro people of America that they do not want a war which would send them back into a new kind of slavery … It is unthinkable that American Negroes would go to war on behalf of those who have oppressed us for generations against a country which in one generation has raised our people to the full dignity of mankind."

Robeson's supporters claimed he had been stitched up by Dynan's false report. They cite other, less damaging versions of his impromptu speech, such as the following, after translation into French and then back again into English:

"We shall not put up with any hysterical raving that urges us to make war on anyone. Our will to fight for peace is strong. We shall not make war on anyone. We shall not make war on the Soviet Union."

There were half a dozen reports of the speech, all different. The closest to Dynan's, in the UK's *Daily Worker*, read:

"It was unthinkable for himself and for the Negro people at

home, that they should go to war in the interests of those who have oppressed them for generations, against a country which had shown there was no such thing as a backward people."

To me, as a reporter who has done hundreds of similar conference reports, the Dynan version is the most plausible. The role of a wire-service reporter is to get an accurate report filed as soon as possible. Dynan went straight from the hall after Robeson spoke, to write and despatch his copy. Dynan was an experienced professional and recent war correspondent in Italy. It's a silly idea that he would delay to concoct a version to damage Robeson. The phrases in Dynan's version are authentic Robeson. I heard some of them on the above-mentioned taped talk in Perth 11 years later. Dynan couldn't invent this Robeson-speak; he must have heard it.

Call it coincidence, but communist leaders elsewhere were expressing similar or more aggressive sentiments than Robeson. In Australia, for example, a month before the Paris conference, CPA general secretary Lance Sharkey said that, "If Soviet Forces in pursuit of aggressors entered Australia, Australian workers would welcome them". Sharkey got a three-year sentence for sedition.

Robeson provided only a muted denial of the AP report, saying that he was referring to Negro people globally as war-averse, not just to US Negroes.

The pro-Soviet advocacy turned US blacks against him, often in harrowing and humiliating ways. In one 1951 incident in a Harlem bar, he told a famous black pitcher for the Brooklyn Dodgers, Don Newcombe, that Newcombe was one of his heroes. Newcombe responded, "I joined the army to fight people like you." They nearly came to blows. One account has Newcombe being led out of the bar by one of Robeson's quasi-bodyguards wielding a switchblade.

In 1952 Robeson received the USSR's highest honour - the Stalin Prize, worth US$25,000, an enormous sum in those days, around $A1 million today.

Even after Khrushchev's denunciation of Stalin's crimes in 1956, Robeson never criticised the dead *vozhd* (boss). When the Soviets invaded Hungary in 1956, Robeson supported them.

The major controversy for half a century was whether Robeson was a Communist Party member or merely a supporter. He lost his US passport from 1950 to 1958 because he refused on principle to answer the question, "Are you now or have you ever been a member of the Communist Party of the USA?" Witnesses who testified that he was a CP member were attacked by Robeson supporters as government shills. Robeson's sympathetic biographer Martin Duberman concluded in 1988, "On the most obvious level, he was never a member of the CP-USA, never a functionary, never a participant in its daily bureaucratic operation …"

But in reality Robeson was a CP-USA member for decades. The party had decided he would be more effective for the cause if his membership remained secret – the threat was that if any party person publicly disclosed Robeson's membership, the person would be expelled. When CP-USA general secretary Gus Hall was serving an eight-year sentence in the 1950s on McCarthy-era charges of conspiracy to advocate the violent overthrow of the US government, Robeson campaigned for his release on civil liberties grounds, without of course disclosing his own party membership.

But in 1998, on the hundredth anniversary of Robeson's birth, party boss Gus Hall announced, "We can now say that Paul Robeson was a member of the Communist Party." Robeson's membership was, he said, "an indelible fact of Paul's life, [in] every way, every day of his adult life". Robeson's most precious moment, Hall said, occurred "when I met with him to accept his dues and renew his yearly membership in the CP-USA. I and other Communist leaders like Henry Winston, the Party's late, beloved national chair, met with Paul to brief him on politics and Party policies and to discuss his work and struggles".

Paul Jnr, himself a CP-USA member from about 1948 to 1962, was a practitioner of dissembling. But when his father was outed - along with himself   he put it succinctly: "If people want a politically correct hero, then Paul Robeson's not the man."

Robeson's reputation has come full circle, from guarded respect up to 1945, vilification for most of the Cold War as a Soviet stooge, and now respect again, especially from the liberal media. A recent profile on America's PBS television gave him a twenty-one-gun salute, managing to make no mention of either Communism or the Soviet Union. I must say the contradictions involved with any assessment of Robeson make him a tough subject to handle.

When my mother died in 2008, my jobs included selecting the funeral music. After batting away numerous well-meant suggestions from third parties, I settled on Robeson singing *"Deep River"*. (I didn't know then that *"Deep River"* had also been the music for Robeson's own funeral). I gave the funeral director a CD including that track, and it played fine. But the funeral director let the CD run on to the next track, which to my horror was Robeson singing *"The Killing Song"*, from his 1935 movie *Sanders of the River*. Given that my mother had spent her life as a peace activist and stalwart of the Australian Peace Council, the lyrics were awful:

On, on, into battle,

Mow them down like cattle!

Stamp them into the dust!

Kill, shoot, spear, smash, smite, slash, fight and sla-a-ay!

I inched as the verses rolled on, but no one was paying attention, they were too busy chatting.

Racism in the lecture room

10 April 1968

Even 50 years later, I find this interview a shock. How far Perth was from the turmoil of US racial politics, and how strange that news of the Afro-American upsurge should be brought to Perth householders by an ex-missionary anatomy lecturer. Almost every paragraph below contains a revelation about turmoil unimaginable in our bland daily lives.

While WA University anatomy lecturer Dr Kingsley Mortimer was lying in a Washington DC hospital after a heart attack, a white man next to him said,

"I have a bit of money. At home I sleep with a shotgun by my side. My wife has a revolver and what we hold, we keep. I would rather be tried for a Negro's murder than have a Negro charged with mine."

By contrast, a white cardiologist who was checking the man over made a point of asking in a Negro colleague for consultation.

During his six months lecturing at Howard University, Dr Mortimer lived the whole time with Negros in the Negro quarter.

Now home in South Perth, he said he never once went out at night except in a car which could leave his doorstep and return him there. He was thought mad to walk alone around the Howard University campus - despite the patrols of guards with revolvers.

The 7,000-student university was started by Abraham Lincoln for freed slaves after the civil war, and is one of the few producing top-quality Negro graduates.

It has become a centre of political education. One of his senior Negro colleagues, lecturing on the backbone of man, referred to differences in the backbone of whales. That reminded the speaker of Moby Dick, the giant white whale.

"What colour did God make the animal in the Antarctic that all men hated it and wanted to destroy it? He made it white!"

The applause of the medical students almost raised the roof. Another time, the man was lecturing on the lips. Negros' lips were full, white men's lips were turned in. He brought in the head of a chimpanzee in a bottle, to show how the ape's thin lips were like those of white men.

Dr Mortimer said two and a half-hour lectures were the rule, with the longest deemed the best. The first thing he said to his class was, "I am going to lecture 50 minutes; if I can't say my piece by then, I never will." Though the students roared approval he never said such a thing again. The staff was not amenable to leg-pulling and any white American who said such a thing would be run off the campus.

In charge of post-graduate training of surgeons and dentists, he asked them about their ambitions. Each said, "I am going out for me."

The affluent professional Negro stayed out of the civil rights issues. "Most Negroes cherish anonymity above all, and want to keep off the files of the police and FBI."

Racialism intruded into even the most formal speech-days of the university. At one ceremony, equivalent to our issuing of honorary degrees, the procession was followed by an orderly group of 40 students. The armed guards hurried over and the senior staff left their seats and gathered protectively around the university president and guests. Students began issuing a pamphlet around the hall. This was a manifestation of Black Power.

(An extract from the leaflet: *"Howard University has traditionally taught its students to suppress their African and Afro-American heritage and to imitate the white beasts who have emasculated black men, raped black women and expected us to finance and construct their capitalist society."*)

As soon as the first citation was read, the group took over the microphone. The president said above the uproar that the other three citations would be read at a dinner that night. One was for a Negro who had given a $20,000 scholarship to a Howard student.

Racial harmony through education would remain a pipedream while teachers were earning $8,000 a year and New York transport men were on strike for $8,000. One hopeless measure had been the implementation of "bussing" – a busload of Negro children would be driven to a good white school. The Negro children were out of their depth while the other Negros noticed that no busloads of white children was delivered to their own run-down schools.

A former medical missionary to Rhodesia, Dr Mortimer said the churches were the only force in the country capable of bringing the races together. But in the well-to-do churches you wouldn't find ten Negros at a service, and in the tumbledown Negro churches you wouldn't see a single white person.

The Negros, through their long suffering, had incorporated religion into their make-up while whites made church-going a social activity.

The churches' failures were in their disunity and their history as a white institution patronising Negros. The question was not how much could be achieved by legislation but how little, and the churches could change people's thinking by setting an example.

Every Negro wore a chip on his shoulder. Some wore it gracefully; some wore it as a weapon.

11,000 dusty letters in the ceiling
29 May 1969

Late on a hot Sunday afternoon in December John Joseph Jones, a curly-headed archivist with the build of a sumo wrestler, arrived at Longreach, Queensland.

He was on the scent of ancient records of the Australian Workers' Union, a collection that federal secretary Tom Dougherty was not even sure existed.

The records were said to relate to the Queensland shearers' strike of 1891, a strike that became to unionism what Gallipoli later became to the nation.

Jones was met by Longreach secretary Alf Kain and over beers they decided to search through the union's little cottage while the light lasted.

It was a rickety weatherboard with a tin gable roof, probably built in the last century (1800s).

They poked around a while, found some mediocre stuff and then the beers persuaded Jones to visit the lavatory out the back. Returning, he noted that the cottage roof jutted backwards, with a spare room sitting under it like a dog under his master's umbrella. Red Longreach dust had blown under the eaves and formed a solid plug above the ceiling.

"What's up there, Alf?"

"I dunno what's up there, I've never been game to shift that plug of dirt."

Jones got a broom handle between his sizable fists, speared the lump, broke off a big flake, and behind it saw some 1896 issues of *The Worker* (Brisbane).

Alf Kain recruited a young assistant to hop on to the ceiling and start moving the mass. The youth stood on top, Alf stood on a table and Jones was debris-catcher at floor level.

"It was like a dust storm in the Mallee," he told me this week as we sat before a wood stove in his Parkerville cottage. "We worked, coughing and spitting our lungs out, covered with red dust from head to foot like Mohawks and the lad on top almost dying of asthma.

"'Oh God, a letters book – 1887!' I'd shout, and Alf on the table would pause to read a ledger book with his assistant whooping-coughing and sputtering above. "'This is just a bit of rubbish - 1902', Alf would say, and drop it on the floor. I didn't mind, the ledger paper was thick as cardboard. But we got down from the loft 11,000 letters written on paper no thicker than cigarette paper. When I touched a blank page it shattered like a car windscreen or a Pharaoh's corpse."

For Jones, the night's work was the finding of the lost continent, the lost chord and Lasseter's Lost Reef all rolled into one. By 1am he got ten tea-chests full of documents dating back to 1884. He said that Australian history won't be the same now they're found.

Each of the 11,000 letters will have a piece of transparent silk organdie glued over it. Restoration work alone will take years.

The records include 16 years of minute books from 1892 of the People's Parliamentary Association of Hughenden - political documents virtually unknown to scholars. There's the minute books of the Central District Strike Council, written in beautiful copperplate by a man named Jackson from Barcaldine, Qld.

He wrote one letter (1891) to the military commander, Brisbane, protesting about the treatment of union prisoners: "The men's arms were first broken, then the men were carried or dragged face-downwards on broken arms and beaten on the neck with truncheons…"

Jackson wrote to a unionist on a station who had complained about the meagre 4/- a week strike pay: "Any man worth his salt would take half as much because this is a great strike and it will have far-reaching effects upon the liberty and the rights of working people …"

Jackson demanded that union ledger books – included in Jones' find – accounted for every farthing of the strike fund. He wrote prophetically: "We should not believe that the public is behind us, otherwise they would have helped us long before this."

Five weeks later: "I have to report, with great sorrow, that the strike has failed because money has not come from Victoria."

There are the first minutes of the Queensland Shearers' Union, gathered from places like Longreach, Blackall, Hughenden, Barcaldine, Ilfracombe and Springsure, and six years' letters of the Queensland Labourers' Union from 1891. The first roll books and cashbooks and minute books not merely recorded motions, but gave all the arguments and names.

None of this would have come to light without a decision by the AWU last year that the entire records to 1957 - hitherto closely guarded – could be made available to the Australian National University. The union had feared that its enemies within and outside would make mischief. Could they trust a university with their records?

It was Jones' job to talk them into the idea. No academic himself, he trained as a toolmaker in England and his first job in Australia was sweeping up wool in the shearing sheds of Tocumwal on the Murray. He had worked through the Northern Territory fixing machinery, and been an engineer on the Labrador railway. Married with four children, he's a trained teacher, arts graduate and journalist, sang at the last Adelaide Festival, has written three plays, one opera and two books on folk music and has issued five recordings.

He got the AWU leaders Tom Dougherty and Edgar Williams to his Parkerville chalet, fed them barbecued steak and chops, yarned with them all day and got their support that night at the Parkerville Hotel.

He started microfilming in Perth a year ago on the spot in the union office, as he wasn't allowed to remove documents. The headache in this method is that one must get, say, 20,000 sheets of records into an order required for scholars, then re-sort them back the union's way.

The records could even show how the Australian language has modified through the decades. Scholars may one day compare the scribes' unedited conference notes with the idiom, say, of Furphy's *Such is Life*, written about the same time.

I asked Mr Jones if the union – often involved in controversy - was prudent in releasing its records. He said the union demanded a security normal in such cases. It kept the right to allow only scholars it approved of to access the records. He said the federal office for many years had kept perfectly thorough records, as though they had no fear of anything in them.

The federal office in Sydney yielded 40,000 frames of microfilm – and other branches are still to be done.

Prague's hall of mirrors

17 January 2018

Fifty years ago, Alexander Dubček began the ill-fated bid to reform the government of Czechoslovakia. In August 1968, the experiment was crushed by Soviet tanks. My story involves a meeting and long interview with a courageous young Czech journalist Ales Benda passing through Perth soon after that Soviet takeover. I wondered how he fared with the Russians and hard-liners when he got back to Prague. The answer was a big surprise. Please read on.

In late 2010, my wife and I were on a slow train from Munich to Prague and got talking to an elderly Czech lady, who gave us her potted life story. Her husband was arrested in the 1960s Communist era and was sentenced to two years hard labour digging out underground coal from seams little more than half a metre thick. On release he couldn't get a normal job anywhere and in desperation he took work in a uranium mine. After a while the uranium dust gave him cancer and he died, she said. Their five children couldn't get higher education or a job because they were tainted by their father's prison record. Four of them got out to West Germany and settled there.

She was talking about the time before the "Prague Spring" of liberalisation that began in early 1968 and ended abruptly in late August when the Soviets and their Polish, Hungarian and Bulgarian allies invaded with 200,000 troops and 2000 tanks. There was only minor resistance but 70 Czechs were killed and about 250 wounded. Passive resistance continued well into 1969.

To suppress any vestige of free speech, the Soviets' first target was the Czech TV, radio and press. Editors were forced to agree to a new 'temporary' censorship regime where the media's prime role was to support the new hard-line Communist leaders. Any dissent led to closure of the media outlet, or worse. By April 1969 censorship became total and continued until the 'Velvet Revolution' ten years later, which brought democracy to the republic.

Forty years before our chat with the lady on the train, I had spent an afternoon interviewing a young Czech journalist who had got stuck in Perth a few days on his way back to Prague. At that point, ten months after the invasion, the last liberties in the Czech republic were being snuffed out by the pro-Soviet regime.

I was 28, he was 25, and being in the same profession, we had a lot in common. But he was braver than me by a giant amount. He talked with total frankness about the Soviet suppression of the Czech people, and was keen that I should publish what he said. He didn't care one jot about consequences. After the piece was published, I just moved on to writing my next article, about teachers' union pay claims. But he would have landed in Prague and faced punishment in terms of career and maybe liberty for telling truths to the bourgeois press. What happened to him? I have no idea. Here's the article.

"Publish all of it!" – Czech journalist

The West Australian, 14 June 1969

Ales Benda is a 25-year-old Czech journalist with an athlete's build, bushy sideboards and a quizzical expression. He is assistant foreign editor of a Prague newspaper Mlada Fronta - at least he thinks he is.

Mr Benda's English is a pleasant drawl, with 'plarz' for 'plus' and 'moof-mends' for 'movements'. With his blue pullover and grey slacks, he looks quite Australian except that his lips are red and he wears socks with sandals. He would often frown, screw up his nose and laugh at the same time - an attitude savouring of 'what the hell'.

To questions about the past and the present he replies volubly: asked about the future he changes the subject.

He has been held up a few days in Perth sorting out a visa hitch and we talked for a few hours on a back lawn in the weekend. After, I asked, "Is it all right if I publish some of this?"

"Publish all of it," he said. He gave his amiable chuckle. A contact had already remarked, "Oh boy, when you get back you will get into big trouble."

Mr Benda's paper swung from conservative to way-out crusading liberalism a few years ago, to the annoyance of the Russians and others.

A few days after the Russians arrived in August 1968, his editor Mr Jelinek got a phone call. "It's General So-and-So here, we'd like you to come to Soviet headquarters for some discussions."

"No thanks," replied the editor. "Our paper is not your paper. Don't give me orders." The editor had been christened 'The Trojan Horse' by Moscow newspapers and had nothing to gain from 'discussions'.

The same morning an armoured car roared into the car park but Mr Jelinek hid successfully in the attic. Three searches later the Russians got tired of hunting Trojan horses.

However, Mr Benda concluded, he had read during his month in Australia that the editor had been sacked, and if that was true his own days as assistant foreign editor were numbered.

On the fatal invasion night of 20-21 August 1968, he was telephoned at 3.30 a.m. about the Russians. He wanted to rush to the paper but was shaking too much to do up his buttons and tie his shoelaces and took half an hour to get dressed. When he arrived the power had been cut off and they couldn't use the presses. They had to wait in the dark, with the sound of gunfire coming nearer and nearer.

"At 5.30 a.m. there came a little Mongolian with an automatic rifle. "What do you want here?" a bloke asked him. He just pointed his rifle. More Russians herded about 60 newspaper people into one room. The Russians were only kids, conscripts, and they were worn out from three days on the road. Whenever they began to sleep we would wake them up and say: 'Hey, you are supposed to be guarding us.' Finally a colonel came down and kicked us out.

"They shut down our paper for three weeks but they didn't know about our provincial presses and we put out underground papers there.

"I sneaked between the tanks and got to our printing presses at Brno and was editor there for a few days - though we didn't even have telephones. The Russians caught up with us, and our main paper was still closed, so I thought it was a good time to take my annual holiday, and I went to London. I kept ringing day after day to see if the paper was going again. On this Australian trip my boss has told me he will dock every reverse charge from my pay."

By now the occupation was largely symbolic and the threat was from Czech officials - either collaborators or those under Russian political pressure.

Inflation was rife. Russian troops would go through the shops spending their accumulated pay, and a soldier might buy ten pairs of shoes in one hit. Czechs, seeing trouble everywhere, were drawing their money out of the bank and buying a washing machine or fridge that would keep its value. There was quite a bit of black marketeering between troops and Czechs who were not loathe to run their cars on petrol from Russian armoured cars.

His most affecting experience was attending the funeral of a 16-year-old lad shot off his motorcycle by Russian guards; the most surprising experience was watching the arguments between Czechs and bewildered young Russians in tanks. Within a week the army had replaced the youngsters with occupation troops from East Germany and other tough professionals. No one argued any more.

"The funniest thing about the business was the invitation we never gave to the Russians to invade us. They'd lined up two blokes to invite them, our minister for communications and someone from the official Czech newsagency. But when they arrived at Radio Prague the technicians refused to broadcast the message and the Russians had to come uninvited.

"The Russians set up a pro-Soviet TV station in the grounds of their embassy. But the two announcers were hopeless - one was a Prague official who was always sozzled, and one was a lady from the Central Committee who had never been before a TV camera in her life, and we split our sides every time she tried to perform. Then the Russians tried to set up a Czech radio in East Germany, but all the Czechs had ferocious German accents…"

Mr Benda is a graduate in economics, and I got a lecture on the needs of the Czech economy. First, the Stalinist stress on heavy industry and steel production had harmed the country's chance in international trade. To make steel, Czechoslovakia imported iron ore thousands of miles from Russia. This made it expensive and it had to be exported at subsidized prices.

Workers had been given a social status with coal miners and foundry workers on top, then factory workers, and people in consumer industries came last. The factories got a stranglehold on the government and decisions were all in their favour.

Things like housing were in a dreadful state – you waited ten years in Prague for a flat, and meanwhile had to live under a bridge, or with your parents, who were probably living with their parents, in a little flat. The overcrowding was even sending the divorce rate up. But construction work was almost all for the confounded factories - each one was a little empire in itself. The only solution would be to freeze investment in industry altogether till consumer shortages were overcome.

Heavy industry was not much use to Czechoslovakia in any case. It should be building up the plastics and chemicals industries and using its concentrated manpower on craftwork like glassware, and labour-intensive production like watch making.

An unpleasant by-product of heavy industry was war equipment. South American juntas were lording it with Czech hardware; both sides used it in Biafra and both sides used it in Egypt.

"Everywhere in the world you can find a Czech machine-gun," he lamented. "Business is business, I suppose."

The country was united against the Russians. But there were violent argument between Czechs about what resistance should be made; whether one should leave the country or not; what constituted collaboration; and whether the government should be influenced from within or opposed.

"Generally it would be good for you to write this," he said, "to show that Communists as a whole are not monsters, that they are not worse or better than other people – that they are just people."

That was how my piece ended in Quadrant OnLine on 17 January 2018. A reader G. Bruno, possibly of Czech background, wrote in saying he'd pulled up a 1992 reference to my friend Ales Benda - in a list of Czech journalists who had subsequently worked for the "StB" Czech secret police!

The Czech news item, via UPI agency, said,

"Among those mentioned on the list are Ales Benda, the former editor of the Czechoslovakian news agency CSTK and now the service's Washington correspondent..."

To which I added my own comment: "Well I'm damned!"

ABORIGINES AND ANTHROPOLOGISTS

On a mule 450 miles to Kalumburu
May 1969

I'd heard a lot about Helmut Petri but hadn't met him till last week. He's a German anthropologist who has learnt most of his English in outback places around the North-West.

In dignified company, he's prone in all innocence to throw in racy colloquialisms. For example, asked if the Aboriginal population in his area was declining, he replied, "The natives are breeding like hell."

He rode a mule about 450 miles from Derby to Kalumburu 30 years ago accompanied by a peanut farmer, Fred Merry, with a camel-train of peanuts. A third member of the party was an American, Douglas C. Fox, who forsook anthropology soon after for public relations work in Washington. [That's some transition!]

They struck into unexplored country from Mt Agnes. They thought they were following the King Edward River to Napier Broome Bay but in fact were on the Lawley River and wound up at Admiralty Gulf. Nothing loth, they trekked north-west and made it to Kalumburu in six weeks.

That was in 1938, and even now some women remember that "incredibly handsome" blue-eyed German.

In 1954 he was back, this time accompanied by one of his girl students, Gisela Odermann. When they arrived at Anna Plains, an Aboriginal from the Njangumarda tribe rushed over, lifted his box camera and took a snap of them.

"Who's studying who?" asked Professor Petri.

Today Gisela is not only his wife; she has a doctorate in her own right.

"Having an anthropologist as wife involves a lot of discussion," said Dr Petri. "On certain subjects we never agree."

He was having breakfast at the Perth hotel, smoked incessantly, and was clad in a duffel jacket, tartan shirt with bulging pockets, slacks and suede shoes. His wife is tall and solidly-built and prefers to stay out of the limelight. She put on what she called "an asbestos face" for the photographer.

Their beat is from Port Hedland to Broome in from the 80-mile beach. Every few years they stay for six months at Pallottine Missions like LaGrange and Anna Plains.

He has a memory for names and knows individually most of the hundreds of natives in the region. Those he hasn't met he knows of by hearsay, and they know about him by bush telegraph.

They have been accepted as members of the Njangumarda tribe, which regards them as their official historians.

One of the magnets drawing the Petris halfway around the world is a revival of tribal beliefs among natives who are more used to mustering sheep than spearing kangaroos. This revival is vaguely linked to a Black Power theme. But whereas Negro militants feel that power is within their grasp physically, Aborigines incorporate the idea into their ritual and spiritual beliefs.

He has discovered beginnings of cargo cults in the region. Natives believe that far in the desert big ships stand waiting. The ships are a cross between the cargo ships that unload desirable things at North-West ports, and the Ark of the Old Testament.

The bible stories of the tribes of Israel in the desert are closest to their own experience, and tend to get rehashed in versions to suit their own mythology.

Hence these arks are filled not with animals two by two, but gold (symbol of white men's wealth) and quartz crystals (associated in their own lore with potency and power). One day, in a few years maybe, big rains will come down and wipe out all the white people who are not sticking to the law of the blackfella. Only the blackfellas will be saved, thanks to their arks.

The myth is reinforced when natives see the mighty ore-carriers arriving – ships of an almost magical size.

The Walmadjari people in the Fitzroy River area have another tradition, he says. They believe they must always move circularly west, and eventually they will reach the centre of the world, which is two salt lakes somewhere near Lake Disappointment. The lakes are the home of two very powerful mythical snakes. When the people finally arrive at the lakes, all will be well once more for the blackfella, though they are fairly vague about what form the millennium will take.

The revivalism started in 1960. In 1966 he first noticed hostility to anthropologists. That was a bad sign as anthropologists are in close touch with them through language and knowledge of their way of life.

The trouble started this way: Many years ago a white woman living in the North-West published an illustrated book on the natives. A very old Pilbara tribesman acquired a copy, and recognized a photo of men taking part in a sacred initiation ceremony. Moreover, it was a ceremony that women should never see. The old man has been creating a lot of ferment around the missions because of this book.

The Aboriginal songs, though they sometimes involve the doings of white men, have so far not taken on the hostile double meanings of some songs further south around Roebourne. Those have references to white cockatoos grabbing everything. They refer in fact to the white man. Most of these anti-white songs are still secret, even to anthropologists.

Dr Petri has described one complex of rituals involving a single series of 500 songs. They tell of the wanderings and achievements of the Two Men. In the dreamtime the Two Men wandered over the country using their sacred boards to hunt game, fight enemies, open waterholes and shape the country. They are now in the sky as stars - strangely enough, the very constellation we call Gemini, the Twins.

The Petris have had narrow squeaks from bushfires on every trip. But both dread the North-West flies even more: "It takes you 50 years to get used to them," he said.

Dr Petri has published three books on the natives of the North-West, all in German. "Our research grants make us publish in the official lingo of whoever puts up the money," he said.

Even in Germany the books – one is called *Dying World in the North-West* - have not aroused much interest. German anthropologists are mostly interested in Africa and the Americas.

At heart a conservative, he doesn't like the student disorders and disrespect. "We have to be back in Germany by November in order to be shot or hanged by our students," he sighed. "Over there, they don't throw tomatoes, they throw Molotov cocktails."

On a smelly camel in quest of native art

19 April 1963

Charles Pearcy Mountford (73), who has spent more than 40 years in quest of Australian native art, now finds his grey hair an advantage when he goes out on desert expeditions.

"The natives equate grey hair with wisdom," he said. "They call me Watitchilpa – Grey Man - and treat me with special respect."

Mr Mountford is in Perth to take part in a North-West expedition by Professor Helmut Petri of the Cologne University and his wife Dr Gisela Petri.

His awards include an OBE, a coveted Franklin L. Burr Prize, several prizes for his films of native life, and others for his documentary photography, mainly of native art.

However, he said he was really just an amateur. He was a retired civil servant and an honorary SA Museum worker.

Lately his native friends and guides had been getting very solicitous. Two years ago he made a trip to west central Australia, where the going was so bad he decided not to take any other white men with him. The country would not support camels so he planned to go over the sand hills by four-wheel-drive car.

One of the natives in his party, a grizzled white-haired old man named Kamanalda, asked him, "No whites?"

"No, just me."

Kamanalda (after a pause): "We look after you proper good, you are proper old b---d."

They did too, he said. The car was full of petrol and water and he had no room for much bedding. He slept on the ground with the natives, with a fire on each side of him, and they always made sure he had the biggest logs.

In all his days he had never had the slightest trouble with natives. He did not even lock up his tobacco and gear – they never took anything.

He had never come to grief in the desert, but he knew that if, for instance, he broke a leg, the natives would undergo great hardships to take him back or get help. They were his main source of information about where the native art sites were. This was often sacred and he always had to win their trust first.

It was not in good taste to walk into their campsite and start asking personal questions. One must set up one's own camp, welcome the natives when they came to look it over, and give them food. They then would often go along with the expedition, as good gifts meant they did not need time to hunt.

He made great use of camels for hard trips. He had ridden more than 1,000 miles perched just above a camel's tail. Of course, he said, the camels did not smell very nice, but then neither did he after three weeks in the desert. He sometimes took a string of 14 camels, several for riding and the rest for water cans and food.

Water always came first in central Australia. There could be 100 miles between water holes and any one of them could have dried up before he got there.

Most of the camels were owned by half-castes and were relatively good-natured. He had never even been spat at – the mildest demonstration of a camel's displeasure – and it was no joke to get a whole mouthful of half-digested grass in the face.

His greatest bane was the tourists who visited sacred native art sites and put their names over the rock paintings with chalk, lipstick or a penknife. They wanted to let people know they had been there. They were the most destructive animals on earth.

Victoria was solving the problem by surrounding the art with a barricade of wire netting. This was also being done in SA but one of the best counter-measures was not to publicise where the sites were. There were some splendid art sites in the Adelaide Hills but only a few responsible people had been told where.

Native art was very simple towards the south, but in the north where there was Indonesian and New Guinea influence, it was often intricate and colourful.

In the art of central Australia the natives used only six sacred symbols, which stood for different things in different places. Concentric circles could mean rock holes, hills or a camp place. Concentric squares, a north-west innovation, meant much the same thing. A wavy line usually stood for a creek.

The natives had four colours – white (from pipe clay), red (red ochre), yellow (yellow rocks or burnt ochre), and black (charcoal or iron ore). Natives would sometimes walk a hundred miles to trade paint during elaborate ceremonies. There was one traditional site for red ochre on the west coast which was so good that a paint company went in and took the lot.

"Aboriginal art is an expression of the deepest thoughts of their origin, their life after death and the meaning of life on earth," he said.

He now had only one bark painting out of more than 500 he had collected since 1948 from the northern coast of Australia (the one exception just suited his study wall).

All the rest he had given to museums. If he kept them, they would be dispersed after his death and within a generation they would be lost.

Thick-set, mild-mannered and slightly deaf, Mr Mountford does not look like the conventional explorer. I found him outspoken on many a controversial topic, but he always remembered to add, "Not for publication."

Perhaps Watitchilpa – Grey or Wise Man – is not a bad name for him.

Note: A month later I interviewed one of Mr Mountford's assistants, as follows.

Tribal Natives Initiate White Woman

Miss Margaret King, a South Australian research worker, let herself be initiated by Port Hedland native women so they could tell her of their sacred love rituals and music.

A Bachelor of Music, she has just returned from a three-month trip to the North-West where she recorded about 250 women's songs.

She worked with Mr C. P. Mountford, who was gathering information on native art.

She said the initiation rite was secret. Only the oldest native women were allowed to know the rituals.

One could hardly stop white people in the street and ask them about their love rituals. In the same way she had to show tact and good manners when interviewing old native women.

To win their confidence she treated their sores and ailments every day - sometimes from 7 a.m. to 11 p.m.

She said the native women had a philosophy which made their lives satisfying and in a way more truthful than ours.

Dr Reim's Marxist apothecary shop for Number One Tucker

December 1968

Dr H. Reim (43) is a big man with red hair and red beard. He said he came from Karl Marx University, Leipzig, and had been studying natives near Wyndham for eight months.

"Just as I expected," I said.

The territory has been the stamping ground of German scholars for more than 30 years. In the late 1930s, when unstudied tribes were getting rare anywhere in the world, German anthropologists swept down on the Kimberleys with whoops of joy. The biggest party was the Frobenius expedition of half a dozen scholars, including Helmut Petri who is there still, working at Anna Plains and La Grange.

Another was Andreas Lommel, now director of Munich Museum. Later comers included Carl von Brandenstein, who probably knows more about the North-West's native songs than anyone else in the world.

Dr Reim has been trying to reconstruct the natives' old way of life by talking to the oldest men.

Most natives there grew up with the Forrest River Mission and now work as station hands or do odd jobs for the Wyndham Shire But in a camp of 40 native pensioners he found three men born to the Walar tribe at the turn of the century. Right up to the Second World War they used to go walkabout from the mission every year, living off the bush. Dr Reim has been filling exercise books with their memories and customs.

He is only just in time. In ten years [by 1980], he said, natives who lived the old way would be dead or too confused to recall it.

He doesn't just talk to them. He teamed up with rubbish carter Ronald Morgan (native name Andomidi) and paid a dollar an hour to join him on walkabout.

Dr Reim's university study was a bit like an apothecary's shop, with lots of bottles and tobacco tins of dried foods and powders that Ron Morgan had found.

One tin contained the dried flesh of bottle-tree nuts, ground to a native flour. "It's got a slight lemon taste," Dr Reim said. "They probably get some Vitamin C from it. I'll get it analysed."

He also had some pandanus nuts but they were not Number One Tucker, he said. They had no flavour. You got a better flour from water-lily roots; they made good damper.

He began sorting his larder. There was stuff like desiccated coconut - made from grass seeds called 'anu', and small yams like potatoes.

He brought back branches of 50 plants, each providing food or 'industrial products' – not the sort Premier Charles Court would be interested in. They were things like 'nimbu', crystals of resin used to glue a stone on a stick to make a tomahawk. Melted down, the crystals are as hard as quartz.

Ronald Morgan sometimes got his dollar an hour just for yarning. Dr Reim says it is untrue that natives get fed up with anthropologists buttonholing them and taking notes.

The two spent weeks living off the bush around the pensioners' camp 15 miles from Wyndham. Ron Morgan would demonstrate how to find food, make things out of twigs, and spear mullet. Ron took only 30 seconds to spear a three-pounder with a rather wobbly old spear. Ron could also teach how to make paint and gather water-lily roots.

Dr Reim made particular friends with the pensioners by rescuing their sacred boards from a hiding place at the old Forrest River Mission. Now they are hidden again nearer the 15-mile camp.

Here's how he did it. He hired an old native named King Peter and got out to the mission by charter plane. They forded the Forrest River at low tide to reach the caves where the 6ft long decorated boards were hidden.

He said the boards are part of a cargo cult - a ritual intended to bring the natives the good things that white people enjoy. Cargo cults reached their highest pitch in New Guinea, where natives were even building jungle airstrips to land non-existent aircraft laden with bully beef and handkerchiefs.

The sacred boards' meaning was "to make white-feller tucker plenty" and also to link the natives with the mythical beings of the North-West. Dr Reim thought that the board cult might be the reason why the natives had stopped doing sacred rock paintings.

Natives thought that the boards were produced by spirits of the Great Sandy Desert and the Western Desert. The boards obviously were made south-east of the Kimberleys – perhaps in the Peterman Range in arid parts of the Northern Territory.

Native songs: making love to your mother-in-law

18 June 1968

Two songs from my school days will be with me forever. One was "Ho Ro, My Nut Brown Maiden" sung with false bonhomie in a nine-year-old treble. The other was an authentic Aboriginal song with piano accompaniment that went, "Jabbin jabbin kiru kaa, aa-aa-aa glaa…"

From memory the words translated, "When we hunt the kangaroo, we will know just what to do."

But it was not till I saw Dr Carl Georg von Brandenstein that I got the inside story on Aboriginal songs. He's a linguist who's been studying the songs from Carnarvon to Port Hedland during the past four years.

He produced a walburra (or spear-thrower) and a mirrimba, a long forked twig. The walburra had about 30 notches cut down one side, and he rasped the twig back and forth, making a noise like Tom Sawyer's stick strumming on a fence. He sang a little melody in plaintive half-tones and tapped the rhythm with his foot.

This sort of song was called a tabi, and was just like the songs of the minstrels of medieval Europe. He said some of those minstrels even used a sort of rattle.

The tabi songs were hard to translate. Some half-castes knew four or five dialects and languages, and filled the songs with imported words, rather like a nightclub singer who would break into a verse or two in French.

The second trouble was that the words had special meanings. For example the Aborigines liked to sing a special song for tourists called "The White Cockatoo". The words go, "He comes in big flocks, he eats up everything, he makes a lot of blah-blah…" Carl knew all along that "white cockatoo" meant "white man" but would listen gravely and not spoil the joke.

One of these personal songs – quite different from corroboree songs – was about the Japanese air attack on Broome on March

3, 1942. "They are coming, they are coming, the blokes with the protruding eyes. Here they come, seven of them, the blokes with the protruding eyes."

The "seven" referred to a flight of seven Japanese aircraft [the total attackers numbered 10]. The natives would not name the Japanese because the magic power of an enemy's name could hit back. Carl isn't sure whether the "protruding eyes" refers to the goggles worn by the pilots.

Another time a middle-aged man began a song and everyone became upset. Suddenly emotion overwhelmed the singer and he shook with silent grief. It turned out that he was singing a song owned by a friend who had died. It was as though you found a song your own dead father used to sing, and you sang it to the family in the lounge room.

The native composer owned his songs and people had to ask for permission to sing them. It was a form of primitive copyright. Some songs died out quickly. Others, by the nyinirri or great songmen, dated back to the turn of the 1900s.

There was one popular song about the first truck that came to Tambrey Station (now derelict): "The giant rattles, his big eyes [headlights] threaten in the dark. His lid in front [bonnet) is shaking - clunk, clunk, clunk - sparks come out and smoke puffs up, and his wheels whirr up the dust. His wheels jump along the rough road. When you sit inside you bump and down, and he takes you to the races."

This went on for 27 verses, full of high spirits and the fun of life.

Most songs were one verse and might have only five words. Those were like verbal shorthand or telegrams.

There was a robust sexuality in many of them. The Aborigines could match the Hindu finesse in sexual matters. Often the songs were a bit wicked, seeming innocent but full of double meanings.

Carl said the most serious offence traditionally was to talk to - or even look at – your mother-in-law. This was no laughing matter. But to his surprise, he heard songs sung with glee about a man who revels and relishes in a detailed affair with his mother-in-law. They were on a par with our James Bond stories - too fanciful to get upset about.

The songs often had a haunting quality. "The man sees his people gather on ration day, gathered on the roadway where all the tyre marks branch off another way. The people sit with their relatives chatting away, and as if in a dream he walks on further. All of a sudden he stands in the cemetery, all alone."

The use of words with multiple meanings was called "kenning" from the Scots word "to ken" or "know". To mention dusk in a song might mean your end was near, or you were going away, or your potency for lovemaking was lost.

A pilot was always called "a clever man" or some such. One song about a plane went, "There he goes, the dust swirling up from the tarmac at Morgana. Now the in-gin (engine) makes a big roar and he screws up into the sky. In the plane sits the clever man, pulling levers. Now he reaches the top and with a gentle puckering of the in-jin he goes straight away into the west."

There were hundreds of songs about having a ride in a motorcar. Singers also took a delight in nature: how a mountain was like a reclining woman or how eagles stretched their wings and flew down with noble strength.

There was one phrase meaning, "the red dusty evening haze, standing up and covering the horizon in brownish mist". That had a host of meanings. Another phrase, "yoola yoola" meant "the special clouds that hang down in the distance and seem to weep". Those clouds promised rain and rain meant everything to that hot spinifex country, where rainmaking was the most important ceremony.

The tabi songs were a strong tradition among the middle-aged and old men. Carl couldn't say if the younger men would carry on the tradition. Sometimes in Port Hedland he would hear a father tell his kids, "Switch that wireless off! I want to sing one of my songs."

The gift of music and poetry could bolster their self-esteem during their arduous and often tragic efforts to cope with white society. It was the opposite of their other outlet, gambling.

Carl said he felt the Kimberley people had not grown old and weary like other races. They had stayed young by their constant freshening of their language.

This interview led to Carl inviting me to collaborate with him on a book of translations of Pilbara song-poetry, which appeared in 1974 as "TARURU: Aboriginal song-poetry of the Pilbara." I wrote the preface and helped tweak his translations to a more musical and fluent prose than Carl's Germanic English.

Which Westerners found Australia?

27 January 1969

Seeing it's Australia Day, see if you can guess which Europeans found Australia? Cook? Marco Polo? Englishmen? Dutchmen? Portuguese?

On the evidence, the prize goes to a pair of Dutchmen called Willem Jansz (skipper) and Jan Lodewycksz van Roossengin (agent), commanding a three-master called the Duyfken, or Little Dove.

Coming from New Guinea in March 1606, the Duyfken charted 200 miles of Cape York peninsular without knowing that it was separate from New Guinea and part of the fabled Southland.

That trip is given the credit because it is the best documented. Historians have been arguing for centuries about shadowy charts, shadowy journals, shadowy reports of some vast continent below Java.

Even Marco Polo about 1289 spoke of a "Greater Java" which was the biggest island in the world and 3000 miles around.

In the learned journals the stately theories sweep down on each other in full sail. The battle erupts in a thunder of mutual criticism and harsh crackle of footnotes; bearded historians with daggers of irony in their teeth swing in the rigging and lock in man-to-man combat.

The fight is over a theory that the Portuguese found Australia a century before the Dutch swarmed onto our coast in the early 1600s.

The Portuguese were secretive about their discoveries and during the Spanish occupation from the 1580s they destroyed a lot of maps and charts. In 1755 Lisbon was wrecked by an earthquake and even more material was lost.

Briefly, here is the case for the Portuguese:

1499: an extraordinary account in Spanish of an animal resembling a kangaroo, in terrain much like our south-west karri forest ("… bearing her whelps about with her in an outward belly, much like unto a great bag or purse … " and with "snout like a fox, ears like a bat, hands like a man.")

1541: the first of nine French maps, probably derived from Portuguese originals, showing a land called Great Java with striking resemblance to parts of our coast and in the right latitudes.

1916: Discovery at Napier Broome Bay, at the top of WA, of two Portuguese carronades (short naval cannon) of the 15th-16th century.

Counter-arguments:

The kangaroo could be a South American opossum, the maps could have been drawn by Portuguese from Malay-Timorese sources, and the cannons could have been carried by late-coming Dutch or English ships.

One historian argues that if a Portuguese ship piled up in Napier Broome Bay and none lived to tell the tale, it wouldn't rank as a 'discovery' in any case.

However evidence for the Portuguese, of a quite new sort and from a totally unexpected source, should cause a little re-writing of the history books, though it has gone almost unnoticed since 1967 in the back pages of a linguistics journal.

The author is Doctor Carl Georg von Brandenstein, a West German linguist now at the WA University working on the native languages of the Pilbara.

In a nutshell his finding is this: In four tribal languages between Cape Keraudren (soon, perhaps, to be A-bombed) and Nickol Bay, there are words which could only have come from the Portuguese, and come in the 16th century long before the Dutch explorers. The chief word is 'tartaruga" for "turtle". It is beyond coincidence that tribal natives and Portuguese should have that nine-letter word independently.

He studied the speech of four tribes - the Kariera and the Ngarluma, and their inland neighbours the Nyamal and the Indyipandi.

More odd combinations:

"Fire" … Portuguese (P), fogueira; Aboriginal (A) pogara or vogara (the tribes are unable to pronounce 'f').

"Flame" … chama (P), tzama (A) - the tribes can't pronounce 'sh'.

"Ashes" … cinza (P), tyinda (A).

Turtle, fire, flame, ashes: could they tie up with the Portuguese landing along the coast, catching turtles maybe with the help of natives, and turtle-cooking when the shell was cut away?

In truth, or should I say 'forsooth', tortoise-shell is named among articles of trade that Portuguese carried around the Indonesian islands in the 16th Century, though their main interest was spices. The favourite turtle-catching spots were around the Celebes, but as intrepid hunters have lately discovered, there are also turtles galore off the North-West coast.

The natives' songs are also unique in Australia, and some resemble minstrel songs of old Europe. Moreover singers use an accompaniment suspiciously like a violin technique, with a bow that makes rattles on the edge of a violin-shaped piece of board. "Could they have seen a sailor playing a fiddle on the beach at night?" Carl asked.

"It's hard to convince people except by producing three complete shipwrecks," he said. "They can't believe one little word could help solve a historical problem. In fact a word-clue could tell you who had visited the coast and also show roughly the length of the coast visited, since people would use the word only over a certain stretch of country.

"The origin of Indian ruling classes was traced by linguistics, not be relics or excavations. In Europe linguists designed a grid showing the movements of races all across the continent. With that theory, archaeologists knew where to dig."

Carl got interested in the four tribes because they didn't speak like most Aborigines, who use a grammar structure like the Incas, the Basques, the Hindi, the Caucasians and other ancient races. The four tribes, however, had picked up some tricks of speech found in modern European languages.

The moderns and the four tribes say, "I shot three ducks". The normal Aboriginal would say, "By me, the shooting concerns three ducks" - putting the speaker in the role of helpless agent of bigger forces. Carl thinks the four tribes may have been influenced by early contact with speakers of Portuguese.

The Portuguese frequented waters to the north of Australia for a hundred years. They would need to have visited our coast regularly before any of their words were imprinted on native languages.

The coast was mainly uninviting. He felt skindivers might be able to find Portuguese wrecks there.

The linguistic discoveries alone are not enough to convince sceptics about a Portuguese discovery of Australia. But they are valuable support for the theory, which has grown like a half-finished jigsaw puzzle from just such scraps of knowledge.

Note: In 2018 Carl's speculation of the Portuguese as discoverers of Australia is regarded as complete bunk.

FOOLING ABOUT IN PROSE

A kiss before Bridge
August 1964

A husband and wife kiss each other good night before they play in bridge tournaments because, afterwards, they won't even be speaking to each other.

This is the sort of thing one learns by talking to hardened bridge players at the current Australian championships at the Subiaco City Hall.

Bridge, two anonymous South Australian women said, was preparation for widow-hood. They were consolidating their future for when their husbands went. It would be better still not to marry at all, but husbands were needed to provide income while the wives played. Once married, a wife should just dispose of him, in a legal fashion, and play on. But never play bridge with him. It was as bad as learning to drive with him. "The sight of my husband at a bridge table maddens me," one said. The bridge clubs were hotbeds of intrigue, jockeying for position and scuttle butting. As for switching husbands, clubs were real merry-go-rounds.

After this, it was only fair to consult a South Australian man for his views.

"I kick the cat every time I lose," he said. "If I lose badly, I kick my wife."

Another player recalled what was claimed to be a true story about a couple who lived in Bennett, USA 20 years ago and invited friends over for a bridge evening. As the guests were leaving, the wife shot her husband. At the trial she told the jury how her husband had bid - and they acquitted her.

I sat by a table for half an hour but did not learn much about bridge.

The four players paid not the slightest attention to one another and neither laughed nor smiled. They laid down their cards one by one and occasionally muttered expressionless words which had something to do with bidding.

The post-mortem on the game was conducted in another language. In the following typical game-analysis, I have translated (in brackets) to English:

> We were playing a couple of Little Old Ladies (novices) in a contract
> which was as Cold as Charity (easy) when the Rabbit (novice) on
> the left Kicks Off (leads) what looks like a Top of Nothing (a suit
> without court cards). Turns out to be a concealed Five Carder (five
> cards including court cards) and wow! Red Rover (it's all over) –
> down three Unclobbered (we did badly).

Bridge players, even the mildest of them, will also 'Dong' and 'Clout' their opponents with no compunction.

Poker faces are compulsory in bridge, a top Australian player Tim Seres (NSW) explained. One did not read faces for clues, as in poker. The bidding and the cards one threw away were the only code allowed. Nor is bridge like rummy, where luck of the draw plays a big part. A team exchanges its hands with rivals after a game.

Mr Seres said bridge brought out people's characters. A solid, cautious businessman could turn into a daredevil gambler with the cards. Similarly a speculator or gambler often proved ultra-cautious at the table.

The dirtiest trick in bridge is called 'Coffee-Housing'. This means hesitating as though two cards are playable, when in fact only one is. Bridge players at European coffee houses apparently had a low reputation.

Mr K McNeil (SA) gave me a parting message. Bridge, he said, was like sex and education – it was here to stay.

Their figures are always fashionable
March 1965

Fashions change fairly often but women are stuck with the one face and figure and when these change, they usually deteriorate. Shop dummies are much better off. An old one has a Roman nose? Tut! Whip it across to the dummy surgery in Hay Street, East Perth and install the latest pert, upturned nose. The head is passé in general? A new head will be provided.

These and a thousand other facts about shoppers' companions I learnt in a slow amble from William-and-Hay to Hay and Pier during which girl shop assistants sighed to me over a particularly nice dummy called Sonia, and display managers fearlessly revealed to me the secrets of their war against males-resistance.

A rather snooty fashion shop confided that the ultimate in dummies had just arrived in a packing case. I could not possibly see it/him/her, it was not 'coming out' till February.

Human evolution from the ape-like stage took possibly 1 million years but dummies can evolve in weeks to keep up with the latest look – be it Bardot or baby-face or ancient Egyptian as portrayed by Elizabeth Taylor.

Today we are in what one manager called the 'super real' era. The eyes can be dessertspoon size, with an iris as big as a shilling. Legs are longer-than-life; mouths can shrink to button size.

Hair ('it's really horse-hair') may be bright orange or a grey that never was on a human head on sea or land. Postures are blatant ham acting but the overall effect is entrancing.

"Once our models were just big clothes-hangers," one man said. "Today they really have to sell the clothes they wear. They must look so right and so chic that a woman can't help seeing herself as the model, and wanting the dress."

When the late John F Kennedy became President, US dummy makers even produced likenesses of him and his wife, which became popular in US clothing stores.

Dummy makers now employ research teams to find out how to make dummies' eyes look real, and see what the latest ideal woman looks like. Venus de Milo with her narrow shoulders and full hips has become unsatisfactory. Dummy makers prefer an ostrich neck, a nipped in waist, a not too full bosom. The New York World Fair shows dummies with a new plastic skin so natural that you could see pore marks.

All this tends to make the clothes-conscious woman buyer a sitting shot. But a shop's lifeblood depends on sales. It cannot afford to fall behind and put dowdy, tarty dummies in the window.

"What happened to the worn-out dummies?" I asked one window dresser. My worst fears were confirmed. "They go into country stores," he said.

By contrast, evolution is slow for male dummies. Most of them still stare stonily straight ahead. But I was escalated up three floors to see the very latest – a male dummy with a modern young man's sulky look.

Sure enough, it sulked. Its hair was cut short in a semi-college cut, it was slim and tanned, and it was bound for the beach, one foot in the air. "He's a little bit of a character," my guide said fondly.

Realism has brought problems. You can't just leave a vibrant young woman dummy naked in the window when you go to get her a new cocktail dress. "If the worst comes to the worst, we pop a shift on her," one shop assistant said. "These lifelike ones can be awful to dress. We have to uncross this one's legs to put her shorts on and then cross them back again, and the shorts always get crumpled."

In the old days when dummies bore no resemblance to anyone living or dead, no one cared if they were clothed or not. "Today we must take greater care," a display man said. "Older women even complain that the nighties on models are too revealing. The modern trend in slumber wear is seduction. If people don't like it, it is just too bad."

Somehow the magic has gone out of store windows for me.

Display people even get up to Frankensteinian tricks like borrowing a bent arm off pretty Miss X to let Miss Y look cute as she lies down on the showroom carpet.

Note: A few years earlier I was junior police roundsman and one Sunday morning I followed the police to a Claremont clothing shop which had been broken into overnight. The owners, police and others talked in huddles in low voices and I felt excluded from these conversations. I did get the various facts needed for a crime report of a few paras. It seemed that this was not the first time the shop had been broken into. At some point later, more worldly colleagues explained that the culprit was not after money. He had fallen in love with a shop dummy and a Saturday night break-in was his substitute for a date. One lives and learns.

Among the folk song set

22 September 1965

I pushed open the door and the coffee-shop patrons stirred uneasily as an importunate flow of cold air got in first. This was folk-song night; the room was packed. Synthetic hurricane lamps eased a mellow ochre light through the smoke and shade, making friends with the chocolate sideboard, the grandfather clock ticking pendulously against the wall and the yellow-striped awning under which coffee machines emitted fitful gleams of chrome. Only a bright-red advertisement for cigarettes was off-key.

"That's be 3/6 for coffees and 10/- for the cover charge for the entertainment," the proprietor said, squirting a star-shaped blob of cream into our cups and using a little torch as a third eye. My pound note departed and I gained some silver coins.

The room was packed with the duffle-jacketed young, curiously inanimate. One girl sat still as an artist's model, her face expressionless and sixpence-pale in its frame of long black hair.

The west corner was the focus of prestige. There sat the entertainers, in manly open-neck shirts or cuddly lambs wool pullovers. Behind them, perched like seagulls on the window ledge, a row of youths paid silent homage.

A young man in brown, forehead gleaming where the hair had receded to prominence. He flapped his right hand on the strings of a banjo, while his left strutted birdlike on the fingerboard. He began to sing:

John Henry was a dirty little man
Carried a razor every day
Killed a man down in Mobile town
You should have seen John Henry get away...
John Henry standing on a top of a hill
So drunk he could not see
Sheriff came up with a warrant in his hand
Said, 'Johnny boy you'd better come with me,

Johnny boy you'd better come with me…"

The tune was plaintive and we all sipped coffee in pleasant melancholy.

Outside the door a group of teenagers wavered uneasily, perhaps deterred by the cover charge. Those at the rear pushed forward, those up front pushed back.

"Come in lads, come in!" shouted the proprietor.

He told us, "Rather than folk singing, it is more entertainment."

The man in brown began singing about a farmer Johnson's ol' yella' cat that wouldn't go away.

The company looked wholesome - fresh faced boys, only two with beards; a couple of washed-out business men; dulled office workers such as myself; a group of about seven girls occupying the south corner, whether segregated by choice or through lack of male initiative being uncertain.

A man with a V-neck jumper and white shirt announced that he was going to give us a song that he was really, really, really fond of. It was quite a good one.

I will seek the desert slush where the scenery is lush

How I long to see that mushroom cloud

Mid the yuca and the thistles I will watch the guided missiles

While the FBI watches me.

I will soon make my appearance

As soon as I get my clearance

Cos the Wild West is where I want to be.

The audience were not the transistor set, certainly, but neither did they seem particularly protest minded. They received this number blankly.

"Coffee break," the singer said after a while. Some people rushed around with jugs of steaming coffee but the sales resistance was fierce.

Uninhibited items by an improvised band came next and they were worth the cover charge. One man played a wooden washboard; another blew through a comb and paper. A youth made raucous noises with a little mouth trumpet, and a recorder twitted with Dolmetsch confidence. Someone came round after with a wicker basket for us to throw money in.

It was getting a bit chilly. The table-load of girls left en masse. The folk singers sang of bums on the railway ('Hear the whistle blow-oh-ohhh') and mournful worksongs ('Yes I work all 'a week in 'a blazin' sun'). Cars swished by outside. The yard of the garage opposite was full of the Holdens, Valiants, Datsuns and odd sports cars of the coffee parlour inmates.

We drove off along the highway. The muted strains of American ballads followed us a little way.

EXTRACTS FROM THE FAMILY FILE

My Mum was no snowflake

Sexual harassment of women subordinates has become a career-destroying matter for any male boss, and rightly so. 'Harassment' now extends to what is called inappropriate behaviour, and not just towards subordinates but to any woman in a work or social context.

In my 50 years as employed reporter I didn't notice any harassment going on except that female colleagues were often the targets of crude banter. In the Canberra Press Gallery, for example, one louche senior reporter stood behind the chair of a hard-working female and said, "Come on, X, give us a f - k. You needn't stop typing." I'm sure that X was not in the least traumatised by the request. The typical female rejoinder of that era was "Why don't you just f - k off!"

However, harassment appeared to be institutionalized in some workplaces, particularly TV studios. I was reading journalist Hugh Riminton's memoirs *Minefields* and was shocked at his account of Channel Nine news boss, the late John Sorell, whom Riminton describes as a 'hideous sleaze'.

Riminton joined Nine in 1989. When the nightly news went to air, Sorell would summon his news team to his office for a full-blooded and booze-fuelled critique. Staff would sit on sofas along one wall. Females were treated as special cases and on one evening three sat side by side on one couch.

Sorell leaned back in his big recliner and bellowed at his favourite foil, the chief editor Grahame 'George' Loutit.

'George!''

'Yes, Admiral!' [Sorell's nickname]

Sorell swung a leery eye at the women on the couch.

'Which one would you fuck first?'

By any measure, even then, this was intolerable behaviour. So why did so many smart young men and women put up with it? One answer is that Sorell's thunderclaps bonded the people who worked underneath him. Great friendships were made because we were all the trenches together.

The other reason is harder to explain. Sorell was a fine judge of what worked on TV, and for all his boorishness was immensely proud of the women he discovered and turned into stars.

Sorell would not survive in a newsroom today. Many might argue that this would be no loss. But good work got done and most people survived.

More than half a century earlier, in the early 1930s, my mother-to-be Joan Allen was copping workplace sexual harassment. She became a clerical junior at *The West Australian* in 1933, the start of her journalistic career. However, her account is devoid of the modern style of self-pity and traumatization. Indeed, she cheerfully admits to valuable quid pro quos in favours from her harassers.

'*The West*' was then in its newly-opened building in St George's Terrace. Joan was a shy 18 year old from the struggling south-west hamlet of Kendenup. She describes herself as a 'dark-eyed country mouse', though photos not much later show a fresh-faced brunette of considerable allure. She owed the job - at the height of the depression - to her glamorous Aunt Gwen, the secret mistress of *The West's* managing editor C.P. Smith. Joan was boarding at the home of Gwen and Gwen's sister Biddie, and well knew what was going on with 'C.P.' and Gwen.

C.P. was notorious for his exploitation of women in Newspaper House and secretaries immediately assumed that Joan was another of his 'protégés', along with a dowdy young typist Ramona on whom he later sired a child. He gave Joan perks including payment for private shorthand lessons. But there was a consequence: at lunchtimes he would summon her to his office for petting sessions.

"As his heavy jowls came closer, gingery eyebrows arched over small shrewd eyes, thick chin divided by a deep cleft, receding reddish hair above a hawkish nose, I felt I was paying a heavy price for my indebtedness," Joan writes in her 1993 autobiography *Anger & Love*.

C.P. would drive Joan at night to his mistress Gwen's home in Subiaco but detour to a lonely spot and start putting his hand up her dress. She could only restrain him by threatening to blab to Gwen.

Worse, she was assumed to be available to other *West* senior managers who would molest her on social occasions…"fatherly old men so eager to put their hands down the front of my dress, desisting only when I looked at Gwen with mute appeal and C.P. shook his head."

Another mum-molester was the mining and smelting magnate W. S. (William Sydney) Robinson, a leader of the Collins House group and one of Australia's top industrialists. 'W.S' arrived on an official visit from Melbourne to the newspaper. Despite his lofty status and age (57, or thrice mum's age) he invited the junior clerk to make a foursome with Gwen and C.P. to a quiet restaurant in the hills, about an hour's drive away.

"In the back of the Nash driving up Greenmount Hill, I squirmed and struggled silently under his roving hands. There was further ignominy when he sent via C.P. an envelope containing a twenty pound note [that's nearly $2,000 in today's money].

"Should I give it back?" I asked Grandma and Gwen, who had received a similar envelope.

"Certainly not!" Grandma said stoutly, to my relief, for I'd never had a twenty pound note before.

Joan had an ugly vision of the downward path to prostitution but banked her windfall anyway. She moved out of her Aunt Gwen's scandal-plagued home to a tiny flat in West Perth, expecting this to restore her own reputation. But she was discomfited to hear the latest Newspaper House calumny, that 'C.P.' was paying the rent and availing himself of her services as mistress.

It seems odd for me to be writing about Mum like this. But who'd want to swap her for today's snowflake woman, who purports to be permanently discombobulated because some man (not necessarily her boss) put his hand on her knee half a decade ago?

Brothers and sisters have I none…

My father Pete Thomas (1914-1988), journalist and historian, could write droll pieces. Here's one of them.

A magazine's section, "Margaret answers your queries" had this exchange in mid-1984.

Q: Could someone explain to me the answer to the riddle: *'Brothers and sisters have I none, but that man's father is my father's son.'* The man saying the words is looking at a portrait. Who is in the portrait? I know the answer is that the man is looking at a portrait of his son, but I don't understand why.

A: In practice it's almost impossible to explain this riddle. We can do no better than reprint a letter sent to us following the question.

From Pete Thomas, Neutral Bay, 30 July 1984.

Dear Margaret,

A few minutes ago I winced massively to hear someone put forward that riddle about 'brothers and sisters'. Then I winced even more to hear a man confidently propound his answer to it because I have a very wry memory of this riddle and an experience relating to it almost half a century ago. In the 1930s, at the callow age of 19 or 20, I was a sub-editor on Perth's morning daily, The West Australian. Each night the sub-editors would take it in turns to stay back for a final check of page proofs, then give the go-ahead for the print run to proceed. The sub-editor, whoever he might be, had total authority.

On this particular night (or rather, early morning) everything had gone normally and then I (who was doing the late turn) spotted something amiss.

In those days there was an 'Answers to Correspondents' column. Readers wrote in with all sorts of queries – legal, real estate, governmental, anything - and reporters would have to burrow around and get replies, which would then be published in the column. This was run on the prestige 'Leader Page' with the editorials and so on.

On this particular night, idly eyeing the 'Answers to Correspondents' column at the very last moment, I came across one bit in which a reader had asked THAT riddle 'Brothers and sisters…' and there was an answer which I, with all my youthful self-assurance, was certain was the wrong one. I issued my edict: that answer had to be changed. Everyone involved with the printing - including men two or three times my age – was aghast but I insisted. And so it was done.

As a result the print run was made inordinately late, all the publishing and distribution arrangements for that morning's issue were disrupted, transport schedules throughout the State for the paper were missed and everything was a total shemozzle. By then I had gone home, serenely feeling that a job had been well and conscientiously done.

Still happily unaware of all these consequences I turned up again for work the next evening and learnt of what had happened. Because of the disruption of the distribution of the paper, during the day there had been a top-level editorial-management meeting to discuss the enormity of it all and what should be done about the perpetrator – me.

At this meeting someone had asked what possible reason I could have had for delaying the paper in that way. The meeting was told of the reason: I had refused to allow the paper to be printed with a 'wrong' answer to some ridiculous riddle. Someone idly asked what was the riddle and what was the answer given. The meeting was told the riddle and the answer. And then (I owe my salvation to this) all the editorial-management top brass at the meeting got into an increasingly heated and unyielding argument among themselves as to what was the right answer. The meeting broke up in a sort of sullen stalemate and never got to any decision about disciplining me. Instead of the firing squad, all that came out of that top-level meeting was a strict instruction – never again was anyone in 'Answers to Correspondents' to essay an answer to that 'Brothers and sisters have I none…'

With best wishes, Pete Thomas.

PS: No, I have not said in this letter what was the original answer given in that column and what I changed it to. I'm not going to invite trouble about it TWICE.

Dad's essay for months caused me mental gymnastics trying to work out why there was more than one plausible answer. The obvious and logical answer (to me) is that the speaker is looking at a picture of his son. Was this answer the one Dad felt obliged to change in proof stage, or was there a different answer in the draft, which Dad felt obliged to change to "his son"? Who knows?

This morning, admitting defeat, I turned to Google where the issues were well thrashed out. Some writers suggested the portrait is of himself but this would mean the speaker was his own son – impossible.

What if "Brothers and sisters have I none" could also mean there was a deceased brother, thus making it a portrait of the speaker's nephew? One contributor revised the rhyme to remove the ambiguity: "Brothers and sisters I have never had. But that man's father is the son of my dad!"

I also discovered the answer can involve theology, namely: "This man's Father (God, Our Father) is my Father's Son (Jesus, our Lord and Saviour). Who is this man? Jesus Christ of course!"

Making a splash with water music
By Geoff Allen, around 1980

My mother's younger brother Geoff, who died in Perth in 2000 aged 76, had a sense of fun exemplified in this account of his war-time bandsman adventures. He was celebrated post-war as a jeweller/silversmith and less so as an artist, though I'm proud to have several of his oils on our living room walls as I write. I bought one when I was about 20 at his joint exhibition with another artist at the WA University. I dropped by as he was packing up and asked how many he'd sold: "None." I knew he was hard-up. So was I but my purchase brought up his sales to one.

I don't know how he acquired such a lucid and wry style in prose. Like many of his generation, he had a working knowledge of the classics and a good memory for poetry. He probably wrote Water Music in the early 1980s, which was when he acquired an electric typewriter.

During the war he was initially in the 44th Battalion's band as a tuba player. The battalion was designated for WA's defence but in July 1944, with the Japanese threat long passed, the unit was broken up to reinforce the 9th Division, which had suffered heavy casualties in both the North African and islands campaigns. The band was assigned to the division's 2/32nd Battalion at its training base at Ravenshoe, in the Queensland tablelands. This training in 1944 was punctuated by divisional and brigade parades addressed by General Blamey (July), Major-General Wootten (September) and Brigadier Porter (December). Geoff's story deals with the September parade for Wootten but he seems to have either muddled or blended details with the much bigger Blamey parade of July. That one, according to the 2/32nd Battalion history[16] involved several divisions, the "30,000 men" Geoff refers to. Wootten's parade involved only the 24 Brigade, about 4,000 men.

Ordinarily I don't particularly care for brass band music. I was learning the clarinet before joining the Army and had the instrument with me to relieve the boredom of camp life. The scene can be imagined, the truck arriving at the 44th Battalion, us getting off and

[16] Tregellis-Smith, S., *Britain to Borneo, A History of the 2/32 Australian Infantry Battalion*. 2/32 Australian Infantry Battalion Association, Victoria, 1993, p. 266.

lining up in ranks at attention; "Does any of youse lot play a musical instrument?" This was the Sergeant Major bellowing. I began to think it may possibly be an offence and might have to surrender the clarinet. There was a particular sort of silence. A couple of crows flew by, one of them squawking manically. "Fall out any men as plays a musical instrument." I suddenly received a violent shove from behind; that was how I became a member of the band.

They received me graciously and I was soon learning the workings of the cornet, then the tenor horn. Then I was moved to the extreme opposite end of the musical spectrum, the Tuba. It wasn't called a Tuba then. We just called it an E flat or a B flat Bass, but I will use the modern name here. I felt rather proud of my role and began to appreciate brass bands. They certainly lend a definite sparkle to parades, marches and ceremonies in the open and of course the effect on troop morale is indisputably a tonic. They are, too, a virtually indestructible weatherproof unit, as I will presently relate. Another point in their favour is that their robust sounds carry exceptionally well and can be heard for miles.

So our serviceable music was available for any and every kind of occasion – such as the nightly mounting of the Guard. Very serious stuff this: boots and instruments polished to transcendental levels, gaiters and belts immaculately whitened for the steely eye of the Duty Officer strutting through our ranks and those of the guard. If we put as much time into musical preparation and improvement as we put into our appearance, we would be a band of some consequence. As it really was, we were a pretty rough lot, not blessed with too much talent or training.

Our principal cornet was an exception; he was a talent if ever there was one. Trained by a famous cornet player of the day, Hughie McMahon, he could play at sight anything you cared to prop up in front of him.

Besides being music-makers, we had rifles and had to learn how to use them. If we saw action, we were to be stretcher-bearers and first-aiders.

Apparently one night in the mess our sergeant was assailed with some insulting words describing us as a bunch of 'softies', and as there was to be a fifteen-mile route-march in a day or so which would have involved the Band sans-instruments, he made a bet with his accuser that we would do the march, with instruments merrily playing. It was a senseless bet as the terrain was hilly and the road corrugated. In the tablelands of Northern Queensland where we now were stationed, we were aware of the effects of the rarefied air at the 3000 feet of altitude, so that blowing a bass on the march had its special difficulties.

We did the best we could in the 15-miler but it was heavy work. I had a fever from a smallpox jab a day or two before. One of the cornet players took over my instrument and rather than drop out, I put his cornet up to my face and faked it on the homeward leg. We survived the ordeal but got no thanks from any quarter.

Not long after the fifteen-mile march, we heard rumours that we were soon to take part in a General Review. General Wootten would wish to review our Division along with the 7th, and part of the 6th. We waited; we were good at waiting. The rumour proved to be true. In due time it was the day before the March Past and so tomorrow the General would review his Battalions, his Brigades and his Divisions under a sparkling Queensland sky. All ranks would be smartly turned out, including campaign ribbons; rifles would be carried at the slope; "hats-slouch" would be worn with side turned up. In columns of six they would pass the saluting base at a brisk 110 paces per minute. Three splendid brass bands would give that final glittering finish to the scene and those thousands of fine young faces would snap smartly to the right as the command 'Eyes Right' was given and the General would respond with a salute and hold salute until the command 'Eyes Front' was given. If those were the thoughts of the General, a certain few details were missing from his imagery.

Digger Bovell and I were wearily Brasso-ing our massive E flats when he remarked, 'I reckon it'll rain like shit tomorrow'. When pressed for his reason he added, "Well, I've got this shoulder pain and it's not from polishing this machine here, besides, look at this." He pointed to a dull patch where he had huffed into the freshly polished bell of the tuba. "That means rain, it should evaporate quicker than that, so, as I say, it'll rain like a bastard."

I pondered this piece of portentous reckoning a moment and with a light laugh suggested that the General ought really to be informed. He said, "You wait, my methods never fail." I caught his smile but still wondered if he was serious.

Thus we and roughly 30,000 others sweated at our preparations of blanco-ing gaiters, polishing the little brass bits on our belts and webbing and not forgetting 30,000 pairs of boots, shining like apples from the vigorous polishing and final burnishing. The parade was to be held on a nearby sports ground.

It was 15 March 1944.[17] I was 20 years and one month old. As we musicians were a little bit important that day, we were driven there and were formed up exactly opposite the saluting platform. The other two bands were disposed to the left and right of us. They were the 2/24th and the 2/48th. We all sat down on the grass and rolled smokes; there was no sight of the thousands as yet.

A brass band is formed up in sixes, the basses and trombones in the first rank, more basses and euphoniums in the second, next baritones and tenor horns, with a mixed blessing of flugel horns and cornets following. The bass drum is centre-rear with two or more side drums flanking that instrument: there may be a cymbalist thrown in there somewhere too.

The other two bands were sitting about when our Drum Major, catching a sound in the distance, blew a short blast on his whistle and we formed up quickly; it was the sound of staff cars arriving. General Wootten and about a dozen high-rankers climbed out and began to mount the platform, some with skyward glances and rolling of the eyes. We could hear now the distant sound of orders shouted and to

---

[17] This date can't be right as the band transferred to the 2/32 much later, on 5 July. Tregellis-Smith, op. cit. p. 265.

our right, the first columns advancing. That was when it started to rain 'like a bastard'. The saluting platform was a respectful 50 feet away and as the band on our left struck the first march at a brisk 110 beats per minute, I saw the General's eyes glance darkly to his left. He was swarthy of complexion and magnificently barrel-chested. Probably a bit of Maori there, thought I, and when he looked to his front I felt that he was always looking directly at me.

The troops were on their way. The rain increased. It was 1:00 p.m. We could be here for the next three hours according to our briefing. It was not a cold rain, but the drops were large and coming straight down. There was no wind.

By now, the first of the Battalions, marching six abreast, was almost about to reach the saluting point. Its Major was proudly strutting several yards ahead of his troop, arms swinging 'tit high', as they insist on expressing it, readying to call above the sounds of the band, "Battalion, EYES RIGHT!" As he gave the command, he threw a smart salute and in unison with the unit, threw his head 45° and maintained that slightly grotesque posture long enough for most of the troop to pass, at which estimated point of time he beefed out the counter-order, "Battalion, EYES FRONT!" In exact unison, every soldier puts his head back in the normal position. The first man in the right file is exempted from these antics as he has to steer. He marches in a straight line or in this case, a slightly curving one around the racetrack or whatever it was. The General of course has to return the salute and I suppose was glad enough to hear the counter-command if his shoulder joints are the same as ordinary men's.

The rain continued. The playing field, I observed, was not soaking up the water, being seemingly composed of heavy loam under the grass. The water was already an inch deep over the entire field. There was a small ungrassed patch just in front of us, which was getting churned up by those hundreds of apple-shiny boots, shiny no longer. The gloss had gone off many things; we were all thoroughly wet with our jungle greens clinging to our bodies. I noticed the General had by now an umbrella, held high up by his driver. Our turn to play; the

Drum Major's mace was up. Six beats of the bass drum and we are launched into 'Colonel Bogey' by K.J. Alford.

The drummers had brought ground sheets to cover their drums but it muffled the crisp sound of the snare drums. We were well into this march when I noticed a Major out in front of his troop stagger badly as he gave the salute. I looked for a cause. The water was draining off the field but as fate would have it, the ungrassed area right in front of us was the drain-off point for the entire field, and every boot with its little horseshoe on the heel loosened a few more ounces of loam to be quickly borne away in the flow. To look at it told you nothing, because everywhere was an even sea of dancing spouts where the robust drops struck. So the 'sea of treachery' as I named it, was deepening by the minute.

In 'Colonel Bogey', there is a rip-roaring bass solo and it would take all of my concentration for this serious work. The other amused front rankers would be similarly engrossed. I love this march. It represents one of the best examples of well-made band music - something for everybody and very full. The tune is so well known in the British Empire that certain ribald lyrics have sprung into being:

"Hitler; he only had one ball,

Goering, oh his were rather small,

Himmler, oh his were similar,

But poor old Goebbels had no balls at all."

We were doing a pretty good job out there under the circumstances, and the total morale must have been raised considerably by our efforts. I did wonder how things would have been without us. I wondered about General Wootten's thoughts about the scene and the water hazard in front of him, but I could judge that like a true commander he had a fine appreciation of the situation. He would see that he was already in the iron grip of a fearsome destiny, which must, like a fever, run to its end. To intervene would be unthinkable.

The rain continued in intensity. The band on our right was sailing into B.B. and C.F., a quite daunting piece as there is some very precise and rapid tongue and finger work for the solo cornets; not too difficult if well practised and beautiful to march to. (The strange title is an acronym for British Bands Contest Final). It all but makes you levitate and there are good bits for all sections. I noticed that the drummer had slowed the beat a little for the benefit of the hard working cornets; they played it beautifully. In sun or rain you do your best. It was a superb band, the 2nd 48th.

All this was good experience. Good for what, I do not know. I made a mental note to write about it in my next letter to my girlfriend, but what could I say? The censor would have deleted any mention of numbers or Reviews or anything of interest for that matter, so I formed the words in my mind:

Dear Betty, it rained all day Saturday and we were playing in it. Apart from that, nothing ever happens - same old grub, same old marching, polishing of the instrument, etc., etc.

When rotating the playing as we were doing here, the inactive bands are still at attention, and being under the eagle-like gaze of the General and the other brass hats we were put on our mettle without respite. We dare not even rub our noses or give way to any desire to scratch, shuffle or shrug. We bass players therefore had to bear the weight of our instruments slung on a hefty leather strap across our shoulders. The same applied to the euphonium players. The trombonists could lower their instruments and let the slide just touch the caps of their boots. The drummers all had to support drums via straps so it was one of those strange and difficult situations, which had to be endured with fortitude, and the rain showed no sign of abating.

The scene to our immediate front was roughly the same as before except for one invisible factor; the hole was deeper. The first half-dozen Majors staggered and recovered as they came to the hazard, but now the later-coming majors would throw the salute and the 'Eyes Right', and then fall on their faces quite reliably.

While it was difficult to stifle our mirth, I was aware of some coarse guffaws behind me. We in the front rank had to remain steely-faced throughout, as we were not obscured from the General's gaze by the passing columns, as the reviewing platform was four feet high. I noticed that the troops, ten or so paces behind the Majors, were possibly alerted by the sound of the fall. Perhaps they passed the warning down the files and made a comparatively graceful passage through the mire. I was also intrigued to note that the Officer, having regained his feet, resumed the salute and the 'Eyes Right' position, maintaining them for the required time before giving the 'Eyes Front' order. None failed to do this, although one Major gave the 'Eyes Front' immediately upon recovering his feet, possibly an initiative calculated to spare his men a similar fate, which would be laudably altruistic of him under the circumstances.

The rain was colder now with smaller drops, about the same volume as before but twice as many drops. A light wind had picked up making moving curtains of water sweep across the ground. The low trees surrounding the playing field were just visible. It was a study in greys with only slight differences between the distant bush, the sky, the teeming lake on the oval and the moving mass of humanity passing. The scarlet epaulettes, collar tabs and cap-bands of the Officers on the stand were no longer such vivid touches as formerly. The General's umbrella, a maroon one, gave a slight warmth and of course the golden bell of my E flat lent an artificial kind of glow. I wondered what it looked like from the General's view. He was glumly saluting in the midst of his sodden Officers and again I wondered what his thoughts might be. Clearly he could do nothing as Major after Major fell down and got up again.

He must have been arm-weary as the intervals between the Battalions were, at the most, twenty seconds. At least he was sheltered. I caught his eye yet again as I achingly hugged my E flat. I think the message he flashed was, 'Yes, we all suffer, we are victims of the litanies of convention and our sufferings are the nobler if borne in silence.'

I was dying for a smoke, but we were only about half-way through the event. The handsome Drum-Major had his mace aloft again - our turn to play. The march that we were playing was *"Sons of the Brave"*, which was our Battalion's official property and by coincidence, here were our troops, about to pass. I hoped that they would be greatly cheered by that bit of clever timing and I hoped with that part of my head not dealing in crotchets and quavers that our officers would fare well through the soup ahead of them.

This piece was so well memorised that I didn't need the music. I looked up and watched. There was the officer of A Company, head up, chest out. But with all his astuteness and undoubted intelligence, he would in fifteen more paces meet the marvellously unexpected. One small comfort if it could be so called, was that being already so wet, the victim's ignominy would be fractionally reduced. He in his imagining would attribute his tumble to unique mischance rather than what we could see. At least the pond by now was not getting any deeper.

There was a touch at my elbow. It was our Band Director. He was doing the rounds of the instruments giving us the nod to decant the water from our Tubas. I tipped about half a gallon out of mine. He went to Digger and the others and of course their yield was similar. It was a welcome break from the standing still like so many shags on rocks. It enabled us to exchange a look, a disgusted groan, and a disbelieving shake of the head. There was a sudden peal of thunder. "Bloody lovely", said Digger into his mouthpiece, megaphoning to me.

The sense of comedy had long ago given way to anxiety and a sense of compassion but then, everybody here was young and very fit so why worry? We were all in it together. The range of feelings among the Band's numbers was from total disgust to rare bemusement at this strange theatre.

There was no more thunder. The band on our right was in action and thoughts of being sizzled by lightning slowly vanished. The General was looking at me or through me - it was a sort of unnerving compliment. I knew that he wasn't staring at Digger or one of the B flats to my right, as we were spaced about six feet apart. I mused on the thought of General Wootten's entry in his diary later at night,

"15 March 1944, Ravenshoe, North Queensland. Review of 3rd Infantry Corps went splendidly, in spite of inclemency of weather. Officers and men did splendid job. 3rd Infantry Corps can cope with anything."

I imagined too, remarks in the Officers' mess later, perhaps a chortling Brigadier addressing a Colonel, "I say, I heard you soaked up more than your fair share today, heh, heh", and the denial, "Oh no, we stayed comparatively dry." Actually no one officer was witness to any other officer's mishap, making the events a mental No Man's Land of conjecture.

I imagined myself home and dry too. I was sick of this dismal scene. At long last there were vehicles towing guns which should mean an end to this endurance test. There was much looking at watches among the Staffers as the last 25 pounder trundled past and, taking a cue from the General, a move off-stage and toward the cars whose drivers, bar one, must have been the only persons completely dry that day.

Jim's mace was up and at the horizontal, which meant Left Wheel as we Quick Marched off, carefully skirting the pond, and as we passed the deserted saluting platform the rain ceased. To the soothing tap of the side drum we were heading for home and a cigarette and a nice mug of tea. Digger threw a long look at me, "I told you", he grinned, "it did rain. Like a bastard."

Lament for Fatherhood Lost

A sad part of my life was that my first marriage failed in 1969, when I was 29. I went East leaving my wife and three-year-old daughter Ros in Perth. Over time I lost touch with Ros while re-marrying twice and creating two other families. By the time I began trying to restore contact with Ros, she was about 32 and understandably wary. It took more than a decade for us to become good friends, and even then there seemed to be a barrier between us. Ros was writing a weekly column for The West Australian's Saturday magazine and one day I suggested, 'Why don't we write each other a letter about our prolonged separation? We'll open them at the same time, sight unseen, and you can publish them both as a column.' Ros liked the idea, both personally and as fodder for another column - finding topics was always a challenge and we journalists have little concern for personal privacy. By coincidence, we opened our letters close to Father's Day and The West gave them a two-page Father's Day feature. In addition, the letter exercise was cathartic and led to a much closer relationship between us. Here's what was published...

Ros Thomas, *The West Australian*, 1-2 September 2012

Reconciled with daughter Ros after abandoning her as a toddler, Tony Thomas shares her column to mark Father's Day. They hope their stories will resonate with other fractured families.

Ros's letter:

A great gulf of loneliness stands between me and my father. And it comes from not knowing. Not knowing who he is, or which parts of me are him. Of not knowing his face and voice by heart. I often catch myself watching my children and their besotted father at their funny games, reliving my childhood vicariously through them. Wistful thinking.

I never had a dad. He is a mythical creature in my life. There is not a single photo of the two of us together. No teary pride with newborn bundle in the delivery suite. No small girl shoulder rides. Nowhere high from where to view the world.

Actually there was one dog-eared snap of us, lost now, but it was only of his hand steadying mine as a laughing toddler in the bath. (I held that photo so many times as a kid, I thought if I looked hard enough, I would see love in that hand.)

It never really mattered to me as a child. My mum was my whole world. But there were always the awkward moments at other people's houses when someone would ask, "Where's your dad?" and I would have to answer stupidly, "I don't know" and by the look on my face, they wouldn't push further.

There were the odd fleeting visits from him, a strange man at the door, whisking me away to an unfamiliar house with new smells and foreign voices. Of another family that was mine, but with no history, for either of us. Studying his face for reflections of my own and finding none. A terrible sense of disconnectedness. The loaded silence on the drive home. An awkward kiss on the cheek on the way out the car door. Floods of tears once safely inside.

Funnily enough, I never pined for him on birthdays or at Christmas, there was always too much other excitement. I don't think I ever looked at friends' fathers with awe or envy either. I just wanted one of my own. A keepsake.

It was the quiet times, playing alone, when I reflected begrudgingly on how different I thought I was, and why it had to be me who had a half missing.

In high school it was my great shame. A reason to feel somehow inferior in the crowd. When the stigma of divorce was an impediment to fitting in. I hated him for it.

By the time I was interested in boys, I already had a thing for men. I was a walking stereotype. There were lovely boyfriends with fatherly kindnesses and affections but they were somehow too simple. I needed the angst-filled, heaving burden of unrequited love. I found it at university in the great novels I studied, and buried myself deep in Oedipus and Electra and became as father-fixated as ever.

How many other fatherless children are out there? How do we reconcile the disappointment of growing up feeling tainted by absent dads, or present ones who can't live up to their responsibilities? Or expectations? Maybe they thought we'd be better off? Maybe we were.

And how do we make a happy life for ourselves despite rough starts? Blame won't help. Nor will anger. Or casting yourself as victim. I decided to take the part of heroine instead and strained to live up to it.

Now in my 40s and a mother, my great hurdle is how to break the cycle of abandonment that is now two generations in the making and was very nearly a third. I feel intense, sometimes overwhelming pressure to ensure my second marriage is a happy union of parenthood and compatibility. Because I cannot fail at delivering my children the unconditional presence of a father.

As a late bloomer, one who didn't really hit her stride until her mid-20s, I have reconciled myself as the abandoned child made good, saved by the love of a mother and later, husband, friends and children. And I now recognise, and more importantly embrace in myself, the fears and self-doubts of a fatherless daughter. For few of us are gifted the perfect childhood.

'Mea Culpa' for the sins of the dad who wasn't there

Tony's letter:

My father returned from the war to find himself supplanted. He flew to Brisbane, for good. The drone of any plane had me rushing out to wave him a six-year-old's welcome home. Who would think, after that, that I too would fail as a father?

I reported for *The West* for 12 years. Ros, you were three when I left my marriage and job in 1970 for Melbourne and then the Canberra Press Gallery. This was for my own good, not yours. On my last night at home, I sat and watched you for hours, asleep in your cot. I marvelled that I could be so selfish.

The following year was the turmoil of marriage separation and break-up and a new wife and plenty of career stress. About a third of my then-modest pay went on maintenance payments to Perth. I could just afford to build a house in Canberra. It was Struggle Street for both estranged families.

I seldom flew back to Perth for access. What is a father meant to do on an afternoon with a daughter who is a stranger? There is only 'activity'. One time we ran around happily, both of us at an eight year old level. But as you grew older, visits became clumsy affairs. After one visit, I howled with grief.

Each gap seemed to lead to a longer gap. When you were about 14, you wrote me a newsy letter about your life and your dog. It was a chance to start building bridges but nothing came of it.

My second marriage had also failed and this time, now in Melbourne, I was determined that I wouldn't lose my son and daughter in Canberra. This issue involved counsellors, barristers and a court. I kept up fatherhood, at least with my toddler son.

But I didn't have emotional energy left for an uphill campaign to generate a fatherly relationship with an adolescent daughter in Perth, who I assumed was busy sorting out local issues.

Maintenance to Perth became less onerous through wage inflation. It is sad that this outflow was the only nexus between our two families, accompanied by its mutual vexations. Divorces are an expensive past-time.

I know this is ridiculous, but next I felt that if I suddenly renewed contact you would interpret it as my wanting to share in your success in radio and television, to which I had contributed zilch.

I eventually became a bit more mature. I had married again and we raised two daughters, happily. I decided to do my damnedest to become some sort of belated father to you, the toddler I left when I was 29. You were suspicious and angry about my decades of absence. I did my best to talk honestly and diplomatically and not to get discouraged by setbacks.

Grandchildren gave me the chance to play a fun role as grandpa, minus baggage. Over the past decade we've finally got to know a bit about each other. I find it hard to express my emotions but I love our odd new relationship.

To other absentee fathers:

"Stay in touch, come what may. Keep showing your face. If you're in another city, it's harder to keep up the contact. Man up and do your best anyway. Don't be a quitter like I was."